Jobseeker's Guide to California State Employment

Myrlys L. Hollis

Columbia Publishers
Sacramento, California

JOBSEEKER'S GUIDE TO CALIFORNIA STATE EMPLOYMENT

Library of Congress Cataloging No.: 90-082078

ISBN: 0-9622514-1-0

Cover design and desktop publishing production by CompuType Communication Arts, Sacramento, California.

First Edition

Printed in the United States of America.

Columbia Publishers
709 Columbia Drive, Suite 1200
Sacramento, CA 95864

To my husband Gregory and my daughter Alysa for their patience and understanding throughout the production of this book.

Contents

Preface

Fired? I couldn't believe it. I was actually being fired. I was working as a Reporter for the Davis, California section of ***Neighbors***, a weekly publication of the Sacramento Bee.

When I returned to work from a two-day illness, the editor called me into her office. She presented me with a check equivalent to three week's pay and asked me to sign an already-prepared resignation.

There was no logical reason for this action, nor was there any warning. The articles I had written were factual, clear, concise and on time. All of them were published—some even after my "resignation."

That was two-and-a-half years ago. Since then, I have closed the private sector chapter of my life and moved into the much more secure public sector. I am now a happily employed member of the California State civil service. California State civil service offers, among other benefits, **job security.**

My experience with state service actually began while I was a student at Howard University. As a college freshman in Washington, D.C. in December 1982, I became a *Student Assistant* for Governor Deukmejian's Washington, D.C. office. (Yes there are California state government offices in other states such as Illinois, New York and Texas.)

I worked during the school year and took leave from my position during the summer months when I returned home to California. During the summer, I was able to work as a "seasonal" state civil service employee.

When I graduated college in May 1986, I applied for and got a civil service job as a *Graduate Student Assistant.* In July of that year I took my first career civil service examination: *Office Assistant II* (entry level clerk-typist), and a few months later got my first job in the state civil service as an *Office Assistant II.* I had no intention of pursuing a career in the secretarial field, but I accepted the first position that was offered because the important thing in California State civil cervice is just getting your foot in the door.

A year later, after taking another examination in February, I accepted a position as a *Worker's Compensation Insurance Representative I (WCIR I)* with the State Compensation Insurance Fund in Oakland, California. Even though I was pregnant and this meant commuting 200 miles a day from Sacramento it was worth it. This was a "professional" classification within civil service and it was my ticket out of the clerical series.

Once I got into the professional series, I was able to "lateral" into a *Staff Services Analyst (SSA)* position because the *WCIR I* classification is comparable—or at the same pay level— as the *SSA*.

In April, 1988, at nine months pregnant,

my big opportunity came when I interviewed for a *Staff Services Analyst* position with the Department of Social Services **in Sacramento**. The week I was offered the job, I went into labor and the Department of Social Services held my position open for seven weeks, until I returned from maternity leave! A far cry from the kind of treatment I'd gotten in the private sector.

I'm still working as an *SSA* with another state agency in Sacramento and I just love my work. And I no longer live with the apprehension of coming to work one morning and finding a "resignation" letter on my desk.

I had to learn about the options available to jobseekers in the California State civil service the hard way. I've written Jobseekers Guide in the hope of making your job search and career planning a lot easier than mine was.

This book was written especially for you. It will take you step-by-step through the process of getting a state job. I've taken the somewhat confusing statutes and regulations and written them in plain English in a handy reference book that will fit in your purse or briefcase. Once you get your state job, this book will also prepare you for what to expect: benefits, vacation, probation and promotion. It will show you how to transfer jobs freely from one department to another, like I have done. Happy job hunting.

Myrlys L. Hollis
Sacramento, California
February, 1990

Foreward

by Lizabeth A. Peralta

Having had the opportunity to work closely with Myrlys Hollis, I welcome the privilege of expressing my personal comments here. It is gratifying to know that Ms. Hollis has written a book that will benefit all of those individuals seeking employment in state service as well as enlightening those individuals who may already be employed by the state, but lack the information they need to advance in their current employment.

Today, more than ever, people are seeking new ways of starting or advancing their careers. They need to know what resources are available to them, what to do with the information once they receive it, and what they can expect in their quest for employment.

Ms. Hollis proves to her readers that they can attain these goals through the use of this guide. This book makes it easier to understand how to get the job! It describes the benefits of numerous resources, teaches us how to utilize them and inspires confidence in our individual potentialities.

Her formula for successful employment with the State is outlined step-by-step allowing you, the reader, to become familiar with all the resources available, alternatives and possible outcomes one might expect. She has also included her own work history which demonstrates that it can be done!

As a State employee, I can vouch for the many benefits jobseekers can derive from **Jobseeker's Guide to California State Employment.** There are many different

As a State employee, I can vouch for the many benefits jobseekers can derive from **Jobseeker's Guide to California State Employment.** There are many different methods a person can use in attempting to obtain employment with the State, but why waste valuable time and needless energy when it is all laid out before you?

Her book tells you where to go, what to expect, what to do and how to do it. In short, this valuable book provides the guidance you need to reach your goal: getting your first state job.

Lizabeth A. Peralta has been a State employee for the past eight years. She entered California State civil service as an Office Assistant II (Clerical) for the Department of Health Services. She worked her way up through the ranks by taking promotional exams and by making lateral transfers, and is currently an Associate Budget Analyst with the California Community Colleges.

Over 100 Employers; Where Do You Want to Work?

The first step in understanding where you will best fit into the State civil service system is to understand the goals of the various employing departments. When I first started exploring job opportunities with the State, I soon discovered that the myth that all state jobs are alike was far from true. California state departments offer a selection of employment opportunities that fit almost every discipline and experience. This chapter includes descriptions of what each of the State's more than 100 potential employers do!

California state government provides services which are vital to the welfare of its 28.5 million residents. To accomplish this, California's 128 State Departments, Boards and Commissions currently employ 175,728 employees statewide and another 314 in other states such as New York and Illinois.

Although the majority of state positions are located in Sacramento, San Francisco and Los Angeles, there are state civil service positions available in all of California's 58 counties (see statewide personnel office addresses in Chapter 7).

Each state department has very specific duties and responsibilities and the job opportunities within them vary accordingly. The program areas range from placing children with adoptive families at the

Department of Social Services to reviewing civil rights violations at the Department of Fair Employment and Housing, to designing bridges and freeways at the Department of Transportation.

In this chapter you will learn more about what each of the state's employer departments does. Take notes as you read about each department's role in state government. These notes will help you to identify the places you'd like to work. It is important to decide early in the job search what areas of government will be your focus.

Administrative Law, Office of

The Office of Administrative Law (OAL) is responsible for the implementation of the *Administrative Procedure Act*. The Act provides procedures for the promulgation of regulations by State agencies and establishes standards with which regulations must comply.

The goals of OAL are to reduce the number of administrative regulations and to improve the quality of those regulations which are adopted. These goals are achieved by: (1) Maintaining the orderly review of regulations promulgated by more than 130 State regulatory agencies; (2) Issuing determinations as to whether or not any guideline, bulletin, manual, instruction, order or other rule is a regulation; and (3) Fostering increased awareness of the regulatory process.

Aging, Commission On

The Commission on Aging is the principal advocate for older persons in California. The objectives are to ensure that the interests of older persons in California are respresented by advising the Governor, Legislature, Department of Aging and agencies at all levels of government regarding the problems and needs of older persons.

The Commission provides coordination and support to local and statewide senior groups relating to program, legislative and policy advocacy activities. The Commission also serves in an advisory capacity to several state programs for the elderly.

Aging, Department of

The Department of Aging serves as both the principal unifying force for services to seniors and as the focal point for the federal, state and local agencies which serve the elderly in California. As the State Unit on Aging, the Department fulfills the goals outlined in the Older Americans Act in creating options for seniors. The Department works with 33 Area Agencies on Aging throughout the State. Under the direction of the Department, the Area Agencies on Aging manage a wide array of services to seniors at the community level, including nutrition porgrams, social services and health insurance counseling. The Department further acts as an advocate for seniors to continue to develop an environment which respects and values California's older citizens.

Agricultural Labor Relations Board

The Agricultural Labor Relations Board (ALRB), which was created in 1975, and is responsible for conducting secret ballot elections to determine collective bargaining representation in agriculture and for investigating and resolving unfair labor practice disputes. The ALRB is divided into two major programs: (1) Board Administration of the *Agricultural Labor Relations Act* and (2) General Counsel Administration of the *Agricultural Labor Relations Act*.

Air Resources Board

The Air Resources Board is responsible for protecting air quality in California. This responsibility includes establishment of ambient air quality standards for specific pollutants, administration of air pollution research studies, evaluation of standards adopted by the U.S. Environmental Protection Agency and development and implementation of the State Implementation Plan for the attainment and maintenance of these standards. The plan includes emission limitations for vehicular and industrial sources established by the Board and local air pollution control districts.

Alcohol and Drug Programs, Department of

The Department of Alcohol and Drug Programs, in partnership with county governments and in cooperation with numerous private and public agencies, organizations, groups and individuals, provides the leadership and coordination in the planning, development, implementation and evaluation of a comprehensive statewide alcohol and drug abuse prevention, intervention, detoxification, recovery and treatment services delivery system. The Department is responsible for the licensing of methadone programs, multiple offender drinking driver programs and alcoholism recovery facilities. In addition, the Department certifies alcohol and drug abuse programs meeting state standards for service quality.

Alcoholic Beverage Control Appeals Board

The objective of the Alcholic Beverage Control Appeals Board, which consists of three members appointed by the Governor, is to provide a remedy of appeal to people who are dissatisfied with a decision of the Department of Alcoholic Beverage Control ordering any penalty or issuing, denying, transferring, suspending or revoking any alcoholic beverage license. Once an appeal is filed, the Board hears oral arguments on the appropriateness of the Department's decision. The Board then prepares, publishes and distributes a formal written opinion. A party seeking review of an Appeal Board order must file a Petition for Writ of Review with the Court of Appeal. The Alcoholic Beverage Control Appeals Fund is supported by a surcharge on license fees of the Department of Alcoholic Beverage Control.

Alcoholic Beverage Control, Department of

The Department of Alcoholic Beverage Control (ABC) administers the provisions of the *Alcoholic Beverage Control Act*, which gives the Department the exclusive right and power to license and regulate the manufacture, sale, purchase, possession and transportation of alcoholic beverages within the state and, subject to certain laws of the United States, to regulate the importation and exportation of alcoholic beverages into and out of the state.

Alternative Energy Source Financing Authority, California

The California Alternative Energy Source Financing Authority provides industry within the state an alternative method of financing the construction and installation of facilities using alternative methods and sources of energy. Such construction can help meet the energy needs of the State in a manner which minimizes degradation of the environment and conserves scarce energy resources. The Authority is empowered to: establish criteria for projects selected for financing; issue revenue bonds; enter into loan agreeements for the sale, construction, installation, or acquisition of projects; and assist small business entities in locating a funding source for projects not approved by the Authority.

Arts Council, California

The California Arts Council was created in 1975. Major statutory mandates to this agency are: to encourage artistic awareness, participation and expression among the citizens of California; to help independent local groups develop their own arts programs; to promote the employment of artists and those skilled in crafts in both the public and private sector; to provide for the exhibition of art works in public buildings throughout California; and to enlist the aid of all state agencies in the task of ensuring the fullest expression of our artistic potential.

Auctioneer Commission, California

The California Auctioneer Commission is a public corporation created in 1982 for the purpose of licensing persons engaged in the practice of auctioneering or operating an auction house or auction company. A seven member Board of Governors has responsibility to set standards, determine license fees, conduct examinations and investigations and inititate disciplinary proceedings.

Auditor General

The Auditor General's Office provides independent audits of the programs and fiscal operations of state government. By performing financial, performance, and investigative audits, and by performing other special studies, the Auditor General provides the Legislature, Governor, and citizens of the state with objective information about the state's financial condition and the performance of the state's many agencies and programs. The Auditor General is in the legislative branch to meet the independence requirements of the Federal government and of professional auditing standards.

Banking Department, State

The State Banking Department was established to protect the public from economic loss resulting from the failure of any of the financial entities it regulates. The Department licenses and regulates: (1) State chartered banks and trust companies including offices of foreign (other state and other nations) banking corporations; (2) Issuers of payment instruments, including companies licensed either to sell money orders or travelers checks or licensed to engage in the business of transmitting money abroad; and (3) Business and industrial development corporations. In addition to encouraging observance of sound banking practices, the Department certifies securities for the State of California and municipalities and other government agencies within California as legal investments. The Superintendent of Banks is the administrator of local agency security. The programs of the Department are supported by an annual assessment of licensees, license and application fees, and charges for specific services.

Board of Control

The primary objectives of the Board of Control are to: (1) Consider and settle claims against the State in an orderly and impartial manner and to reduce the number of items requiring legislative review or judical adjudication; (2) Provide equitable allowances to state officials for travel, relocation expenses and other reimbursements specifically assigned to its jurisdiction; (3) Protect the public against arbitrary or capricious acts of state agencies in the procurement of supplies and equipment; and (4) Compensate innocent victims of violent crimes for documented financial losses associated with the crime.

Board of Equalization, State

The State Board of Equalization administers 13 tax programs for support of state and local government activities, more tax programs than any other state department. They are: Sales and Use Taxes; Motor Vehicle Fuel License (Gasoline) Tax; Use Fuel Tax; Alcoholic Beverage Tax; Cigarette Tax; Insurance Tax; Energy Resources Surcharge; Emergency Telephone Users Surcharge; Hazardous Waste Tax; Hazardous Substance Tax; Solid Waste Disposal Site Fee; Private Railroad Car Tax; and Timber Yield Tax.

The Board also assesses utility property for local property tax purposes, and guides local government in the administration of the property tax. The Board has more than 60 offices throughout California as well as offices in New York, Chicago, and Houston.

Boating and Waterways, Department of

The program objectives and responsibilities of the Department of Boating and Waterways are to develop and improve boating facilities throughout the state, to promote safety of persons and property connected with the operation of vessels on state waters and promote uniformity of the laws relating thereto, and to conduct a beach erosion control program in cooperation with the federal government and local governmental agencies.

The Department makes loans for small craft harbor development and grants for boat launching facilities; plans and provides funding for capital outlay projects; licenses yacht and ship brokers and for-hire vessel operators, and conducts a program of boating safety and regulation. The Department also participates with the U.S. Corps of Engineers and local agencies in the construction of beach erosion control projects.

Government Organization and Economy, Commission on State

The Commission, also known as the Little Hoover Commission, was created in 1961. Its objective is to provide assistance to the Governor and the Legislature in promoting economy, efficiency and improved service in State government. The Commission pursues that objective by conducting studies and making recommendations to the Governor and the Legislature concerning the organization, operation and performance of state agencies.

California State University

The program objectives of the California State University are to provide: (1) Instruction in the liberal arts and sciences, the professions, applied fields which require more than two years of college education, and teacher education-both for undergraduate students and graduate students through the master's degree; (2) Public services to the people of the State of California; (3) Services to students enrolled in the California State University; (4) Institutional services to support the primary functions of instruction, research, public services, and student services in the California State University and to ensure that legal obligations related to executive and business affairs are met.

California-Mexico Affairs, Office of

The Office of California-Mexico Affairs was establised in 1982. The office ensures that California participates in the four-state Southwest Regional Conference where the State is represented by the Governor or his designee.

The basic functions of the Office of California-Mexico Affairs are to: (1) Develop and further favorable economic, educational and cultural relations with the State of Baja California, the State of Baja California Sur, other Mexican states bordering on the United States, and other states and territories of the Republic of Mexico; (2) Cooperate with similar organizations situated within the United States or Mexico; and (3) Carry out the ongoing responsibilities of the Commission of the Californias and the Southwest Border Regional Conference, and to report to the Governor and the Legislature annually on plans and programs.

Child Development Programs Advisory Committee

The Child Development Programs Advisory Committee was established to provide policy recommendations to the Governor, the Superintendent of Public Instruction, the Legislature and other relevant state agencies concerning child care and development. The Committee also reviews and evaluates the effectiveness of child development programs and the need for children's services.

Chiropractic Examiners, Board of

The Board of Chiropractic Examiners was established in 1922. The Board is responsible for assuring California consumers that providers of chiropractic services are adequately trained and meet recognized standards of performance for treatment and practice. The Board uses licensing, continuing education and disciplinary procedures to maintain standards. It also sets educational standards for recognized chiropractic colleges, reviews complaints and investigates possible violations of the *Chiropractic Act*.

Coastal Commission, California

The California Coastal Commission was established through the *California Coastal Act of 1976*. The Act established policies with which "coastal zone" conservation and development decisions must comply. The zone extends three miles seaward and generally about 1,000 yards inland. In particulary important and generally undeveloped areas where there can be a considerable impact on the coastline from inland development, the coastal zone extends as much as five miles inland.

The Commission's jurisdiction does not extend into or around San Francisco Bay, where development is regulated by the San Francisco Bay Conservation and Development Commission.

The policies of the Act deal with public access to the coast, coastal recreation, the marine environment, coastal land resources and coastal development of various types, including energy facilities and other industrial development.

Coastal Conservancy, State

The State Coastal Conservancy was created in 1976 to develop and implement programs to protect, restore and enhance resources in the coastal zone within the policies and guidelines established pursuant to the *California Coastal Act of 1976*.

Colorado River Board of California

The principal objective of the Colorado River Board is to protect California's rights and interests in the water and power resources of the Colorado River system. This is accomplished through investigations and through working with the other Colorado River Basin states, federal agencies, the Congress, and the courts. Activities include analyses of the engineering, legal and economic matters concerning the Colorado River resources of the seven Basin states (Arizona, California, Colorado, Nevada, New Mexico, Utah, and Wyoming) and all factors involved in the 1944 U.S.-Mexico Water Treaty obligation to deliver Colorado River water to Mexico. The Board develops a single position among the California agencies having the major established water and power rights in the Colorado River. The Board also collaborates with other California agencies, primarily the Department of Water Resources, Water Resources Control Board, and Department of Fish and Game, and works closely with the Attorney General.

Commerce, Department of

The Department of Commerce serves as the primary state agency for promoting business development and job creation efforts in California. The Department works closely with domestic and international businesses of all sizes, economic development corporations, chambers of commerce, regional visitor and convention bureaus, and the various permit-issuing state and municipal government agencies to improve California's economic climate.

Community Colleges, California

The Board provides statewide leadership to the public community college segment of California higher education.

The objectives of the Board are to: (1) Give direction, coordination, planning, and leadership to California's Community Colleges; (2) Promote quality education in community colleges; (3) Improve district and campus programs through information and technical services on a statewide basis, while recognizing the cummunity oriented aspect of California's network of 106 community colleges; and (4) Seek adequate financial support while ensuring the most prudent use of public funds.

Conservation Corps, California

The California Conservation Corps (CCC) is a disciplined work force which assists federal, state, local agencies and nonprofit entities in conserving and improving California's natural resources while providing employment, training, and educational opportunities for the young men and women of the State.

In addition to tree planting, stream clearance, trail building, park development, landscaping, home weatherization, and wildlife habitat restoration, the CCC responds to emergencies such as fires, floods, earthquakes, and other natural disasters. In addition to physical work, the CCC provides programs to enhance corpsmembers' employability and increase access to educational opportunities. Major areas of concentration are literacy, education at the high school and community college level, conservation awareness, and career development.

Conservation, Department of

The Department of Conservation is responsible for promoting the development and management of the state's land, energy, and mineral resources. The Department provides services and disseminates information in the following areas: geology and seismology, mineral resources, geothermal and petroleum resources, agricultural and open space land, and container recycling and litter reduction.

These services and information are critical to the public and private sectors for land use decisions, siting of facilities, regulation and conservation of petroleum resources, protection of agricultural and open space land, optimum utilization of mineral resources consistent with sound conservation practices, and conservation of soil resources.

Consumer Affairs, Department of

Provides licensing, monitoring and other services through 30 Boards and Commissions: Board of Accountancy; Board of Architectural Examiners; Athletic Commission; Bureau of Automotive Repair; Board of Barber Examiners; Board of Behavioral Science Examiners; Cemetery Board; Bureau of Collection and Investigative Services; Contractors' State License Board; Board of Cosmetology; Board of Dental Examiners; Bureau of Electronic and Appliance Repair; Bureau of Personnel Services; Board of Funeral Directors and Embalmers; Board of Registration for Geologists and Geophysicists; Board of Guide Dogs for the Blind; Bureau of Home Furnishings; Board of Landscape Architects; Board of Medical Quality Assurance; Board of Examiners of Nursing Home Administrators; Board of Optometry; Board of Pharmacy; Polygraph Examiners Board; Board of Registration for Professional Engineers; Board of Registered Nursing; Certified Shorthand Reporters Board; Structural Pest Control Board; Tax Preparers Program; Board of Examiners in Veterinary Medicine; Board of Vocational Nurse and Psychiatric Technicial Examiners.

Controller, State

The State Controller is an elected state fiscal officer. The primary objectives of this office are to: (1) Provide sound fiscal control over receipt and disbursement of public funds; (2) Report the financial operations and conditions of the state and local government; (3) Assure that money due the State is collected and to provide equitable, effective and economical tax administration; (4) Provide fiscal assistance and guidance to local government; (5) Administer the State's unclaimed property laws; and (6) Serve as a member of fiscally oriented State boards and commissions.

Corporations, Department of

The principal objectives of the Department of Corporations are to regulate the offer and sale of securities; provide for the licensing and regulation of investment brokers and agents; and regulate securities advertising. In addition, the Department is charged with regulating franchises, various types of financial institutions and health care service plans. Department activities include: (1) Providing appropriate controls over the solicitation, marketing and sale of securities and franchises to California residents; (2) Providing deterrents and safeguards against unfair or unscrupulous promotional schemes; (3) Providing regulatory surveillance over companies engaged in lending money or receiving funds from the public in a fiduciary capacity and companies engaged in the business of providing health care to its enrollees; and (4) Instituting appropriate enforcement action when violations of law occur.

Corrections, Board of

The Board of Corrections establishes standards for the construction and operation of local jails and inspects them biennially; establishes standards for employment and training of local corrections and probation personnel and funds the training; and administers the County Correctional Facility Capital Expenditure Funds. At the request of the Governor, the Board also conducts special studies in penology and corrections.

Corrections, Department of

The principal objectives of the Department are the control, care and treatment of men and women who have been convicted of serious crimes, or those admitted to the civil narcotics program, and committed to State correctional facilities. The Department's objectives also include the supervision of men and women who have been paroled from correctional facilities and returned to the community.

The Department is organized into five divisions: Institutions Division, Evaluation and Compliance Division, Planning and Construction Division, Parole and Community Services Division and the Administrative Services Division.

Criminal Justice Planning, Office of

The goal of the Office of Criminal Justice Planning (OCJP) is to improve the criminal justice system in California by providing financial and technical assistance to local governments, state agencies and the private sector; education and training for the citizens of California; and technical and research support for the Administration and the Legislature. The services provided by OCJP include: (1) Grant funding to local agencies and organizations; (2) Technical assistance to ensure effective program management; (3) Development of state-of-the-art approaches for justice systems, crime prevention and victim services programs; (4) Dissemination of information on successful program models; (5) Promotion of information exchange, including interdisciplinary approaches and mutual support among criminal justice agencies, public and private organizations; and (6) Development of publications on crime prevention and victim services for statewide distribution.

Debt Advisory Commission, California

The purpose of this Commission is to: (1) Assist the Housing Bond Credit Committee; (2) Assist, upon request, issuers in planning, preparing, marketing and selling new debt issues; (3) Collect and provide information on debt authorizations; (4) Serve as a statistical center for all State and local debt issues; (5) Undertake studies on the methods to reduce costs and improve the credit ratings of State and local issues; (6) Collect and summarize specific information concerning the use of proceeds of local housing revenue bonds; (7) Collect information on local refunding bonds sold at negotiated or private sale; and (8) Provide verification to the State Treasurer in his certification of housing bonds.

Debt Limit Allocation Committee, California

The California Debt Limit Allocation Committee was created in response to the enactment of the *Federal Tax Reform Acts of 1984 and 1986.* These Acts limit the dollar volume of federally tax-exempt "private activity" bonds which may be sold in any one state during a calendar year. The term "private activity," as applied to tax-exempt bonds, generally includes industrial development bonds, housing bonds and student loan bonds. The *Tax Reform Act of 1986*, in addition to further limiting the purposes for which federally tax-exempt "private activity" bonds may be issued, reduces the dollar volume limit of such bonds to approximately $1.3 billion ($50 per capita) for California after 1987.

The Committee oversees the State's allocation system for the issuance of "private activity" bonds.

Developmental Disabilities, Area Boards on

The Area Boards on Developmental Disabilities protect and advocate the legal, civil and service rights of persons with developmental disabilities. There are thirteen Area Boards throughout the state which are responsible for regional monitoring and coordination, and there is an Organization of Area Boards in Sacramento which resolves common problems, improves coordination and promotes the exchange of information.

In addition to protection and advocacy activities, the Area Boards also review the policies and practices of publicly funded agencies; conduct or cause to be conducted public information programs; encourage and assist in the establishment of citizen advocacy organizations; encourage the development of needed services of good quality; coordinate services to prevent duplication, fragmentation and unnecessary expenditures; and assist the State Council on Developmental Disabilities in preparation of the State Plan.

Developmental Disabilities, State Council on

The California State Council on Developmental Disabilities is responsible for the planning, coordination, monitoring and evaluation of services for persons with developmental disabilities and for establishing a system to ensure the legal, civil and service rights of such individuals.

Developmental Services, Department of

The Department of Developmental Services administers the *Lanterman Developmental Disabilities Services Act*. The intent of this Act is to ensure coordination of services to persons with developmental disabilities; to ensure that such services are planned and provided as part of continuous care which is sufficiently complete to meet the needs of those who are developmentally disabled at each stage of their lives, regardless of their ages or the degree of their handicaps; and, to the extent possible, accomplish these goals without dislocating persons with developmental disabilities from their home communities.

The Department sets broad policy for the delivery of developmental services statewide; establishes priorities, standards and procedures within which the Developmental Services Program operates; monitors, reviews and evaluates the actual operation of the services; and oversees the correction of faulty procedures and practices brought to light by the evaluation and review process. Services are delivered directly, through seven state developmental centers and indirectly through a statewide network of 21 private, nonprofit, locally based community agencies.

Economic Opportunity, Department of

The Department of Economic Opportunity administers programs to assist the low-income residents and communities of California in the following areas: Low-Income Home Energy Assistance Program, Community Services Block Grant and the federal Department of Energy Weatherization Program. Services are provided by the Department through a network of approximately 200 community agencies. The goal of the programs is to assist the low-income population of California to become self-sufficient.

Education, Department of

California's public education system is administered at the state level by the Department of Education, under the direction of the State Board of Education and the Superintendent of Public Instruction, for the education of students from preschool age to adulthood. The primary goal of the Superintendent and the Department is to provide education policy direction to local school districts, and to work with the educational community to improve academic performance.

The state administration aspects of the program are managed through six branches of the Department: the Executive Branch, the Public and Governmental Affairs Branch, the Field Services Branch, the Department Management Services Branch, the Curriculum and Instructional Leadership Branch and the Specialized Programs Branch.

Emergency Medical Services Authority

The Emergency Medical Services (EMS) Authority coordinates EMS statewide, develops guidelines for EMS systems, regulates the education, training, certification of EMS personnel/trauma care systems and coordinates the State's medical response to any disaster.

The overall responsibilities and goals of the EMS Authority are as follows: (1) Assessing statewide EMS needs, effectiveness and coordinating services; (2) Providing technical assistance to existing agencies, cities and counties; (3) Developing implementation and planning guidelines for EMS systems and disaster medical response; (4) Reviewing and approving local EMS agency plans on an annual basis; (5) Coordinating medical and hospital disaster preparedness and response and assisting the Office of Emergency Services in the preparation of the medical component of the State Emergency Plan; (6) Establishing minimum standards for the education, training and certification of specified emergency medical care personnel; (7) Establishing minimum standards for designating and monitoring Poison Control Centers; and (8) Receiving, awarding and monitoring implementation of federal, state and local EMS-related grants.

Emergency Services, Office of

The Office of Emergency Services (OES) coordinates emergency activities to save lives and reduce property losses during disasters and expedites recovery from the effects of disasters, such as the October, 1989 northern California earthquake. On a day-to-day basis, the office provides leadership, assistance and support to state and local agencies in planning and preparing for the most effective use of federal, state, local and private sector resources in emergencies. This emergency planning is based upon a system of mutual aid in which a jurisdiction relies first on its own resources, then calls for assistance from its neighbors. The Office of Emergency Services' plans and programs are coordinated with those of the federal government, other states, and the state agencies and political subdivisions of California.

During an emergency, OES functions as the Governor's immediate staff to coordinate the state's responsibilities under the *Emergency Services Act* and applicable federal statutes, and it acts as the conduit for federal assistance through natural disaster grants and federal agency support.

Employment Development Department

The mission of the Employment Development Department is to contribute to a stable California economy by helping California employers meet their labor needs; helping California job seekers to attain gainful employment; assisting disadvantaged persons become self-sufficient; aid unemployed and disabled workers by maintaining benefit payment programs based on insurance principles; and collecting payroll taxes to support state activities and benefit programs. To further serve the people of California, the Department also administers the *Job Training Partnership Act* program, assists employment, training and vocational education program planners by providing economic and labor market data, and coordinates activities performed by the Department with other organizations that provide employment, training, tax collection and benefit payment services.

Energy Resources Conservation and Development Commission

The Energy Resources Conservation and Development Commission is working to ensure the continuance of a reliable supply of energy at a level consistent with California's needs, while complying with environmental, safety and land use goals. The Commission's programs are aimed at processing applications for siting new power facilities, encouraging measures to reduce wasteful and inefficient use of energy and monitoring alternative ways to conserve, generate and supply energy.

Exposition and State Fair, California

The objective of the California Exposition and State Fair is to provide a medium for the education, commercial interaction, personal interaction and recreation of the citizens of California by providing a forum for the competitive and non-competitive exhibition of the State's industrial and agricultural accomplishments.

Fair Employment and Housing Commission

The Fair Employment and Housing Commission is a quasi-judicial body responsible for the enforcement of State civil rights laws against discrimination in employment, housing and public accommodations. The seven members of the Commission are appointed by the Governor. The Commission issues decisions on accusations prosecuted before it by the Department of Fair Employment and Housing, interprets civil rights statutes through regulations and provides a forum for civil rights concerns. The objective of the Commission is to improve social tensions and guarantee equal opportunity in employment, housing and public accommodations by preventing and eliminating discrimination based on race, religious creed, color, national origin, ancestry, sex, marital status, physical handicap, medical condition and age over 40.

Fair Employment and Housing, Department

The mission of the Department of Fair Employment and Housing is to protect and enforce the civil rights of all persons as provided by the civil rights laws of the State of California. The goals of the Department are to: (1) Maximize the efficient use of state resources in the delivery of services, ensuring that equal employment opportunity and affirmative action are promoted (2) Process and resolve complaints in a primary manner and (3) Emphasize education, communication and cooperation among all sectors for the purpose of preventing discriminatory activities.

Fair Political Practices Commission

The Fair Political Practices Commission has primary responsibility for the impartial administration and implementation of the *Political Reform Act of 1974*. The objectives of the Act are to: (1) Ensure that election campaign expenditure data is fully and accurately disclosed so that the voters may be fully informed and to inhibit improper financial practices; (2) Regulate the activities of lobbyists and disclose their finances to prevent any improper influencing of public officials; (3) Provide for the disclosure of assets and income of public officials which may affect their official actions to avoid any conflicts of interest; (4) Ensure that the state ballot pamphlet contains useful and adequate information so that the voters will not be entirely dependent upon paid advertising for information concerning state measures; (5) Eliminate laws and practices that unfairly favor incumbents to provide for fair elections; and (6) Provide adequate mechanisms to public officials and to private citizens to ensure vigorous enforcement of the Act.

Finance, Commission on State

The objective of the Commission is to aid the Legislature and the Governor in establishing an appropriate, timely and coordinated fiscal policy for the state by providing them and the public with independent forecasts of State revenues, expenditures and the surplus or deficit at least four times a year.

The Commission also has the responsibility to produce an annual long-range forecast of General Fund revenues and expenditures extending ten years into the future. The Commission prepares semi-annual reports assessing the impact of selected federal government expenditures on California's economy, revenues and employment. The Commission also computes the California Necessities Index which is used to determine the annual cost of living adjustments for various health and welfare programs.

Finance, Department of

By statute, the Director serves as the Governor's chief fiscal policy advisor with emphasis on the financial integrity of the state and maintenance of a fiscally sound and responsible Administration. The objectives of the Department are to: (1) Prepare, present and support the annual financial plan for the State; (2) Assure a responsible and responsivestate resource allocation within resources available; (3) Foster efficient and effective state structure, processes, programs and performance; and (4) Establish integrity in state fiscal data bases and systems.

Fire Marshal, Office of the State

The mission of the State Fire Marshal's office is to foster, promote and develop ways and means of protecting life and property from fire and related perils through direct action, and coordination of the California Fire Service. To accomplish this mission, the State Fire Marshal assists local and state authorities in the enforcement of all laws and ordinances; prepares, adopts and enforces minimum statewide fire and panic safety standards; prepares, adopts and enforces standards for the use and control of hazardous materials; is liaison to the film industry for fire and life safety procedures of special effects; and disseminates information and material relative to new technological developments in the field of public fire safety.

Fish and Game, Department of

The program objectives of the Department of Fish and Game are to ensure that fish and wildlife are preserved to be used and enjoyed by the people in the State, now and in the future. The specific objectives of the Department are to: (1) Maintain all species of fish and wildlife for their natural and ecological values as well as for their direct benefits to the public; (2) Provide for varied recreational use of fish and wildlife; (3) Provide for an economic contribution of fish and wildlife in the best interests of the people of the state; and (4) Provide for scientific and educational use of fish and wildlife.

All of the programs of the Department are directed towards the accomplishment of these objectives through the protection, conservation, enhancement, and restoration of fish and wildlife resources and habitats and the regulation of resources used.

Food and Agriculture, Department of

The objectives of the Department of Food and Agriculture are: to serve the citizens of California and protect the consumer by maintaining a viable food system which assures delivery of an abundant supply of wholesome food; to provide leadership in the development of policy on issues important to California food and agriculture; to develop policy and provide assistance in areas such as marketing and exporting; to protect public and worker health and safety related to pesticide use by registering and regulating chemicals; to prevent or eradicate intrusions of harmful plant and animal pests and diseases; to develop and enforce weights and measures standards for all levels of commerce; and to provide support to district, county and citrus fairs in areas of planning, budgets, exhibits, vocational education, events, construction and maintenance.

Forestry and Fire Protection, Department of

The Department of Foresty and Fire Protection, under the policy direction of the State Board of Forestry, is responsible for providing fire protection and watershed management services for private and State-owned watershed lands. The primary objectives of the Department are to: (1) Maintain a fire prevention program that minimizes fire losses due to human causes; (2) Provide an efficient fire control system that holds damages from wildlife to a level that will not seriously impair the use or benefits received from department-protected lands; and (3) Maintain and improve the quality of land and vegetative resources in order to maximize the economic and social benefits that are derived from these resources now and in future generations.

In addition, the Department provides fire protection services for some local governments on a cost reimbursement basis.

Franchise Tax Board

The objective of the Franchise Tax Board is to fairly, effectively and efficiently administer those programs and functions delegated to the Board by the Administration and mandated by law, including self-assessed income tax programs, programs to distribute benefits to the public and functions that contribute to the State's operational effectiveness.

The Franchise Tax Board administers the Personal Income Tax and Bank and Corporation Tax Laws through programs which include self-assessment, audit, collection and filing enforcement activities.

General Services, Department of

The objectives of the Department of General Services are to: (1) Meet the varied responsibilities for management review, control and support assigned to it by the Governor and by statute; (2) Provide support services to operating departments with greater efficiency and economy than they can individually provide for themselves; and (3) Increase effectiveness and economy in the administration of state government by establishing and improving statewide policies and guidelines.

Hastings College of the Law

The College was founded in 1878, and was provided affiliation with the University of California. Policy for the college is established by the Board of Directors and carried out by the Dean and other officers of the college. Vacancies on the Board are filled by the Governor and approved by a majority of the Senate.

Health and Welfare Agency Data Center

The primary objectives of the Health and Welfare Agency Data Center are to: (1) Ensure the effective, efficient and economical use of agency electronic data processing (EDP) resource by providing EDP services at reduced cost by eliminating unnecessary duplication and by ensuring optimum utilization; (2) Ensure the EDP resources are available to meet Agency needs by providing the necessary computer capability and capacity to meet those needs; (3) Promote the appropriate use of EDP resources to assist in the achievement of Agency goals and objectives by identifying potential EDP-related applications and by formulating and recommending policies on the appropriate use of EDP in the Agency.

Health Planning and Development, Office of Statewide

The goal of the Office of Statewide Health Planning and Development is to develop a State health policy to assure the accessibility of needed, appropriate and affordable health services. To accomplish this goal, the Office is responsible for: (1) Developing the State Health Plan and the Statewide Health Facilities and Services Plan; (2) Assuring that construction plans and specifications for all major health facilities are in compliance with state building codes; (3) Assuring that available federal and state financial assistance is provided for development of needed health facilities; (4) Recommending changes in health facility licensing laws and regulations based upon the outcomes of privately conducted State monitored demonstration projects; (5) Conducting health profession staff planning activities; and (6) maintaining uniform systems of accounting and reporting for the disclosure of health facility costs.

Health Services, Department of

The goals of the Department of Health Services are to: (1) Promote an environment that will contribute to human health and well-being; (2) Assure the availability of equal access to comprehensive health services using public and private resources; (3) Emphasize prevention-oriented health care programs.; (4) Promote the development of knowledge concerning the causes and cures of illness and the means of delivering health services to the public; (5) Assure economic expenditure of public funds to serve those persons with the greatest health care needs.

These goals are carried out through eleven programs: Preventive Medical Services, Toxic Substances Control, Laboratory Services, Environmental Health, Acquired Immune Deficiency Syndrome, Family Health Services, Rural and Community Health, Medical Care Services, Licensing and Certification Audits and Investigations and Administration.

Highway Patrol, California

The principal objective of the California Highway Patrol is to ensure the safe, convenient, and efficient transportation of people and goods across the state's highway system.

Horse Racing Board, California

The purpose of the Board is to regulate parimutel wagering for the protection of the betting public, to promote horse racing and breeding industries and to maximize state tax revenues.

Principal activities of the Board include: protection of the betting public; licensing of racing associations; sanctioning of every person who participates in any phase of horseracing; designating racing days and charity days; acting as a quasi-judicial body in matters pertaining to horseracing meets; collecting the State's lawful share of revenue derived from horseracing meets; and, enforcing laws, rules and regulations pertaining to horseracing in California.

Housing and Community Development, Department of

The objectives of the Department of Housing and Community Development are to guide, support and, where appropriate, direct the public and private sectors in the provision of a decent home and living environment for every Californian. To accomplish these objectives, the Department engages in two major activities: (1) The analysis and implementation of building codes and the enforcement of standards for the construction of manufactured homes, and (2) The administration of various housing development and rehabilitation programs, with particular attention paid to meeting the needs of low-income and other disadvantaged groups.

The Department provides both technical assistance in housing development through its staff, and direct grants or loans to local government and nonprofit housing agencies.

Housing Finance Agency, California

The primary purpose of the California Housing Finance Agency is to meet the housing needs of persons and families of low and moderate income. The primary functions of the Agency are to sell tax-exempt bonds and use the proceeds to finance housing at below-market interest rates by: (1) Making construction loans and mortgage loans to qualified borrowers to finance housing developments, or purchasing such loans from qualified mortgage lenders, and (2) Purchasing loans originated and serviced by qualified mortgage lenders.

In addition to increasing the supply of affordable housing, the Agency's financing activities provide a stimulus to the state's economy which results in additional employment opportunities and increased income to California residents.

The Agency may: (1) Provide technical services in connection with the financing of housing developments; (2) Act as a State representative in receiving and allocating federal housing subsidies; and (3) Under certain circumstances, make grants to housing sponsors, provided that grants are not made with the proceeds of the sale of bonds or notes.

Housing Insurance, California

The goal of the California Housing Insurance program is to encourage and facilitate the preservation of existing housing and improve housing opportunities for persons of low and moderate income. In 1977, a program was established for bond and loan insurance. The program was initially funded with a $5 million appropriation and a $5 million loan. The loan has since been fully repaid. All money in the fund is continuously appropriated for the purposes of insuring loans and bonds pursuant to the program.

To fill the void created for mortgage insurance for the low and moderate income housing market, the fund currently insures California Housing Finance Agency's single family loans and has earned a claims-paying ability credit rating equivalent to that of a private mortgage insurance company.

Industrial Development Financing Advisory Commission, California

The California Industrial Development Financing Advisory Commission was created in 1980. The legislation which enacted this agency allows cities and counties to establish industrial development authorities which are empowered to issue industrial development revenue bonds under certain terms and conditions. Bonds issued for this purpose are subject to the State's "private activity" bond ceiling, as specified in the *Federal Tax Reform Act of 1986*, and allocated by the California Debt Limit Allocation Committee.

The program is intended to benefit economically distressed areas within the state. The proceeds of the bonds provide industry with an alternative method of financing capital outlay required to acquire, construct or rehabilitate facilities which will increase employment or otherwise contribute to economic development.

Industrial Relations, Department of

The objective of the Department is to protect the workforce in California, improve working conditions and advance opportunities for profitable employment. The Department is continually working toward this objective by enforcing the compulsory Workers' Compensation Insurance Law and adjudicating workers' compensation insurance claims, by working to prevent industrial injuries and deaths; by promulgating and enforcing laws relating to wages, hours, and conditions of employment; by promoting apprenticeship and other on-the-job training; by assisting in negotiations with parties in dispute when a work stoppage is threatened; and by analyzing and disseminatng statistics which measure the condition of labor in the state.

Insurance, Department of

The principal objective of the Department of Insurance is to protect insurance policyholders in the state. To accomplish this objective, the Department conducts examinations of insurance companies and producers to ensure that operations are consistent with the requirements of the Insurance Code.

In addition to the current objectives of the Department, the passage of Proposition 103 in November 1988, places additional responsibility on the Department. This measure makes major reforms on business conducted in the State by the insurance industry and requires the Department to implement and monitor these reforms.

Justice, Department of

The constitutional office of the Attorney General, as chief law officer of the state, has the responsibility for seeing that the laws of California are uniformly and adequately enforced.

The Justice Department is responsible for providing skillful and efficient legal services on behalf of the people of California. The Attorney General represents the people in all matters before the Appellate and Supreme Courts of California and the United States; serves as legal counsel to state officers, boards, commissions and departments; represents the people in actions to protect the environment and to enforce the consumer, antitrust and civil rights laws; and assists district attorneys in the administration of justice.

The Justice Department also coordinates efforts to address the statewide narcotics enforcement problem; assists local law enforcement in the investigation and analysis of crimes; provides person and property identification and information services to criminal justice agencies; supports the telecommunications and data processing needs of the California criminal justice community; and pursues projects designed to protect the people of California from fraudulent, unfair and illegal activities such as special efforts to prosecute organized criminal activity conducted in California.

Lands Commission, State

The State Lands Commission administers policies established by the Legislature and the Commission in the management and supervision of all statutory lands which the State has received from the federal government. Statutory lands include the beds of all naturally navigable waterways such as major rivers, streams and lakes; tide and submerged lands in the Pacific Ocean which extend from the mean high tide line seaward to the three-mile limit; swamp and overflow lands; vacant state school lands; and granted lands.

The Commission authorizes the use of land subject to reasonable rules and regulations and the determination of fair and adequate compensation. These decisions are reached at public hearings and are based upon environmental, health and safety, and public benefit consideration.

Law Revision Commission, California

The primary objective of the California Law Revision Commission is to study the statutory and decisional law of this state, to discover defects and anachronisms and to recommend legislation to effect needed reforms.

The Commission assists the Legislature in keeping the law up to date by studying complex and controversial subjects, identifying major policy questions for legislative attention, gathering the views of interested persons and organizations and drafting recommended legislation for legislative consideration. The efforts of the Commission permit the Legislature to determine significant policy questions rather than to concern itself with the technical problems in preparing background studies, resolving intricate legal problems and drafting needed legislation. The Commission thus enables the Legislature to accomplish legal reform that otherwise might not be made because of the heavy demands on legislative time.

Legislative Counsel Bureau

The Legislative Counsel Bureau provides legal assistance to the two houses of the Legislature and their members and committees in resolving a large volume of complex legal problems arising in connection with the legislative process, all of which must be resolved within a critical time span. The legal services furnished include rendering opinions, drafting bills, counselling, attendance as Counsel at meetings of legislative committees, and representing the Legislature in litigation. The attorney client relationship is maintained, and all work is confidential.

In addition, the Bureau prepares and provides necessary indices and appropriate tables necessary to identify legislative measures, and compiles and indexes statutes and codes.

Lieutenant Governor, Office of the

The Lieutenant Governor is a constitutional officer who becomes Governor when a vacancy occurs in the Office of the Governor. He is President of the Senate and provides leadership in the administration of programs assigned to him by statute and administrative directive.

The Lieutenant Governor chairs the Commission for Economic Development which provides support and guidance for the development of California's economy through advice and recommendations given to the Governor and the Legislature. He also serves on the three-member State Lands Commission.

Lottery, California State

Proposition 37, approved by California voters on November 6, 1984, amended the California Constitution to authorize the establishment of a statewide lottery, and enacted an initiative statute, the *California State Lottery Act of 1984*, which created the California State Lottery Commission, and gave it broad powers to oversee the operations of a statewide lottery. The primary purpose of the Act is to provide additional monies to benefit public education without the imposition of additional or increased taxes.

Mandates, Commission on State

The principal objectives of the Commission on State Mandates are: (1) Through its Administration program, to adjudicate differences between local entities and the State over the existence of a reimbursable state mandates in a particular statute or executive regulation, and (2) Through its Payments for Mandated Costs program, to ensure that funding is provided for the ongoing costs of activities which have been determined by the Commission, by the courts or by the mandating legislation itself to be reimbursable.

Maritime Academy, California

The California Maritime Academy was established in 1929 to educate officers for the United States Merchant Marine. The program has been broadened to provide well-trained, college-educated officers for the maritime industry.

The Academy offers a four-year academic program. Inherent in the goal of the Academy are the following objectives: (1) To educate each student in an accredited college program in marine transportation, marine engineering and related fields; and (2) To train each student in the skills and knowledge essential to licensing in the American Merchant Marine.

Medical Assistance Commission, California

The purpose of the Commission is to negotiate contracts with health care service providers to deliver health care services to Medi-Cal beneficiaries. The Commission's objective is to promote efficiency and cost-effectiveness in the Medi-Cal program through a system of negotiated contracts which fosters competition and maintains access to quality health care for beneficiaries.

The major activities of the Commission and its staff are the: (1) Negotiation of contracts with hospitals for inpatient services statewide; (2) Development and negotiation of contracts with county health systems; and (3) Development and negotiation of contracts with health care plans in selected areas for the provision of all covered health services to Medi-Cal beneficiaries on a per capita basis.

Mental Health, Department of

The Department of Mental Health, as the state's mental health authority, administers the *Lanterman-Petris-Short Act,* the *Short-Doyle Act* and other state and federal statutes and is responsible for the direct operation of Atascadero, Metropolitan, Napa and Patton State Hospitals. In addition, the Department manages all treatment programs for mentally disabled patients at Camarillo State Hospital.

Within the Department's overall goal of upgrading, balancing and integrating community and State-operated services, the objective of the State Hospital Services program is to complement mental health services in the community. The program provides specialized inpatient services which are, for the most part, not available in local communities.

The Department promotes access to appropriate statewide mental health services for California residents. The Department invites the participation of numerous persons and organizations such as: the California Conference of Local Mental Health Directors; the California Council on Mental Health; Local Mental Health Advisory Boards; California Mental Health Association; California Alliance for the Mentally Ill; private psychiatrists; primary health care providers; and individuals in informal networks of local support systems.

Military Department

The Military Department is responsible for protecting life and property during periods of civil emergency and natural disaster by furnishing trained units for federal mobilization and for State missions as required by the Military and Veterans Code or as directed by the Governor.

The Department is organized into a command element and three functional staff divisions to accomplish the command and management responsibilities of the Adjutant General. The Department is organized in accordance with Department of the Army and Department of the Air Force staffing patterns.

Mortgage Bond and Tax Credit Allocation Committee, California

The California Mortgage Bond Allocation Committee approves mortgage revenue bond allocations for qualified cities, counties and state agencies. The Committee also certifies specific census tracts as areas of chronic economic distress.

Motor Vehicles, Department of

The Department's objectives are to: (1) Protect the public interest in vehicle and vessel ownership, to provide various revenue collection services for state and local agencies and to provide miscellaneous registration-related services through the vehicle and vessel registration and titling process; (2) Promote highway safety and financial responsibility by regulating the issuance and retention of driver licenses and to provide personal identification services to drivers and nondrivers; and (3) Provide public protection by licensing and regulating occupations and businesses related to the manufacture, transport, sale and disposal of vehicles and occupations and businesses related to the instruction of drivers in the safe operation of vehicles on the highways.

Museum of Science and Industry

The Museum of Science and Industry is an educational, scientific and technological center administered by a nine-member board of directors appointed by the Governor. It is located in Exposition Park, a 104-acre tract just south of the central part of Los Angeles, which is owned by the State in the name of the museum. In a number of state-owned buildings, it presents a series of exhibits and conducts associated programs centering on the scientific and industrial development of the state. In addition, it has reponsibility for maintenance of the park, the museum and parking facilities for visitors to the park and museum.

Native American Heritage Commission

The Legislature created the Native American Heritage Commission in 1976 to preserve and protect California Native American cultures. The Commission's powers and duties include: identifying and cataloging geographic sites of importance to Native Americans; helping Native Americans to obtain access to these sites when necessary; protecting Native American burials and sacred sites; and ensuring that remains are treated appropriately when burials are discovered. The Commission is empowered to make recommendations to the Legislature and to other public agencies, request their services, receive grants and donations, and bring legal action when necesary to accomplish these objectives.

Occupational Informational Coordinating Committee, California

The Committee is required by statute to report, annually, to the State Job Training Coordinating Council on the design and implementation of the occupational information system in California. The Committee is responsible for fostering coordination between users and producers of occupational information and for coordinating the development of the California Occupational Information System, which provides labor market information to employment/ training program planners, career counselors, and economic developers.

Osteopathic Examiners, Board of

The Board of Osteopathic Examiners, which has existed since 1922, sets and enforces standards for licensure of California osteopathic physicians and surgeons. By conducting examinations, investigations and disciplinary proceedings, the Board ensures that recognized standards of practice and treatment are maintained by its licentiates.

Parks and Recreation, Department of

The Department of Parks and Recreation acquires, designs, develops, operates and maintains units of the State Park System. The Department is also responsible for administering both federal and state local assistance programs. These activites are directed toward the accomplishment of eight principal objectives: (1) To secure and preserve elements of the state's outstanding landscape, cultural and historical features; (2) To provide the facilities and resources which are required to fulfill the recreational demands of the people of California; (3) To provide a meaningful environment in which the people of California are given the opportunity to understand and appreciate the state's cultural, historical and natural heritage; (4) To maintain and improve the quality of California's environment; (5) To prepare and maintain a statewide recreational plan that includes an analysis of the continuing need for recreational areas and facilities and a determination of the levels of public and private responsibility required to meet those needs; (6) To encourage all levels of government and private enterprise throughout the state to participate in the planning, development and operation of recreational facilities; (7) To meet the recreational demands of a highly accelerated, urban-centered population growth, through the acquisition, development and operation of urban parks; and (8) To encourage volunteer services in the State Park System through the establishment of a recognition program of such services.

Peace Officer Standards and Training, Commission on

The Commission on Peace Officer Standards and Training is responsible for raising the level of competence of law enforcement officers in California by establishing minimum selection and training standards, improving management practices and providing financial assistance to local agencies relating to the training of their law enforcement officers.

Personnel Administration, Department of

The Department of Personnel Administration is the agency responsible for managing the nonmerit aspects of the state's personnel system. The goal of the Department is to ensure the proper administration of existing terms and conditions of employment for the state's civil service employees and to represent the Governor as the employer in all matters concerning state employer-employee relations.

It is also the responsibility of the Department to administer the personnel classification plan, and to provide for the compensation, terms and conditions of employment, as well as the development and training of the State's management team and employees not represented in the collective bargaining process.

Personnel Board, State

The State Personnel Board manages and oversees the merit apects of the civil service system for state government and is responsible for serving the personnel needs of state agencies and improving personnel practices and procedures.

The Board, within the framework of a merit system, oversees all aspects of the merit employment system, conducts recruitment efforts, develops examining techniques to select and rank qualified applicants, receives and resolves appeals on medical issues, discrimination complaints and adverse action; and provides leadership in personnel management, practices and procedures. The Board also coordinates and evaluates affirmative action/ equal employment opportunity efforts within state departments. In addition, the State Personnel Board administers the Career Opportunities Development Program, a program which is designed to provide public service jobs for welfare recipients.

Pilot Commissioners, Board of

The Board of Pilot Commissioners (for the Bays of San Francisco, San Pablo and Suisun) is responsible for providing qualified pilots for vessels entering or leaving those bays. The seven member board is appointed by the Governor and administers the program of licensing and regulating pilots by training pilots, conducting examinations and acting on complaints.

Planning and Research, Office of

The Office of Planning and Research assists the Governor and his Administration in planning, research and liaison with local government, education and community interest and to facilitate implementation of the decisions made within the Administration. In addition, the office has statutory responsibilities relating to state planning, permit assistance, and environmental and federal project review procedures.

Postsecondary Education Commission, California

The California Postsecondary Education Commission is responsible for planning for and coordinating education beyond high school. The Commission provides policy analyses, advice and recommendations to the Legislature and the Governor on statewide policy and funding regarding colleges, universities and other postsecondary institutions. Among its major responsibilities are the review of proposed new academic and vocational education facilities and programs, recommendations on the need for and location of new campuses and off-campus centers, identification of potential barriers to diversification of students and faculty, the operation of a statewide postsecondary information system, selective evaluation of segmental budget requests, the development and annual update of a five-year plan for postsecondary education, publication of reports on the condition of independent institutions and other issues.

Prison Terms, Board of

The Board considers parole release and establishes the length and conditions of parole for all persons sentenced to prison under the Indeterminate Sentence Law, persons sentenced to prison for a term of less than life under Penal Code section 1168 (b), and for persons serving sentence of life with possibility of parole. The Board also reviews the sentences of all determinately sentenced prisoners and may recommend to the court that the sentence be recalled and the prisoner resentenced.

The Board may suspend or revoke the parole of any prisoner who has violated parole. The Board determines the necessity for recission or postponement of parole dates for persons sentenced to prison for life, persons sentenced under Penal Code section 1168, and persons sentenced to prison under the Indeterminate Sentence Law. The Board may waive parole for any prisoner and may discharge any prisoner prior to the expiration of the statutory maximum parole period. Upon request of persons determinately sentenced, the Board reviews the length and conditions of parole imposed by the Department of Corrections and the Department's denial of good time credit, and may modify the Department's decision. The Board also advises the Governor on applications for clemency.

Public Defender, State

The Office of the State Public Defender was created in July 1976 to represent those entitled to representation at public expense. The State Public Defender has offices in Sacramento, San Francisco and Los Angeles to provide a statewide capability to represent indigents in the State appellate courts.

The State Public Defender, in conjunction with court appointed legal counsel, represents persons who are financially unable to employ counsel in the following matters: (1) An appeal, petition for hearing or rehearing to an appellate court or petition for certiorari to the United States Supreme Court or a petition for executive clemency from a judgment relating to criminal or juvenile court proceedings; (2) Petitions for an extraordinary writ or action for relief relating to a final judgment of conviction or wardship; (3) Proceedings after a judgment of death; (4) Proceedings in which an inmate of a State prison is charged with an offense where the county public defender has declined to represent the inmate; and (5) Any proceeding where a person is entitled to representation at public expense.

Public Employees' Retirement System

The Public Employees' Retirement System (PERS) administers a group of separate, but related, benefits for more than 800,000 past and present public employees in California. This grouping consists of retirement, disability and death benefits; administration of Social Security coverage for state employees; and the development negotiation and administration of contracts with a number of health maintenance organizations, group hospital and medical insurance plans.

Participants in the system's programs include constitutional officers of the State, members of the Legislature, judges, State employees, most school employees who are not teachers, volunteer firefighters and any other public employees whose employer has contracted for benefits administration by PERS.

Public Employment Relations Board

The objective of the Public Employment Relations Board is to promote the improvement of personnel management and employer-employee relations by working to: (1) Prevent and remedy unlawful acts and conduct of employers and employee organizations; and (2) Determine and implement, through secret ballot elections, the free, democratic choice by employees as to whether they wish to be represented by a union in dealing with public school employers (pre-kindergarten-community colleges), the State of California, the University of California, the California State University and Hastings College of Law.

Public Utilities Commission

The objectives of the Public Utilities Commission are to: (1) Provide the public with the lowest reasonable rates for services by utility and transportation companies; (2) Make certain that utility and transportation companies render adequate service and have sufficient facilities to meet the needs of the public; (3) Ensure that the public has stable, efficient utility and transportation services by controlling and limiting entry into the field of those applicants with financial responsibility and demonstrated capability to render adequate service; (4) Promote public safety and accident reduction by establishing and enforcing safety regulations for utility and transportation companies, as well as for railroad highway grade crossings; and (5) Determine the just compensation for the acquisition of utility or transportation company property by political subdivisions of the state.

Real Estate, Department of

The primary objectives of the Department of Real Estate are to: (1) Protect the public in offerings of subdivided property; (2) Guarantee that licensed individuals conducting real estate transactions are competent and qualified; (3) Prevent fraud, deceit and misrepresentation in the real estate marketplace by assisting the public through the investigation of complaints; and (4) Educate the public and professional communities regarding the laws and regulations governing the handling of real estate transactions.

Rehabilitation, Department of

The Department of Rehabilitation is the principal state agency that helps people with disabilities reach social and economic independence. The primary goal of the Department is to rehabilitate and place into suitable employment, persons with physical and mental handicaps.

The objectives of the Department are to: (1) Provide restorative, educational and supportive services to clients through vocational rehabilitation counselors; (2) Advocate for the rights and opportunities of the disabled; (3) Develop small business opportunities for the blind and severely disabled; (4) Eliminate architectural, transportation and attitudinal barriers to social and economic integration; (5) Support services and programs provided by community rehabilitation facilities and other local level resources; and (6) Provide prevocational services to persons with disabilities who are not ready for vocational rehabilitation programs.

San Francisco Bay Conservation and Development Commission

The San Francisco Bay Conservation and Development Commission was created in 1965 to provide a regional approach to protecting the public interest in the San Francisco Bay; to ensure the beneficial use of the most valuable single natural resource of the entire region and to provide a democratic and politically responsive process through which the bay and its shoreline can be managed as a single unit.

Santa Monica Mountains Conservancy

The Santa Monica Mountains Conservancy was created in 1979, to implement the Santa Monica Mountains Comprehensive Plan by developing programs for full fee or less than fee acquisition, and restoration or consolidation of lands in the Santa Monica Mountains Zone for park, recreation or conservation purposes.

Savings and Loan, Department of

The principal objectives of the Department of Savings and Loan are to protect the public's savings and investment funds held by state associations, to assure compliance by associations with laws and regulations including those involving consumer protection and anti-discrimination, and to assure the continued financial growth of these associations consistent with public need and convenience.

Secretary of State

The Secretary of State, a constitutional office, is the Chief Election Officer of the State and is responsible for the administration and enforcement of election laws. The office is also responsible for the administration and enforcement of laws pertaining to filing documents associated with corporations, limited partnerships and perfection of security agreements. In addition, the office is responsible for appointment of notaries public, enforcement of notary laws and preservation of documents and records having historical significance. All documents filed are a matter of public record and of historical importance. They are available through prescibed procedures for public review and certification as to authenticity.

Seismic Safety Commission

The purpose of the Seismic Safety Commission is to improve earthquake safety in California. To accomplish this, the Commission works with federal, state and local agencies, as well as the private sector, on a variety of activities including issuing policy studies, sponsoring legislation, and coordinating seismic safety activities through oversight and leadership. The Commission is also responsible for: (1) Annually revising the California Earthquake Hazards Reduction Program; (2) Implementing a program which requires local governments to inventory hazardous buildings, develop a mitigation plan, and report to the Commission; (3) Reviewing the state's progress in preparing for the inevitable earthquakes; and (4) Pursuing programs to strengthen state-owned buildings that lack seismic resistance.

Social Services, Department of

The Department of Social Services administers four major program areas: Welfare Program Operations, Social Services, Community Care Licnesing and Disability Evaluation.

The goals of the Department are to: (1) Ensure the delivery of payments and benefits and provide services to foster self-sufficiency, with human dignity and equity, to welfare recipients, with effectiveness in terms of accuracy of payments and with efficiency in terms of the lowest possible administrative costs; (2) Provide social services to California's elderly, blind, disabled and other adults and children, to protect them from abuse, neglect, exploitation and to help families stay together; (3) Regulate group homes, nurseries and preschools, foster homes, half-way houses, day care centers and homes to assure the public that all such California facilities meet established standards for health and safety; and (4) Evaluate the disability of applicants for various *Social Security Act* programs and State disability programs, in an efficient, effective and equitable manner, to ensure that eligibility exists.

Status of Women, Commission on the

The Commission was established in 1971 as a permanent state agency to eliminate inequities in laws, practices and conditions which affect women. The Commission implements its mandate by examining bills introduced in the Legislature which affect women's rights; maintaining and distributing information to the public on needs of women; developing and maintaining liaison with government agencies and advisory bodies; and providing technical and consultative assistance to organizations which assist women.

Emphasis is on economic issues, employment, child care/support/custody, health services, problems of violence against women, minority/older women and homemakers' rights.

Stephen P. Teale Data Center

The Stephen P. Teale Data Center is the State's general purpose computing service bureau, assisting state agencies in achieving program objectives through the application of advanced information systems technology. Since the Center's establishment in 1972, it has continually experienced growth in the overall demand for information processing services and an increase in the number of client departments it serves.

Student Aid Commission

The primary purpose of the Commission is to ensure the effective and efficient administration of federal and state authorized financial aid programs including grant, work study and loan programs for students attending California postsecondary educational institutions. The Commission has a responsibility to provide leadership on financial aid issues and make public policy recommendations concerning financial aid programs.

To meet these responsibilities, the Commission compiles information on student financial aid issues, evaluates the effectiveness of its programs, conducts research assessing California's financial aid needs, engages in long-range planning as a foundation for program improvement and disseminates information to parents, students and education institutions throughout California.

Summer School for the Arts, California State

The California State Summer School for the Arts was created to provide California high school students who have demonstrated exceptional talent and excellence in the arts with intensive instruction through a multi-disciplinary, residential summer training program.

The School allows students to choose from six major disciplines of study: Creative Writing, Dance, Film/Video, Music, Theatre Arts and Visual Arts. The program provides a training ground for future artists aspiring to careers in the state's arts and entertainment industries.

Tahoe Conservancy, California

The California Tahoe Conservancy was established in 1984. It's objective is to develop and implement programs to maintain an equilibrium between the natural endowment and the man-made environment of the Lake Tahoe region. This involves a program of acquisition and management of land for the purposes of protecting the natural environment, provision of public access and recreational facilities and preservation of wildlife habitat areas. The Conservancy is designated as the principal agency for implementation of the Lake *Tahoe Acquisitions Bond Act.*

Task Force to Promote Self-Esteem, and Personal and Social Responsibility

The California Task Force to Promote Self-Esteem, and Personal and Social Responsibility was created in 1986. The 25 member task force is mandated to study and make findings concerning the relationships between health, self-esteem, personal responsibility and social problems. The task force is also required to recommend ways in which study findings can be incorporated into public policy and programs, non-governmental institutions and personal awareness. The task force is scheduled to become inoperative on July 1, 1990.

Teacher Credentialing, Commission on

The Commission was established in 1970, with the specific charge of ensuring excellence in education by encouraging high standards of quality and diversity. The Commission carries out its program of standards for the preparation and licensing of teachers through six program elements: Credential Issuance/Information; Certification Standards/Program Approval; Program Monitoring and Evaluation; Examinations; Professional Standards; and Agency Administration.

Teachers' Retirement System, State

The State Teachers' Retirement System (STRS) was formed in 1963 and has exclusive control over the investment and administration of the Teachers' Retirement Fund, makes rules, sets policies and has the power and authority to hear and determine all facts pertaining to application for benefits under the retirement system. STRS is responsible for the determination, computation and payment of benefits to members, retirees, and beneficiaries, and for the distribution of information to all members, employers and other interested groups. STRS also provides for survivor, disability and death benefits under specific conditions.

Traffic Safety, Office of

The Office of Traffic Safety (OTS) was established in 1967 to administer the California Traffic Safety Program. Under the provisions of State law, the OTS carries out a wide range of activities designed to reduce deaths, injuries and property damage that result from traffic accidents. The activities include: (1) Developing the California Highway Safety Plan which identifies major traffic safety problems, appropriate grant agreements; and (2) Coordinating statewide traffic safety programs and activities.

The major areas of traffic safety activity are alcohol and drugs, police traffic services, occupant protection, traffic records, traffic engineering and emergency medical services.

Transportation Commission, California

The California Transportation Commission advises and assists the Secretary of the Business, Transportation and Housing Agency and the Legislature in formulating and evaluating state policies and plans for California's transportation programs. The Commission is also an active participant in the initiation and development of state and federal legislation that seeks to secure financial stability for the State's transportation needs.

Transportation, Department of (CALTRANS)

The Department of Transportation has four primary programs: Aeronautics, Highway Transportation, Mass Transportation and Transportation Planning.

The Aeronautics program is concerned with airport and heliport safety, better ground access to airports, funding for improvements to airports and noise control. The program also helps small and medium-sized communities acquire and maintain air services.

The Highway Transportation program's highest priorities are maintaining and rehabilitating roads and highways and building new projects as set forth in the five-year State Transportation Improvement Program

The Mass Transportation program assists local government in providing public transportation, and funds certain commuter and intercity rail services and local guideways.

The Transportation Planning program plans for future development and integration of the elements of the state's transportation systems.

Treasurer, State

The State Treasurer, a constitutional office, provides banking services for State government with a minimum interest and service cost and a maximum yield on investments. The Treasurer is responsible for the custody of all money and securities belonging to or held in trust by the State; investment of temporarily idle State monies; administration of the sale of State bonds, their redemption and interest payments; and payment of warrants drawn by the State Controller and other state agencies. The Treasurer is also responsible for reviewing the financial soundness of certain local district construction financing proposals.

University of California

The University of California conducts higher education programs in four major areas: (1) Instruction of qualified individuals, by sharing with them knowledge and skills and by helping them to experience with their instructor the processes of developing and testing new hypotheses and fresh interpretations of knowledge; (2) Research directed toward advancing the understanding of arts and sciences and the interpretation of human history; (3) Education for professional careers-education grounded in the understanding of relevant sciences, literature, and research methods by which the boundaries of knowledge are pushed back; and (4) Public service contributing to the fulfillment of the university's obligation to disseminate knowledge and bringing to faculty and students the stimulation of applying their knowledge and special skill to the problems of modern life.

Veterans Affairs, Department of

The Department of Veterans Affairs has a threefold overall objective to: (1) Provide comprehensive assistance to veterans and dependents of veterans in obtaining benefits and rights to which they may be entitled under State and federal laws; (2) Afford California veterans the opportunity of becoming homeowners through the long-term low-interest loans available under the Cal-Vet farm and home loan program; and (3) Provide support for the Veterans Home of California where eligible veterans may live in a retirement community and where complete nursing care and hospitalization are provided.

Vocational Education, California State Council on

The Council is responsible for: (1) Evaluating the adequacy and effectiveness of statewide vocational education programs and services; (2) Advising the State Board of Education, the Board of Governors of the California Community Colleges, the Governor, the Legislature, and other agencies on matters relevant to vocational education policy, programs, and plans; and (3) Analyzing and reporting to the Governor and Legislature on the distribution of spending for vocational education in the state and the availability of vocational education services within the state.

Waste Management Board, California

The purpose of the California Waste Management Board is to establish and maintain a comprehensive waste management and resource recovery policy for nonhazardous waste. The Board's major objectives are to protect the public health and safety, to preserve the environment, to reduce the volume of landfill disposal of nonhazardous wastes and to encourage the timely planning and siting of adequate solid waste facilities.

These objectives are accomplished through enforcement of state standards at waste facilities by Board designated local agencies; technical assistance to local governments and to private entities; review and approval of county solid waste management plans; studies and investigation of new or improved methods of solid waste handling, disposal or reclamation; public awareness and education programs; studies of methods to reduce and control litter; development and implementation of a statewide information and retrieval system; and promotion of alternatives to landfill disposal.

Water Resources Control Board, State

The objectives and responsibilities of the State Water Resources Control Board and the nine Regional Water Quality Control Boards are to preserve and enhance the quality of California's water resources and to assure their proper allocation and effective utilization. These objectives are achieved through two action programs: water quality and water rights.

Water Resources, Department of

The role of the Department of Water Resources is to protect, conserve, develop and manage California's water. The Department has a major responsibility for supplying suitable water for personal use, irrigation, industry, recreation, power generation and fish and wildlife. The Department also has major responsibilities for flood management and dam safety.

Wildlife Conservation Board

The Wildlife Conservation Board is involved in acquiring, conserving developing, improving and providing access to our natural resources to accommodate the needs of the people who use and enjoy the state's fish and wildlife resources and compatible activities.

Through its staff, the Board conducts necessary investigations and studies to determine the areas within the state most essential and suitable for wildlife production and preservation and which will provide recreational advantages. As a result of such studies, the Board determines which lands or rights in lands or waters should be acquired by the State to further the wildlife conservation and recreation program. The Board develops fishing piers and fishing access sites at lakes, on the ocean and along the state's waterways and aqueducts.

World Trade Commission, California State

The objective of the Commission is to encourage international trade and development. The Commission is governed by leading representatives of

California government and private industry, and promotes policies and programs that expand opportunities for California's firms doing business internationally.

Youth Authority, Department of the

The primary mission of the Youth Authority is to protect society from the consequences of criminal activity by: (1) Providing a broad range of services to youthful offenders committed to the Department, directed towards the permanent reduction of criminal behavior; (2) Assisting local criminal justice agencies with efforts to combat crime and delinquency; (3) Encouraging the development of local crime and delinquency prevention programs.

Youthful Offender Parole Board

The Youthful Offender Parole Board is the paroling authority for young persons committed by the courts to the Department of the Youth Authority. The Board uses a classification system which designates young offenders by categories of offense. The categories guide the Board in setting parole consideration dates, that is, the presumptive period of incarceration after which a person can be released to parole without being a danger to society.

The hearings have been categorized as follows: Initial Hearings; Referrals to Parole which includes approval, denial or requests for parole plans; Miscellaneous Hearings which include annual reviews, disciplinary hearings and other hearings conducted in the institutions or in the locale where wards are on parole; and Parole Hearings which include probable cause violation/disposition, rescission and discharge hearings.

State Organization Chart

Figure 1

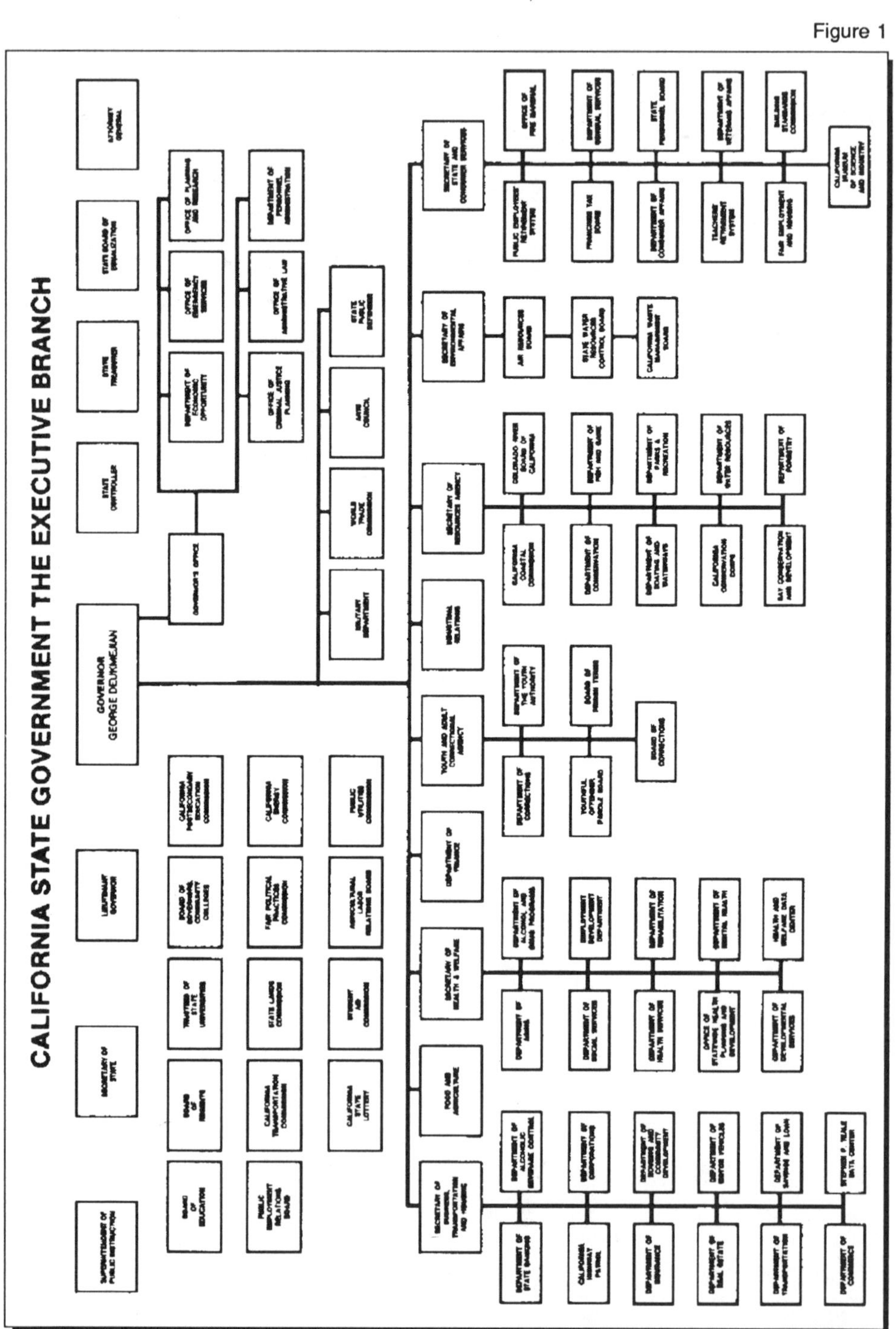

Chapter 2:

What Kind of Work Do You Want to Do?

Where Do You Start?

Now that you've made a list of departments you'd like to work for, the next step is to test for the position you want. The myth that all state jobs are just alike is totally untrue. There are hundreds of very different and sometimes specialized civil service classifications. As you have seen from the preceding chapter, state employees work among some 128 Departments, Boards and Commissions and no two are alike in terms of their purpose and the segment of the California population they serve.

Before you can apply for any permanent civil service job with the State of California, you must first successfully compete in an examination. Once you obtain at least the minimum passing score, you will be placed on an *employment* (or hiring) *list.*

In order to maximize your job search efforts and not waste time filling out applications for tests you don't yet qualify for, carefully review each classification's specifications and ONLY apply to take exams in civil service classifications which you believe you can qualify to take.

You've got literally hundreds to choose from! Review the listings that start on page 44 carefully, and with an open mind. Don't limit yourself to classification titles that simply sound interesting or familiar; on the other hand, don't disregard those that sound boring either. For example, even though classification titles such as *Office Assistant* and *Staff Services Analyst* are generic and non-descript, they are actually entry level, upwardly mobile positions that do not require specialized areas of education or experience.

Your primary goal is to take all of the civil service examinations that you can qualify for—anything just to get your foot in the door!

Each of the listed classifications has a *specification* which lists the required qualifications for an individual to participate in examinations to establish an employment list for that classification.

The State Personnel Board (SPB) will provide these specifications at your request. You can walk into one of the SPB offices and request the particular specifications you're interested in and the SPB staff will give them to you, or you may telephone the offices at either 916-322-2530 or 213-620-2770, and request up to five specifications. The SPB will mail up to five specifications to you. Make sure you have the correct name and spelling of the classifications before you call. You may also mail your request for specifications to:

State Personnel Board
General Files
801 Capitol Mall
P.O. Box 944201
Sacramento, CA 94244-2010

Some Classifications Don't Require Testing

There are some positions in state service that do not require a civil service test: Seasonal positions; Student Assistant positions and Graduate Student Assistant positions. These are paid positions. Even though they are not permanent, they can be an excellent way to become familiar with state service, meet people, and make contacts within the state civil service system for future reference. This is how I got my start in civil service.

Seasonal

Every year, there are about 10,000 *seasonal positions* available in California state government. Although most coincide with summer and school vacations, some positions are available throughout the year. These are italicized in the alphabetical listing of civil service classifications on beginning on the next page.

To apply for a seasonal position, contact the personnel office of the department you're interested in to find out if there are any seasonal positions available. You should make these contacts very early in mid April or May, since other students and returning seasonals will also be seeking employment during this peak season.

If you worked in a seasonal position during any 12-month period, you will have hiring perference over all other applicants who did not work as seasonals during the previous year. If you fall into this category, call your former supervisor or the personnel office in the department where you worked to get further information.

In many seasonal positions, jobseekers who are receiving Aid to Families with Dependent Children (AFDC) have hiring preference over those who are not receiving AFDC. State departments are required to inform the Employment Development Department (EDD) of all openings for seasonal positions, and request that EDD refer applications of jobseekers receiving AFDC benefits. If you are receiving AFDC benefits and are interested in applying for a seasonal position, contact your local EDD office (check listing on page 182 to find where the nearest office is located).

Student Assistants and Graduate Student Assistants

Student Assistant and *Graduate Student Assistant* positions exist in a number of state departments throughout the state. They can be either full time or part time, and are usually from three to nine months duration, and some are longer.

To qualify for a Student Assistant position, you must be enrolled in a college or university. Your hourly pay will be based on the number of semester/quarter units you have completed.

To qualify for a Graduate Student Assistant position, you must have applied for or be enrolled in a graduate studies program at a college or university. To apply for either position, you'll need to contact the personnel office(s) of the department(s) you're interested in to find out about potential job openings.

A

Able Seaman
Account Clerk II
Account Manager, California Exposition and State Fair
Accountant I (Specialist)
Accountant I (Supervisor)
Accountant Trainee
Accounting Administrator (Specialist)
Accounting Administrator (Supervisor)
Accounting Administrator II & III
Accounting Analyst
Accounting Officer (Specialist)
Accounting Officer (Supervisor)
Accounting Specialist, Fair Political Practices Commission
Accounting Technician
Activity Coordinator, Veterans Home and Medical Center
Actuarial Statistician
Actuary
Actuary, Public Employees Retirement System
Actuary, State Compensation Insurance Fund
Adaptive Drive Evaluation Specialist, Department of Rehabilitation
Adaptive Equipment Supervisor
Administrative Advisor II (CEA)
Administrative Advisor to State Controller(CEA)
Administrative Assistant, California State Fair and Exposition
Administrative Assistant I & II
Administrative Assistant, Fair Political Practices Commission
Administrative Law Judge I, Department of Social Services
Administrative Law Judge I, Office of Administrative Hearings
Administrative Law Judge I & II, Public Employment Relations Board
Administrative Law Judge I & II, Public Utilities Commission
Administrative Law Judge I & II, State Personnel Board
Administrative Law Judge II (Specialist), Department of Social Services
Administrative Law Judge II (Specialist), Office of Administrative Hearings
Administrative Law Judge II (Supervisor), Department of Social Services
Administrative Law Judge II (Supervisor), Office of Administrative Hearings
Administrative Law Judge, Department of Health Services

Administrative Law Judge, Unemployment Insurance Appeals Board
Administrative Officer IV, Department of Water Resources
Administrative Officer, California Museum of Afro-American History and Culture
Administrative Officer, District Agriculture Association
Administrative Program Manager, California Housing Insurance Fund (CEA)
Administrative Service Officer I & II
Administrative Services Intern
Administrator for Academic Planning and Development, California Community Colleges
Administrator for Facilities Planning and Utilization, California Community Colleges
Administrator for Fiscal Planning and Administration, California Community Colleges
Administrator for Student Services Planning and Development, California Community Colleges
Administrator for Vocational Education, California Community Colleges
Administrator I, II, III & IV, Franchise Tax Board
Administrator I & II, Fair Employment and Housing
Administrator of School Apportionments, Grants and Fiscal Assistance
Administrator, Orientation Center for the Blind
Administrator, Veterans Home and Medical Center
Administrator, Economics Program, Museum of Science and Industry
Administrator, Industrial Education Program, Museum of Science and Industry
Administrator, Science Program, Museum of Science and Industry
Adoptions Caseworker
Adoptions Caseworker (Hispanic)
Adoptions Supervisor I & II
Adult Education Administrator I
Adult Education Consultant
Aging Programs Analyst I & II
Agricultural Aide (Seasonal)
Agricultural Biological Technician
Agricultural Biologist
Agricultural Chemist I & II
Agricultural Chemist III (Specialist)
Agricultural Chemist III (Supervisor)
Agricultural Education Administrator
Agricultural Education Consultant
Agricultural Inspector I, II & III (Seasonal)
Agricultural Inspector II & III (Permanent Intermittent)
Agricultural Laboratory Microscopist
Agricultural Marketing Technician
Agricultural Pest Control Specialist
Agricultural Pest Control Supervisor
Agricultural Services Technician I & II
Agricultural Survey Interviewer I, II & III
Agriculture Program Supervisor I & II (Inspection Services)
Agriculture Program Supervisor II (Market News)
Agriculture Program Supervisor II, III & IV (Pest Management)

Agriculture Program Supervisor III (Chemistry Laboratory Services)
Agriculture Program Supervisor III & IV (Pest Prevention)
Air Operations Officer I, II, & III
Air Operations Officer I, II, & III (Maintenance)
Air Pollution Research Specialist
Air Pollution Specialist
Air Resources Engineer
Air Resources Engineering Associate
Air Resources Field Representative I, II, & III
Air Resources Technician I & II
Aircraft Mechanic
Alcohol & Drug Program Analyst I & II
Alcohol & Drug Program Manger
Alcohol & Drug Program Specialist
Alcohol & Drug Program Supervisor
Alcohol & Drug Program Administrator
Alcohol Program Analyst I, II, III & IV
Alcohol Program Specialist
Alcohol Treatment Counselor Veterans Home and Medical Center
Alcoholic Beverage Control Counsel I, II & III
American Indian Education Assistant
American Indian Education Consultant
Animal Technician I, II, III & IV
Appeals Assistant
Appeals Supervisor I & II, Unemployment Insurance Appeals Board
Apprenticeship Consultant
Aquatic Specialist
Archeological Aide (Seasonal)
Archeological Project Leader (Seasonal)
Archeological Specialist (Seasonal)
Architectural Assistant
Architectural Associate
Architectural Associate, Health Facilities
Architectural Designer

Classifications Requiring a High School Education or Less

Attendant, Resident Schools
Audiologist Aide
Bookbinder I
CalTrans Highway Maintenance Worker
CalTrans Landscape Maintenance Worker
Correctional Officer
Dispatcher-Clerk
Drafting Aide I
Fairground Aide, District Fairs
Fire Fighter I
Food Service Worker I
Heavy Equipment Mechanic Apprentice
Hospital Peace Officer
Hospital Worker
Junior Engineering Technician
Key Data Operator
Laboratory Assistant
Laborer
Office Assistant
Park Maintenance Assistant
Security Guard
State Police Officer Cadet (Female)
State Police Officer Cadet (Male)
State Traffic Officer Cadet (Female)
State Traffic Officer Cadet (Male)
Teaching Assistant

Architectural Project Production Analyst
Architectural Senior
Archivist I & II
Area Administrator, Division of Apprenticeship Standards
Area Manager, Exclusion and Detection
Area Manager, CAL/OSHA Consultation Service
Area Office Administrator, Property Tax Division
Area Operations Supervisor, California State Fair
Area Supervisor I & II, Office Machine Service
Area Supervisor, Rehabilitation Bureau
Armory Custodian I, II & III
Arson and Bomb Investigator
Arson and Bomb Investigator Assistant
Arts Program Administrator, Department of Corrections
Assistant Consultant in Teacher Preparation
Assistant Administrative Analyst, Accounting Systems
Assistant Agricultural Economist
Assistant Aircraft Parts Manager/Mechanic
Assistant Area Supervisor, Office Machine Service
Assistant Arts Grants Administrator
Assistant Aviation Consultant
Assistant Boating Administrator
Assistant Boundary DeterminationOfficer
Assistant Box Office Manager, Cow Palace
Assistant Bridge Engineer
Assistant Bureau Chief, Division of Law Enforcement, Department Of Justice
Assistant CalTrans Administrator (Specialist)
Assistant CalTrans Administrator (Supervisor)
Assistant Chancellor, Programs, California Community Colleges (CEA)
Assistant Chemical Testing Engineer
Assistant Chief Administrative Law Judge, Public Utilities Commission
Assistant Chief Athletic Inspector
Assistant Chief, Buildings & Grounds Division
Assistant Chief, Central Program Services
Assistant Chief, Central Program Services (Educational)
Assistant Chief Counsel
Assistant Chief Counsel, Department of General Services
Assistant Chief, Division of Accounting, State Controller's Office
Assistant Chief, Division of Apprenticeship Standards
Assistant Chief, Division of Industrial Accidents, (CEA)
Assistant Chief, Division of Local Government Fiscal Affairs, State Controller's Office
Assistant Chief, Legal Division, Department of Transportation
Assistant Chief of Education, Correctional Program
Assistant Chief, Public Utilities Counsel
Assistant Chief, Rehabilitation Facilities Development
Assistant Chief, Transportation Division, Public Utilities Commission
Assistant Chief, Vector Control Section
Assistant Chief, Business Enterprise Program
Assistant Chief, CAL/OSHA Consultation Service
Assistant Chief, California Highway Patrol
Assistant Chief, Conservation and Liquidation Division, Department of Insurance

Assistant Chief, Division of Corporate Filing and Services
Assistant Chief, Division of Labor Standards Enforcement
Assistant Chief, Division of Occupational Safety and Health
Assistant Chief, Division of Tax Administration, State Controller's Office
Assistant Chief, Division of Unclaimed Property, State Controller's Office
Assistant Chief, Elections and Political Reform Division, Secretary of State's Office
Assistant Chief, Extractive Development Program, State Lands Commission
Assistant Chief, Food and Drug Branch
Assistant Chief, Local Environmental Health Programs
Assistant Chief, Producer Licensing, Department of Insurance
Assistant Chief, Sanitary Engineering Section
Assistant Chief, Telecommunications Division
Assistant Civil Engineer
Assistant Civil Maintenance Superintendent, Water Resources
Assistant Clerk
Assistant Commissioner, California Highway Patrol (CEA)
Assistant Commissioner, Legal Programs, Department of Corporations (CEA)
Assistant Control System Engineer
Assistant Criminal Justice Specialist
Assistant Development Specialist
Assistant Director (Finance), Public Utilities Commission
Assistant Director (Medical), Department of Health Services (CEA)
Assistant Director, Commission on Peace Officer Standards and Training
Assistant Director of Child Development
Assistant Director of Dietetics
Assistant Director, Health Training Center Department o Mental Health
Assistant Director, Public Utilities Commission
Assistant Division Chief/Program Manager, Department of Motor Vehicles
Assistant Division Chief/Regional Executive Officer, Water Resources Control Board
Assistant Division Chief, Air Resources Board
Assistant Energy Facility Siting Planner
Assistant Engineer, Water Resources
Assistant Engineering Specialist (Civil)
Assistant Engineering Specialist (Electrical)
Assistant Engineering Specialist (Sanitary)
Assistant Engineering Specialist (Utilities)
Assistant Equipment Engineer
Assistant Estimator, California Housing Finance Agency
Assistant Examination Proctor
Assistant Executive Director, California Transportation Commission
Assistant Executive Director, Commission on Peace Officer Standards & Training (CEA)
Assistant Executive Officer I & II, Professional & Vocational Regulation

Assistant Executive Officer, Wildlife Conservation Board
Assistant Executive Officer, Standards & Training,
Board of Corrections
Assistant Executive Officer, State Athletic Commission
Assistant Executive Secretary, California
Law Revision Commission
Assistant Executive Secretary, Districts Securities Commission
Assistant Executive Secretary, Fish & Game Commission
Assistant Field Representative I, School Administration
Assistant Field Representative II,
School Administration (Specialist)
Assistant Field Representative II,
School Administration (Supervisory)
Assistant Finance Budget Analyst
Assistant Fish and Game License Officer
Assistant Food Manager (Correctional Facility)
Assistant Forest Property Appraiser
Assistant General Counsel I & II, Agricultural Labor
Relations Board
Assistant Geologist
Assistant Head Group Supervisor
Assistant Health Care Service Plan Analyst
Assistant Health Physicist
Assistant Hospital Administrator
Assistant Industrial Hygiene Specialist, State Compensation
Insurance Fund
Assistant Industrial Hygienist
Assistant Industrial Superintendent,
Prison Industries (Agriculture)
Assistant Industrial Superintendent,
Prison Industries (Bakery)
Assistant Industrial Superintendent,
Prison Industries (Bindery)
Assistant Industrial Superintendent,
Prison Industries (Concrete Construction)
Assistant Industrial Superintendent,
Prison Industries (Detergent)
Assistant Industrial Superintendent,
Prison Industries (Fabric Products)
Assistant Industrial Superintendent,
Prison Industries (Key Entry)
Assistant Industrial Superintendent,
Prison Industries (Knitting Mill)
Assistant Industrial Superintendent,
Prison Industries (Laundry)
Assistant Industrial Superintendent,
Prison Industries (Mattress and Bedding)
Assistant Industrial Superintendent,
Prison Industries (Meatplant Operations)
Assistant Industrial Superintendent,
Prison Industries (Metal Products)
Assistant Industrial Superintendent,
Prison Industries (Micrographics)
Assistant Industrial Superintendent,
Prison Industries (Optical Products)
Assistant Industrial Superintendent,
Prison Industries (Paper Products)

Assistant Industrial Superintendent,
Prison Industries (Poultry Abattoir)
Assistant Industrial Superintendent,
Prison Industries (Poultry Production)
Assistant Industrial Superintendent,
Prison Industries (Printing)
Assistant Industrial Superintendent,
Prison Industries (Shoe Manufacturing)
Assistant Industrial Superintendent,
Prison Industries (Swine Abattoir)
Assistant Industrial Superintendent,
Prison Industries (Swine Production)
Assistant Industrial Superintendent,
Prison Industries (Textile Mill)
Assistant Industrial Superintendent,
Prison Industries (Vehicle Reconditioning and Servicing)
Assistant Industrial Superintendent,
Prison Industries (Wood Products)
Assistant Information Officer
Assistant Investment Officer, Retirement Systems
Assistant Laboratory Chief, Public Health Laboratories
Assistant Land Agent
Assistant Land Surveyor
Assistant Landscape Architect
Assistant Leasing Officer
Assistant Legislative Coordinator, Department of Education
Assistant Manager, Land Operations
Assistant Medi-Cal Field Office Administrator
Assistant Medical Officer, State Compensation Insurance Fund
Assistant Medical Officer, State Personnel Board
Assitant Meteorologist
Assistant Mobile Equipment Superintendent
Assistant Operations Security Officer
Assistant Parking Operations Supervisor
Assistant Physical Testing Engineer
Assistant Principal Claim Auditor
Assistant Procurement Engineer
Assistant Program Chief, Administrative, Department of
Health Services
Assistant Program Review Analyst
Assistant Program Specialist, California Debt Advisory
Commission
Assistant Property Agent
Assistant Property Appraiser
Assistant Property Auditor-Appraiser
Assistant Public Health Biologist
Assistant Railroad Equipment Inspector, Public Utilties
Commission
Assistant Railroad Track Inspector, Public Utilities Commission
Assistant Rehabilitation Engineering Consultant
Assistant Right of Way Agent
Assistant Risk Analyst
Assistant Safety Engineer
Assistant Sanitarian
Assistant Seamer
Assistant Small Business Officer
Assistant Space Planner

Assistant State Park Resource Ecologist
Assistant Steel Inspector
Assistant Superintendent of Public Instruction, Director of Vocational Education (CEA)
Assistant Superintendent of Public Instruction for Child Development (CEA)
Assistant Superintendent of Public Instruction for General Education (CEA)
Assistant Superintendent of Public Instruction for Special Education (CEA)
Assistant Superintendent, Psychiatric Services, Correctional Facility
Assistant Tax Service Specialist
Assistant Telecommunications Engineer
Assistant Tourism Specialist
Assistant Transportation Engineer
Assistant Transportation Engineer, CalTrans
Assistant Transportation Operations Supervisor, Public Utilties Commission
Assistant Treasury Program Officer
Assistant Utilities Engineer
Associate Accounting Analyst
Associate Administrative Analyst (Accounting Systems)
Associate Agricultural Biologist
Associate Agricultural Economist
Associate Air Pollution Specialist
Associate Air Resources Engineer
Associate Airport Engineer
Associate Architect
Associate Arts Administrator, Department of Corrections
Associate Arts Grants Administrator
Associate Automotive Equipment Standards Engineer
Associate Aviation Consultant
Associate Boating Administrator
Associate Boundary Determination Officer
Associate Bridge Engineer
Associate Budget Analyst
Associate Business Equipment Analyst
Associate Business Management Analyst
Associate CalTrans Administrator (Specialist)
Associate CalTrans Administrator (Supervisor)
Associate Casualty Actuary
Associate Chemical Testing Engineer
Associate Chief Deputy Commission, Board of Prison Terms
Associate Civil Engineer
Associate Construction Analyst
Associate Control System Engineer
Associate Corporations Investigator
Associate Corrosion Engineer
Associate Cost Estimator, Water Resources
Associate Data Processing Analyst (Specialist)
Associate Data Processing Analyst (Supervisor)
Associate Design Officer, California Housing Finance Agency
Associate Development Specialist
Associate Direct Marketing Specialist
Associate Director, California Postsecondary Education Commission (CEA)

Associate Economic Entomologist
Associate Editor of Publications
Associate Electric Utilities Engineer
Associate Electrical Engineer
Associate Electrical Engineer, Hydraulic Structures
Associate Electrical Engineer, CalTrans
Associate Electrical Testing Engineer
Associate Electronics Engineer
Associate Engineering Geologist
Associate Engineering Personnel Examiner
Associate Environmental Hazards Scientist
Associate Environmental Planner
Associate Environmental Planner (Archeology)
Associate Environmental Planner (Architectural History)
Associate Environmental Planner (Cultural Resources)
Associate Environmental Planner (Natural Sciences)
Associate Environmental Planner (Socio Economic)
Associate Equipment Engineer
Associate Estimator of Building Construction
Associate Estimator, California Housing Finance Agency
Associate Finance Budget Analyst
Associate Fish Pathologist
Associate Fishery Biologist
Associate Forest Property Appraiser
Associate General Counsel, Unfair Labor Practices, Agricultural Labor Relations Board
Associate Geochemist
Associate Geologist
Associate Geophysicist
Associate Governmental Program Analyst
Associate Governmental Program Analyst, Fair Political Practices Commission
Associate Hazardous Materials Specialist
Associate Health Care Service Plan Analyst
Associate Health Physicist
Associate Health Planning Analyst
Associate Health Program Advisor
Associate Highway Electrical Engineer
Associate Hydraulic Engineer
Associate Industrial Hygiene Specialist, State Compensation Insurance Fund
Associate Industrial Hygienist
Associate Insect Biosystematist
Associate Insurance Examiner
Associate Insurance Investigator
Associate Insurance Policy Officer
Associate Insurance Rate Analyst
Associate Investment Analyst, California Housing Finance Agency
Associate Land Agent
Associate Land and Water Use Analyst
Associate Land Surveyor
Associate Landscape Architect
Associate Leasing Officer
Associate Life Acutary
Associate Management Analyst

Associate Management Auditor
Associate Marine Biologist
Associate Materials Analyst
Associate Materials and ResearchEngineer
Associate Mechanical Engineer
Associate Mechanical Engineer, Hydraulic Structures
Associate Mechanical Engineer, CalTrans
Associate Mechanical Testing Engineer
Associate Medical Coordinator (PesticideUse and Worker Health and Safety)
Associate Meteorologist
Associate Mineral Resources Engineer
Associate Motor Vehicle Pollution Control Engineer
Associate Oil and Gas Engineer
Associate Park and Recreation Specialist
Associate Personnel Analyst
Associate Personnel Analyst, Fair Political Practices Commission
Associate Pesticide Review Scientist
Associate Pipeline Safety Engineer
Associate Planner
Associate Plant Nematologist
Associate Plant Pathologist (Diagnostician)
Associate Plant Pathologist (Field)
Associate Power Operations and Maintenance Engineer
Associate Printing Plant Superintendent
Associate Procurement Engineer
Associate Program Review Analyst
Associate Program Specialist, California Debt Advisory Commission
Associate Programmer Analyst (Specialist)
Associate Programmer Analyst (Supervisor)
Associate Project Engineer, CalTrans
Associate Property Agent
Associate Property Appraiser
Associate Property Auditor-Appraiser
Associate Public Health Biologist
Associate Railroad Equipment Inspector, Public Utilities Commission
Associate Railroad Track Inspector, Public Utilties Commission
Associate Rehabilitation Engineering Consultant
Associate Right of Way Agent
Associate Risk Analyst
Associate Safety Engineer
Associate Safety Engineer (Construction)
Associate Safety Engineer (Electrical)
Associate Safety Engineer (Elevators)
Associate Safety Engineer (Industrial)
Associate Safety Engineer (Mining, Tunneling & Mineral Industries)
Associate Safety Engineer (Pressure Vessels)
Associate Sanitary Engineer
Associate Seed Botanist
Associate Seismologist
Associate Small Business Officer
Associate Space Planner
Associate Specification Writer, Hydraulic Structures
Associate State Park Resource Ecologist

Associate Steel Inspector (Specialist)
Associate Steel Inspector (Supervisor)
Associate Superintendent of Public Instruction (CEA)
Associate Systems Software Specialist (Supervisory)
Associate Systems Software Specialist (Technical)
Associate Tax Auditor, Board of Equalization
Associate Tax Research Specialist
Associate Telecommunications Engineer
Associate Tourism Specialist
Associate Transportation Engineer
Associate Transportation Engineer, CalTrans
Associate Transportation Engineer, CalTrans (Registered)
Associate Transportation Engineer, CalTrans (Supervisor)
Associate Transportation Operations Supervisor, Public Utilities Commission
Associate Transportation Planner
Associate Transportation Representative
Associate Treasury Program Officer
Associate Utilties Engineer
Associate Vocational Education Analyst, California Advisory Council for Vocational Education
Associate Waste Management Engineer
Associate Waste Management Specialist
Associate Water Quality Biologist
Associate Water Quality Engineer
Associate Water Resources Control Engineer
Associate Wildlife Biologist
Associate Wildlife Pathologist
Athletic Inspector
Attendant, Resident Schools
Attorney General Investigator
Attorney General Investigator, (Supervisor)
Attorney General Investigator-In-Charge
Audio-Visual Assistant
Audio-Visual Equipment Technician
Audio-Visual Specialist (Supervisory)
Audio-Visual Specialist (Technical)
Audio-Visual Technician, Museum of Science and Industry
Audiologist Aide
Audiologist I & II
Adiologist License Applicant
Auditor I
Auditor I (Hispanic)
Automated Test Systems Inspector I, II & III
Automobile Mechanic
Automobile Mechanic, Correctional Facility (Female)
Automobile Mechanic (Female)
Automobile Mechanic, Correctional Facility
Automobile Mechanic Supervisor
Automobile Mechanic Trainee
Automotive Emission Test Specialist I, II & III
Automotive Emission Test Supervisor
Automotive Equipment Operator I & II
Automotive Equipment Operator I, Correctional Facility (Female)
Automotive Equipment Operator I (Female)
Automotive Equipment Operator I & II, Correctional Facility

Automotive Equipment Standards Engineer
Automotive Pool Attendant I, II & III
Automotive Pool Manager I & II
Automotive Pool Manager I, Correctional Facility
Automotive Technician I, II & III
Automotive Technician I (Female)
Automotive Technician Trainee
Automotive Technician Trainee (Female)

B

Baker I & II
Baker I & II, Correctional Facility
Bank Examiner
Bank Examiner IV (Specialist)
Bank Examiner IV (Supervisor)
Barber, Correctional Facility
Barbershop Manager
Bay Development Design Analyst, San Francisco Bay Conservation and Development Commission
Bay-Delta Fishery Project Manager
Beaty Shop Manager
Bilingual/Migrant Education Administrator I
Bilingual/Migrant Education Assistant
Bilingual/Migrant Education Consultant
Biological Scientific Illustrator
Biomedical Engineer
Biostatistician II, III & IV
Board Coordinating Parole Agent, Youthful Offender Parole Board
Board Counsel I & II, ALRB
Boat Operator
Boating Facilities Manager I, II & III
Boating Programs Trainee
Book Repairer
Bookbinder I, II, III & IV
Bookkeeping Machine Operator I & II
Boundary Determination Technician
Box Office Manager, Cow Palace
Brace Maker
Branch Chief I & II, Inspection Services
Branch Chief, Animal Health
Branch Chief, Chemistry Laboratory Services
Branch Chief, Livestock Identification
Branch Chief, Marketing Services
Branch Chief, Measurement Standards
Branch Chief, Meat Inspection
Branch Chief, Milk and Dairy Foods Control
Branch Chief, Pest Management and Prevention
Brand Inspector
Bridge Architectural Assistant
Bridge Architectural Associate
Bridge Archictectural Trainee
Bridge Painting Inspector I
Budget Officer, Department of Water Resources
Budget Technician I & II
Building Maintenance Worker
Building Maintenance Worker, Correctional Facility (Female)

Building Maintenance Worker (Female)
Building Maintenance Worker, Correctional Facility
Bureau Chief, Consumer Policy Issues, Department of Insurance
Bureau Chief, Division of Law Enforcement, Department of Justice
Bureau Manager, Investigations, Department of Motor Vehicles
Business Education Administrator I
Business Education Consultant
Business Enterprise Consultant I & II
Business Equipment Analyst
Business Equipment Service Supervisor
Business Equipment Service Technician
Business Equipment Service Technician, Electronic
Business Equipment Service Technician Trainee
Business Management Trainee
Business Manager, Correctional Facility
Business Manager I & II
Business Service Assistant
Business Service Officer I & II (Specialist)
Business Service Officer I & II (Supervisor)
Business Service Officer III & IV
Business Taxes Administrator I, II, III, IV & V
Business Taxes Compliance Specialist
Business Taxes Compliance Supervisor I,II & III
Business Taxes Representative
Business Taxes Representative I & II
Butcher-Meat Cutter II, Correctional Facility
Buyer I & II

C

CEA I, II, III, IV & V
CalTrans Electrician I (Female)
Calculating Machine Operator (Key Driven)
California Indian Housing Manager I & II
California Indian Housing Representative I & II
California Maritime Academy Business Manager
CalTrans Bridge Maintenance Supervisor
CalTrans Electrical Superintendent I, II, & III
CalTrans Electrical Supervisor
CalTrans Electrical Technician
CalTrans Electrical Technician (Female)
CalTrans Electrician I & II
CalTrans Electrician II (Female)
CalTrans Equipment Operator
CalTrans Equipment Operator (Female)
CalTrans Heavy Equipment Operator
CalTrans Highway Maintenance Leadworker
CalTrans Highway Maintenance Worker
CalTrans Highway Maintenance Worker (Female)
CalTrans Landscape Maintenance Worker
CalTrans Landscape Maintenance Worker (Female)
CalTrans Landscape Maintenance Leadworker
CalTrans Landscape Program Administrator
CalTrans Landscape Specialist
CalTrans Maintenance Office Systems Technician
CalTrans Maintenance Superintendent I, II & II

CalTrans Maintenance Supervisor
Capital Outlay Program Manager
Captain Firefighter/Security Officer
Captain, Fish and Game Patrol Boat
Captain, Office of California State Police
Captain, State Fair Police
Carpenter Apprentice
Carpenter I & II
Carpenter I & II, Correctional Facility
Carpenter I & II, Correctional Facility (Female)
Carpenter Supervisor
Carpenter Supervisor, Correctional Facility
Case Service Assistant, Department of Rehabilitation
Case Service Supervisor, Department of Rehabilitation
Casework Specialist, Youth Authority
Catholic Chaplain
Catholic Chaplain, Intermittent
Central Laboratory Services Administrator
Certification Officer I, II & III
Certification Technician
Chapel Musician
Chief Actuary, Department of Insurance
Chief Administrative Law Judge, Department of Health Services
Chief Administrative Law Judge, Department of Social Services (CEA)
Chief Administrative Law Judge, Public Employment Relations Board (CEA)
Chief Administrative Law Judge, Public Utilities Commission (CEA)
Chief Administrative Law Judge, Unemployment Insurance Appeals Board (CEA)
Chief, Air and Industrial Hygiene Laboratory
Chief Arson and Bomb Investigator
Chief Assistant Attorney General (CEA)
Chief Athletic Inspector
Chief, Branch Public Health Laboratory
Chief, Bureau of Exhibits
Chief, Bureau of Maternal and Child Health
Chief, Central Program Services
Chief Chemist, Pesticide Evaluation
Chief, Clinical Chemistry Laboratory
Chief Compliance Officer, Health Facilities Construction
Chief, Concessions Division, Department of Parks and Recreation
Chief, Construction Branch, Department of Water Resources
Chief Construction Supervisor
Chief Cost Estimator, Water Resources
Chief Counsel, Department of General Services (CEA)
Chief Counsel I & II (CEA)
Chief Counsel, Department of Industrial Relations (CEA)
Chief Dentist
Chief Deputy Attorney General (CEA)
Chief Deputy Legislative Counsel (CEA)
Chief Deputy State Oil & Gas Supervisor (CEA)
Chief, Division for the Blind
Chief, Division of Corporate Filing and Services

Chief Engineer and Production Consultant, Television Communications Center
Chief Engineer, Fisheries Vessel
Chief Engineer I & II
Chief Engineer I & II, Correctional Facility
Chief Engineer, Reclamation Board
Chief Engineering Geologist, Department of Water Resources
Chief, Field Division, Department of Water Resources
Chief, Fire and Rescue Division, Office of Emergency Services
Chief, Food and Drug Laboratory
Chief, General Services Section, Board of Equalization
Chief Geologist, State Lands Division
Chief Hearing Advisor, California Energy Commission
Chief Hearing Officer/Executive Secretary, New Motor Vehicle Board
Chief Hearing Reporter, Public Utilities Commission
Chief, Highway Outdoor Advertising Program
Chief Hydroelectric Plant Operator
Chief Investigator, California Horse Racing Board
Chief Investigator, Department of Insurance
Chief Investigator, Fair Political Practices Commission
Chief Investigator, MediCal Fraud Unit, Department of Justice
Chief, Laboratory Field Services
Chief, Law Enforcement Division, Office of Emergency Services
Chief, Legal Division, Department of Transportation (CEA)
Chief Lottery Agent
Chief Medical Consultant, Deparment of Rehabilitation
Chief Medical Consultant, Board of Medical Quality Assurance
Chief Medical Officer, Correctional Institution
Chief Medical Officer, Veterans Home and Medical Center
Chief, Medical Services Correctional Program (CEA)
Chief Meteorologist, Air Resources Board
Chief Microbial Diseases Laboratory
Chief Museum Security Officer
Chief of Archives
Chief of Education, Correctional Program
Chief of Facilities Planning
Chief of Flood Operations, Water Resources
Chief of Interpretive Services
Chief of Investigations, Board of Prison Terms
Chief of Land Surveys
Chief of Library Services (CEA)
Chief of Litigation (CEA)
Chief of Medicine, Veterans Home and Medical Center
Chief of Mobile Equipment Operations
Chief of Operations, Secretary of State's Office
Chief of Plant Operations I, II & III
Chief of Plant Operations I, II & III, Correctional Facility
Chief of Plant Operations III (Water Treatment)
Chief of Professional Education, Mental Hospital
Chief of Professional Education, Developmentally Disabled Hospital
Chief of Program Evaluation, Department of Education (CEA)
Chief of Public Health Nursing (Contract Counties)
Chief of Racing
Chief of Research, Correctional Program
Chief of Utility Operations, Water Resources

Chief, Officer of Governmental Affairs, Department of Education
(CEA)
Chief Petroleum Engineer
Chief Physician and Surgeon
Chief Planning Officer, San Francisco Bay Conservation and Development Commission
Chief Psychiatrist, Correctional Facility
Chief Public Health Veterinarian
Chief, Rehabilitation Facilities Development
Chief Reservoir Engineer, State Lands Division
Chief, Sanitation and Radiation Laboratory
Chief Savings and Loan Examiner
Chief Specification Writer, Water Resources
Chief, Vector Control Section
Chief, Viral and Rickettsial Diseases Laboratory
Chief Water and Power Dispatcher
Chief, Aerometrics Data Division, Air Resources Board
Chief, Alcohol Treatment Service
Chief, Bureau of Fraudulent Claims, Department of Insurance
Chief, Business Enterprise Program
Chief, Child Health and Disability Prevention Branch
Chief, Compliance Division, Air Resources Board
Chief, Correctional Case Records Services
Chief, Crime Prevention Center (CEA)
Chief, Crippled Children Services Section
Chief, Division of Hazardous Liquid Pipeline Safety and Enforcement
Chief, Division of Personnel and Patrol Services, State Controller's Office
Chief, Division of Unclaimed Property, State Controller's Office

Classes Requiring a 2 Years of College

Accountant Trainee
Accounting Analyst
Agricultural Biological Technician
Auditor I
Bank Examiner
Computer Operator
Construction Inspector Technician
Criminal Identification Specialist I
Criminal Intelligence Specialist I
Data Processing Technician
Drafting Aide II
Editorial Aide
Electrical Engineering Technician I
Employment and Claims Assistant
Fish and Game Warden Cadet (Female)
Fish and Game Warden Cadet (Male)
Fish and Wildlife Assistant I
Forestry Assistant I
Forestry Technician
Groundskeeper
Group Supervisor
Investigator Assistant
Library Technical Assistant I
Licensing Registration Examiner, DMV
Management Services Technician
Pharmacy Assistant
Photocomposition Machine Operator
Programmer I
Rental Agent Trainee
Special Agent, DOJ
State Park Cadet (Ranger)
Television Assistant
Worker's Compensation Insurance Technician

Chief, Domiciliary Services
Chief, Elections Division, Secretary of State's Office
Chief, Emergency Assistance Programs Division, Office of Emergency Services
Chief, Environmental Health Division
Chief, Extractive Development Program, State Lands Commission (CEA)
Chief, Family Health Services Section
Chief, Firefighter/Security Officer
Chief, Food and Drug Branch
Chief, Forensic Services, Department of Mental Health
Chief, Governmental Affairs Office, State Energy Resources Conservation and Development Commission
Chief, Haagen-Smit Laboratory Division, Air Resources Board
Chief, Habilitation Services
Chief, Hazardous Materials Laboratory Section
Chief, Hazardous Waste Management Branch Chief, Health and Safety, Department of Health Services
Chief, Infectious Disease Section
Chief, Laboratory Services Branch
Chief, Local Environmental Health Programs
Chief, Marketing Branch, Prison Industries
Chief, Medical Administrative Services
Chief, Mobile Service Division, Air Resources Board
Chief, Mobility Barriers, Department of Rehabilitation
Chief, Office for the Deaf, Department of Social Services
Chief, Office of Children Services, Department of Mental Health
Chief, Office of County Health Services
Chief, Office of Long-Term Care and Aging
Chief, Office of Prevention Services, Department of Mental Health
Chief, Office of Program Planning, Evaluation and Control, Air Resources Board
Chief, Planning and Construction
Chief, Preventive Medical Services Branch
Chief, Producer Licensing, Department of Insurance
Chief, Quality Assurance, Prison Industries
Chief, Radiological Health Section
Chief, Rate Regulation Division, Department of Insurance
Chief, Rehabilitation Bureau
Chief, Research and Development, Extractive Development Program, State Lands Commission
Chief, Restorative Care Service
Chief, Sanitary Engineering Section
Chief, Special Investigator, Employment Development Department
Chief, Technical Assistance and Analysis Division, Fair Political Practices Commission
Child Care Practitioner
Child Development Administrator I & II
Child Development Assistant I & II
Child Development Consultant
Child Nutrition Administrator (CEA)
Child Nutrition Assistant
Child Nutrition Consultant

Civil Defense Signal Officer
Civil Engineering Associate
Civil Engineering Technician I & II
Civil Maintenance Apprentice, Water Resources
Civil Maintenance Journeyworker, Water Resources
Civil Maintenance Superintendent, Water Resources
Civil Maintenance Supervisor, Water Resources
Claim Auditor
Claims Auditor, Welfare Programs
Claims Specialist, Victims of Crime Program
Claims Supervisor, Victims of Crime Program
Clerical Trainee
Clerk, California Conservation Corps
Clients'/Patients' Rights Advocate
Clinical Administrator
Clinical Dietitian
Clinical Dietitian (Hispanic)
Clinical Laboratory Technologist
Clinical Psychology Intern
Clothing Center Manager
Coastal Program Analyst I, II & III
Codes and Standards Administrator I, II, & III
Collection Agent
Collections Manager
Commercial Vehicle Inspection Specialist I & II
Communicable Disease Manager I, II & III
Communicable Disease Representative
Communicable Disease Specialist I & II
Communications and Warning Officer, Office of Emergency Services
Communications Operator I & II, California Highway Patrol
Communications Operator, California State Police
Communications Supervisor I & II, California Highway Patrol
Community College Program Assistant I & II
Community Liaison Representative, State Hospitals
Community Program Administrator I & II
Community Program Specialist I, II, III & IV
Community Resources Development Specialist
Community Resources Manager, Correctional Institution
Community Services Consultant
Compensatory Education Consultant
Compensatory Education Research and Evaluation Specialist, Youth Authority
Compliance Officer, Health Facilities Construction
Composing Technician I & II
Composing Technician Trainee
Compositor (Imposition and Paste-up)
Compositor (Video Display Terminal Operator)
Comptroller, Department of Water Resources
Computer Equipment Technician
Computer Equipment Technician Supervisor
Computer Operations Specialist I & II
Computer Operations Supervisor I & II
Computer Operator
Conciliator, Department of Industrial Relations
Conservancy Project Development Analyst I, II & III
Conservancy Project Development Analyst I (Hispanic)

Conservation Administrator I & II, California Conservation Corps
Conservation and Liquidation Officer, Department of Insurance
Conservationist I & II, California Conservation Corps
Construction Financing Administrator
Construction Financing Representative
Construction Financing Specialist
Construction Inspector
Construction Inspector Technician, Water Resources
Construction Management Supervisor
Construction Office Manager I & II
Construction Project Inspector (Various Sites)
Construction Project Specialist I (Various Sites)
Construction Supervisor I, II & III
Construction Supervisor I, II & III, Water Resources
Construction Supervisor, Correctional Program
Consultant and Medical Examiner, Division of Industrial Accidents
Consultant in Behavioral Sciences, Department of Health Services
Consultant In Intergroup Relations
Consultant In Mathematics Education
Consultant In Occupational Therapy For Physically Handicapped Children
Consultant In Pupil Personnel Services
Consultant In Teacher Preparation (Examination and Research)
Consultant In Teacher Preparation, (Program Evaluation and Research)
Consultant On Hospital Administration
Consulting Communicable Disease Representative
Consulting Optometrist I & II, Department of Health Services
Consulting Psychologist
Consulting Sanitarian
Consumer Affairs Manager, Public Utilities Commission
Consumer Affairs Representative, Public Utilities Commission
Consumer Affairs Supervisor, Public Utilities Commission
Consumer Assistance Technician
Consumer Liaison Officer (Consumer Affairs)
Consumer Liaison Officer (Health Facilities)
Consumer Liaison Officer (Rehabilitation)
Consumer Protection Assistant
Consumer Services Coordinator
Consumer Services Representative
Control Cashier (Motor Vehicle Services), Department of Motor Vehicles
Control Cashier (Vehicle Registration), Department of Motor Vehicles
Control System Technician I, II & III
Cook I & II
Cook I & II, Correctional Facility
Cook, California Conservation Corps
Coordinator, Radiological, Office of Emergency Services
Coordinator, Communications, Office of Emergency Services
Coordinator, Fire Services, Office of Emergency Services
Coordinator, Law Enforcement, Office of Emergency Services
Coordinator Marine Fisheries Management Program
Coordinator of Activities (Kinsey Auditorium)

Coordinator of Graphic Services
Coordinator of Nursing Services
Coordinator of Volunteer Services
Coordinator, Services to the Deaf, Department of Rehabilitation
Coordinator, Indian Health
Coordinator, Legislative Information System
Coordinator, Office of Family Planning
Copyholder
Corporation Assistant
Corporation Documents Examiner
Corporation Examiner
Corporation Examiner IV (Specialist)
Corporation Examiner IV (Supervisor)
Corporations Counsel
Corporations Counsel (Hispanic)
Corporations Investigator
Correctional Administrator, Department of Corrections
Correctional Captain
Correctional Case Records Assistant
Correctional Case Records Manager
Correctional Case Records Specialist
Correctional Case Records Supervisor
Correctional Counselor I, II & III
Correctional Counselor I (Hispanic)
Correctional Counselor II (Specialist)
Correctional Counselor II (Supervisor)
Correctional Health Services Administrator I & II
Correctional Lieutenant
Correctional Officer
Correctional Sergeant
Corrections and Probation Consultant, Board of Corrections
Cosmetology Examiner I & II
Counsel, Multistate Tax Affairs, Franchise Tax Board
Counselor, Department of Education Special Schools
Counselor, Orientation Center for the Blind
Counselor, School for the Deaf
Crew Leader, Youth Conservation Corps
Crime Prevention Program Supervisor
Crime Prevention Specialist
Crime Studies Technician I & II
Crime Studies Technician Trainee
Criminal Identification and Intelligence Assistant
Criminal Identification and Intelligence Supervisor
Criminal Identification Specialist I, II & III
Criminal Identification Specialist (Hispanic)
Criminal Intelligence Specialist I, II & III
Criminal Justice Specialist I & III
Criminal Justice Specialist II (Supervisory)
Criminal Justice Specialist II (Technical)
Criminalist
Criminalist I & II
Criminalist Manager
Criminalist Supervisor
Criminalist Trainee
Customer Services Manager

D

Dairy Foods Specialist
Dairy Laboratory Technologist
Dairy Microbiologist
Dairy Program Coordinator
Data Communications Specialist
Data Entry Manager
Data Processing Manager I, II, III & IV
Data Processing Technician
Data Processing Technician Specialist I & II
Datat Processing Technician Supervisor I & II
Deckhand, Ferryboat
Deckhand, Fish and Game Boat
Delineator
Dental Assistant
Dental Consultant I & II, Department of Health Services
Dental Health Consultant, Department of Health Services
Dental Hygienist
Dental Hygienist Auditor
Dental Hygienist Consultant
Dental Laboratory Technician
Dental Program Consultant, Department of Health Services
Dentist
Department of Justice Administrator I, II & III
Departmental Construction and Maintenance Supervisor
Departmental Food Administrator
Departmental Food Administrator, Special Schools
Departmental Safety Coordinator
Deupty Attorney General
Deputy Attorney General III & IV
Deputy Attorney III & IV, CalTrans
Deputy Attorney, CalTrans
Deputy Chancellor, California Community Colleges (CEA)
Deputy Chief, Legal Division, Department of Transportation (CEA)
Deputy Chief Surplus Property Officer
Deputy Chief, California Highway Patrol
Deputy Chief, Investigations and Staff Services, Department of Consumer Affairs
Deputy Chief, Legal Division, Department of Personnel Administration (CEA)
Deputy Commissioner I, II & III, Department of Real Estate
Deputy Commissioner, Board of Prison Terms
Deputy Comptroller, Department of Water Resources
Deputy Director for Programs, CaliforniaState Summer School for the Arts
Deputy Director, Alcohol Programs
Deputy Director, Educational Programs, California Museum of Science and Industry (CEA)
Deputy Director, Grants (CEA)
Deputy Director, Legislative, Governmental and Public Affairs, California Coastal Commission
Deputy Director, Loans (CEA)
Deputy Director, Public and Environmental Health Division
Deputy Director, Public Health (CEA)
Deputy Division Chief, Alcoholic Beverage Control
Deputy Division Chief, California Energy Commission

Deputy Executive Secretary, California Pollution Control Financing Authority
Deputy General Counsel, Public Employment Relations Board (CEA)
Deputy Labor Commissioner I, II, III & IV
Deputy Legislative Counsel I, II, III & IV
Deputy Program Director (Rental), California Housing Finance Agency
Deputy Regional Director, State Parks
Deputy Registrar of Charitable Trusts
Deputy Registrar of Contractors I, II, III & IV
Deputy Registrar, Structural Pest Control Board
Deputy State Fire Marshal
Deputy State Fire Marshal III (Specialist)
Deputy State Fire Marshal III (Supervisor)
Deputy State Public Defender
Deputy Superintendent, Clinical Services, Correctional Facility
Deputy Workers' Compensation Appeals Board (CEA)
Developmental Specialist
Diagnostic Education Supervisor
Dietetic Technician
Direct Marketing Specialist
Director of Dietetics
Director, Administration, Planning and Program Development, California Housing Finance Agency
Director, California Specialized Training Institute
Director, Division of Law Enforcement, Department of Justice (CEA)
Director, Legislation and Communication,California Community Colleges (CEA)
Director, Legislation and External Affairs, California Postsecondary Education Commission (CEA)
Director, Television Communications Center
Director, Vocational Education, California Community Colleges
Disability Evaluation Analyst
Disability Evaluation Analyst II
Disability Evaluation Analyst III (Specialist)
Disability Evaluation Analyst III (Supervisor)
Disability Evaluation Services Administrator I, II & III
Disability Evaluation Technician
Disability Insurance Program Manager I, II & III
Disability Insurance Program Representative
Disability Insurance Program Supervisor
Disability Insurance Specialist I, II & III
Disaster Worker Clerical Services (Various Disasters)
Disaster Worker Management Services (Various Disasters)
Disaster Worker Speciality Services (Various Disasters)
Disaster Worker Staff Services (Various Disasters)
Dispatcher Clerk Supervisor
Dispatcher Clerk
Dispensary Attendant
District Administrator, Alcoholic Beverage Control
District Fair Assistant Manager
District Fair Business Assistant I & II
District Manager, California State Lottery
District Manager, Division of Occupational Safety and Health
District Medical Director, Division of Industrial Accidents

District Representative Apprentice, Housing and Community Development
District Representative I & II, Division of Codes and Standards
District Sales Representative, California State Lottery
District Structural Engineer
Diversion Program Administrator
Diversion Program Compliance Specialist I & II
Division Chief, Department of Insurance (CEA)
Division Chief, Retirement Systems
Division Chief, Secretary of State's Office
Document Preservation Technician
Drafting Aid I & II
Drafting Services Aid
Drafting Services Manager
Drawbridge Operator
Drawbridge Operator (Female)
Driver Improvement Analyst
Driver Improvement Manager I, II & III
Drug Program Analyst I, II, III & IV
Drug Program Specialist
Dry Cleaning Plant Supervisor

E

Economic Entomologist
Editor of Publications, California Postsecondary Education Commission
Editorial Aid
Editorial Assistant, Department of Education
Editorial Technician
Education Administrator for Special Programs
Education Administrator I & II
Education Program Supervisor, Youth Authority
Education Programs Assistant I & II (Various Projects)
Education Programs Specialist I, II & III (Various Projects)
Education Research and Evaluation Administrator I & II
Education Research and Evaluation Assistant
Education Research and Evaluation Consultant
Egg and Poultry Quality Control Inspector
Election Official, Public Employment Relations Board
Elections Assistant, Office of the Secretary of State
Electric Generation System Program Specialist I, II & III
Electric Generation System Specialist I, II & III
Electric Transmission System Program Specialist I, II & III
Electric Transmission System Specialist I, II & III
Electrical Construction Inspector
Electrical Construction Supervisor I & II
Electrical Drafting Technician
Electrical Engineer
Electrical Engineer (Hispanic)
Electrical Engineering Technician I, II & III
Electrical Estimator I, II & III
Electrical Inspector I & II
Electrical Project Inspector (Various Sites)
Electrical-Mechanical Testing Technician I, II & III
Electrician Apprentice
Electrician I & II

Electrician I (Female)
Electrician I & II , Correctional Facility
Electrician I & II, Correctional Facility (Female)
Electrician Supervisor
Electrician Supervisor, Correctional Facility
Electrician/Power Line Worker
Electroencephalographic Technician
Electronics Specialist, Fruit and Vegetable Quality Control
Electronics Technician
Electronics Technician, Correctional Facility
Elevator Operator
Emergency Management Coordinator/ Instructor I & II, Office of Emergency Services
Emergency Services Coordinator, Office of Emergency Services
Emergency Services Project Specialist I, II & III (Various Projects)
Employment and Claims Assistant
Employment Development Administrator
Employment Development Planner I, II & III
Employment Development Specialist I, II & III
Employment Program Assistant
Employment Program Counselor
Employment Program Manager I, II & III
Employment Program Representative
Employment Program Supervisor I & II
Employment Program Techncian
Energy Analyst
Energy and Mineral Resources Engineer
Energy Program Specialist I, II & III, (Building/Appliance Efficiency)
Energy Program Specialist I, II & III, (Conservation)
Energy Program Specialist I, II & III, (Economics/Statistics)
Energy Program Specialist I, II & III, (Forecasting)
Energy Program Specialist I, II & III, (Fuels)
Energy Program Specialist I, II & III, (Technology Assessment)
Energy Program Specialist I, II, III, IV & V (Various Projects)
Energy Resource Specialist I & II
Energy Resource Specialist III (Managerial)
Energy Resource Specialist III (Supervisory)
Energy Specialist I, II & III (Building/Appliance Efficiency)
Energy Specialist I, II & III (Conservation)
Energy Specialist I, II & III (Economics/Statistics)
Energy Specialist I, II & III (Forecasting)
Energy Specialist I, II & III (Fuels)
Energy Specialist I, II & III (Technology Evaluation and Development)
Engineering Geologist
Engineering Manager I, II & III (CEA)
Environmental Biochemist
Environmental Hazards Scientist
Environmental Health Specialist
Environmental Planner
Environmental Planner (Archeology)
Environmental Planner (Architectural History)
Environmental Planner (Cultural Resources)
Environmental Planner (Natural Sciences)
Environmental Program Manager I & II

Environmental Services Intern
Environmental Specialist I, II & III
Environmental Specialist IV (Specialist)
Enviromental Specialist IV (Supervisory)
Epidemiologic Interviewer I & II
Epidemiologist
Equal Employment Opportunity Analyst
Equestrian Center Manager
Equipment Maintenance Supervisor
Equipment Maintenance Supervisor, Correctional Facility
Equipment Management Supervisor
Equipment Parts Coordinator
Equipment Parts Manager I, II & III
Equipment Parts Worker
Equipment Parts Worker (Female)
Event Coordinator, Cow Palace
Events Services Supervisor
Examination Proctor
Examination Proctor, Department of Insurance
Examiner I, II & III, Laboratory Field Services
Examiner in Barbering
Examiner in Electrology
Executive Assistant
Executive Assistant, California Museum of Science and Industry
Executive Assistant, California Unemployment Insurance Appeals Board
Executive Director, Hospital for the Developmentally Disabled (CEA)
Exective Director, Hospital for the Mentally Disabled (CEA)
Executive Secretary, Districts Securities Commission
Executive Secretary I &II
Executive Secretary, Research Advisory Panel
Exhibit Designer-Installer
Exhibit Designer-Coordinator
Exhibit Representative I & II
Exhibit Specialist
Exhibit Superintendent I & II
Exhibit Supervisor
Exhibit Technician
Expert Examiner
Exposition Assistant I, II & III

F

Fair Employment and Housing Consultant I & II
Fair Employment and Housing Consultant III (Specialist)
Fair Employment and Housing Consultant III (Supervisor)
Fair Employment and Housing Counsel
Fair Employment and Housing Counsel III
Fair Political Practices Commission Counsel-Enforcement
Fairground Aid, District Fairs
Fairground Aid, District Fairs (Female)
Fairground Attendant, District Fairs
Fairground Attendant, District Fairs (Female)
Fairs Horseracing Consultant
Fairs Management Consultant
Farm Hand

Feed, Fertilizer and Livestock Drugs Inspector
Feed, Fertilizer and Livestock Drugs Supervisor
Ferry Operator I & II
Field Agent, Wildlife Conservation Board
Field Examiner I, II & III, Agricultural Labor Relations Board
Field Representative, Board of Funeral Directors and
Embalmers
Field Representative I, Office of Local Assistance
Field Representative Surplus Property Agency
Field Representative, Board of Correction
Field Representative, Bureau of Electronic and Appliance Repair
Field Representative, Department of Justice
Field Representative, School Administration (Specialist)
Field Representative, School Administration (Supervisory)
Financial Adviser, Department of Water Resources
Financial Forecasting Analyst, Commission on State Finance
Financial Forecasting Specialist, Commission on State Finance
Financial Management Auditor II & III
Fire Apparatus Engineer
Fire Apparatus Engineer (Paramedic)
Fire Chief
Fire Chief, Correctional Facility
Fire Control Aid
Fire Fighter
Fire Fighter, Correctional Facility
Fire Fighter I & II
Fire Fighter II (Paramedic)
Fire Lookout (Seasonal)
Fire Prevention Assistant
Fire Prevention Engineer
Fire Prevention Officer I & II
Fire Service Training Specialist
Fire Service Training Specialist III
Fire Service Training Supervisor
Firefighter/Security Officer
Fiscal Officer I & II
Fish and Game License Officer
Fish and Game Patrol Captain
Fish and Game Patrol Lieutenant
Fish and Game Warden Cadet (Female)
Fish and Game Warden Cadet (Male)
Fish and Game Warden, Department of Fish and Game
Fish and Wildlife Assistant I & II
Fish and Wildlife Interpreter I, II & III
Fish and Wildlife Manager
Fish and Wildlife Resources Information and Education Officer
Fish and Wildlife Scientific Aid
Fish and Wildlife Seasonal Aid
Fish Culturist
Fish Habitat Assistant
Fish Habitat Supervisor I & II
Fish Hatchery Manager I & II
Fish Virologist
Fisheries Management Supervisor
Fishery Biologist
Flammability Research Test Engineer
Fluid Milk Testing Coordinator

Folk Arts Specialist
Food Administrator I
Food Administrator I & II, Correctional Facility
Food and Agriculture Management Development Trainee
Food and Drug Investigator
Food and Drug Program Coordinator
Food and Drug Regional Administrator
Food Manager
Food Manager, Correctional Facility
Food Service Supervisor I & II
Food Service Worker I & II
Food Service Worker I & II, Correctional Facility
Food Technology Specialist
Forensic Scientist Toxicologist I, II, III & IV
Forensic Scientist Toxicologist Trainee
Forest Geneticist
Forester I, II & III
Forestry Aid
Forestry and Fire Protection Administrator
Forestry Assistant I & II
Forestry Construction and Maintenance Supervisor
Forestry Cook I & II
Forestry Equipment Manager I, II, III & IV
Forestry Field Trainee
Forestry Pilot (Helicopters)
Forestry Technician
Foster Grandparent Field Supervisor
Foster Grandparent/Senior Companion
Foster Grandparent/Senior Companion Program Coordinator
Foster Grandparent/Senior Companion Project Coordinator
Foundation Driller
Foundation Driller (Female)
Foundation Driller Leadworker
Free Venture/Private Industries Specialist, Department of Youth Authority
Fruit and Vegetable Quality Control Inspector
Fruit and Vegetable Quality Control Supervisor I & II
Fusion Welder
Fusion Welder, Correctional Facility
Fusion Welder, Correctional Facility(Female)

G

General Auditor II & III
General Counsel, Board of Osteopathic Examiners
General Counsel, Fair Political Practices Commission (CEA)
Genetic Disease Program Specialist I, II, III & IV
Geologic Aid
Geological Drafting Technician
Geothermal Energy Program Specialist I, II & III
Geriatric Nursing Assistant
Glazier
Glazier, Correctional Facility
Glazier, Correctional Facility (Female)
Governmental Auditor II & III
Graduate Legal Assistant
Graduate Legal Assistant, Fair Political Practices Commission

Graduate Student Assistant
Grain and Commodity Inspector
Grain and Commodity Supervisor I & II
Graphic Artist
Graphic Services Supervisor
Groundskeeper
Groundskeeper, Correctional Facility (Female)
Groundskeeper (Female)
Groundskeeper, Correctional Facility
Group Supervisor
Group Supervisor Trainee
Guide I, Historical Monument
Guide II, Historical Monument (Specialist)
Guide II, Historical Monument (Supervisor)
Guide Trainee, Historical Monument
Gunsmith

H

Hazardous Materials Specialist
Hazardous Materials Specialist (Hispanic)
Head Group Supervisor I & II
Health Analyst
Health and Safety Program Specialist I, II & III
Health and Safety Specialist I, II & III
Health Education Consultant I & II
Health Education Consultant III (Specialist)
Health Education Consultant III (Supervisor)
Health Facilities Evaluator I & II
Health Facilities Evaluator Manager I & II
Health Facilities Evaluator Nurse
Health Facilities Evaluator Nurse (Hispanic)
Health Facilities Evaluator Specialist
Health Facilities Evaluator Supervisor
Health Facilities Evaluator Trainee
Health Planning Manager I & II
Health Planning Specialist I & II
Health Program Audit Manager I, II & III, Department of Health Services
Health Program Auditor II, III & IV, Department of Health Services
Health Program Coordinator, Correctional Facility
Health Program Manager I, II & III
Health Program Specialist I & II
Health Program Technician I & II
Health Record Technician I & III
Health Record Technician II (Specialist)
Health Record Technician II (Supervisor)
Health Services Counsel I, II & III
Health Services Specialist
Health Training Consultant
Hearing Advisor I & II, California Energy Commission
Hearing Assistant, Department of Social Services
Hearing Conservation Specialist
Hearing Officer I & II, Agricultural Labor Relations Board
Hearing Officer I & II, New Motor Vehicle Board

Hearing Officer I & II, Occupational Safety and Health Appeals Board
Hearing Reporter
Hearing Reporter, Public Utilities Commission
Hearing Transcriber/Typist
Hearing Transcriber/Typist, Public Utilities Commission
Heavy Equipment Bodyworker/Painter
Heavy Equipment Electrician
Heavy Equipment Mechanic
Heavy Equipment Mechanic, Correctional Facility
Heavy Equipment Mechanic, Correctional Facility (Female)
Heavy Equipment Mechanic (Female)
Heavy Equipment Mechanic Apprentice
Heavy Equipment Mechanic Apprentice (Female)
Heavy Fire Equipment Operator
Heavy Truck Driver
Heavy Truck Driver, Correctional Facility
Highway Equipment Cleaner
Highway Equipment Superintendent I, II, III & IV
Highway Field Office Assistant
Highway Mechanic Supervisor I & II
Highway Outdoor Advertising Inspector
Homemaking Education Administrator I
Homemaking Education Consultant
Hospital Administrative Resident I, II, III & IV
Hospital Administrator
Hospital Aid
Hospital Coordinator of Forensic Services
Hospital General Services Administrator I & II
Hospital Health and Safety Coordinator
Hospital Peace Officer I, II & III
Hospital Social Worker I & II
Hospital Worker
Housekeeper
Housekeeper, Correctional Facility
Housing and Community Development Finance Advisor
Housing and Community Development Manager I, II & III
Housing and Community Development Representative I & II
Housing and Community Development Specialist I & II
Housing Construction and Rehabilitation Specialist
Housing Construction Inspector, California Housing Finance Agency
Housing Finance Assistant (Construction Services)
Housing Finance Assistant (General)
Housing Finance Assistant (Rental)
Housing Finance Associate (Affirmative Action)
Housing Finance Associate (Construction Services)
Housing Finance Associate (General)
Housing Finance Associate (Management Services)
Housing Finance Associate (Rental)
Housing Finance Associate (Single Family)
Housing Finance Chief (Construction Services)
Housing Finance Chief (Management Services)
Housing Finance Chief (Rental)
Housing Finance Chief (Single Family)
Housing Finance Officer (Affirmative Action)
Housing Finance Officer (Construction Services)

Housing Finance Officer (Management Services)
Housing Finance Officer (Rental)
Housing Finance Officer (Single Family)
Housing Finance Specialist (Affirmative Action)
Housing Finance Specialist (General)
Housing Finance Specialist (Management Services)
Housing Finance Specialist (Rental)
Housing Finance Specialist (Single Family)
Housing Finance Trainee (General)
Housing Maintenance Inspector, California Housing Finance Agency
Housing Program Specialist, Department of Fair Employment and Housing
Human Rights Officer
Hydroelectric Plant Electrical Supervisor
Hydroelectric Plant Electrician Apprentice
Hydroelectric Plant Electrician I & II
Hydroelectric Plant Maintenance Superintendent
Hydroelectric Plant Mechanic Apprentice
Hydroelectric Plant Mechanic I & II
Hydroelectric Plant Mechanical Supervisor
Hydroelectric Plant Operations Superintendent
Hydroelectric Plant Operator
Hydroelectric Plant Operator Apprentice

I

Industrial Education Administrator I
Industrial Education Consultant
Industrial Engineer, Office of State Printing
Industrial Relations Counsel I & II
Industrial Relations Counsel III (Specialist)
Industrial Relations Counsel III (Supervisor)
Industrial Relations Representative
Industrial Superintendent, Prison Industries (Agriculture)
Industrial Superintendent, Prison Industries (Bakery)
Industrial Superintendent, Prison Industries (Bindery)
Industrial Superintendent, Prison Industries (Coffee Roasting and Grinding)
Industrial Superintendent, Prison Industries(Concrete Construction)
Industrial Superintendent, Prison Industries (Detergent)
Industrial Superintendent, Prison Industries (Egg Production)
Industrial Superintendent, Prison Industries (Electronic Components)
Industrial Superintendent, Prison Industries (Fabric Products)
Industrial Superintendent, Prison Industries (Fiberglass Products)
Industrial Superintendent, Prison Industries (Furniture Refurbishing)
Industrial Superintendent, Prison Industries (Key Entry)
Industrial Superintendent, Prison Industries (Knitting Mill)
Industrial Superintendent, Prison Industries (Laundry)
Industrial Superintendent, Prison Industries (Mail Presort Operations)
Industrial Superintendent, Prison Industries (Maintenance and Repair)

Industrial Superintendent, Prison Industries (Mattress and Bedding)
Industrial Superintendent, Prison Industries (Meat Plant Operations)
Industrial Superintendent, Prison Industries (Metal Products)
Industrial Superintendent, Prison Industries (Micrographics)
Industrial Superintendent, Prison Industries (Optical Products)
Industrial Superintendent, Prison Industries (Paper Products)
Industrial Superintendent, Prison Industries (Poultry Production/Abattoir)
Industrial Superintendent, Prison Industries (Printing)
Industrial Superintendent, Prison Industries (Shoe Manufacturing)
Industrial Superintendent, Prison Industries (Swine Production/Abattoir)
Industrial Superintendent, Prison Industries (Telemarketing)
Industrial Superintendent, Prison Industries (Textile Mill)
Industrial Superintendent, Prison Industries (Vehicle Reconditioning and Servicing)
Industrial Superintendent, Prison Industries (Wood Products)
Industrial Supervisor, Prison Industries (Bakery)
Industrial Supervisor, Prison Industries (Bindery)
Industrial Supervisor, Prison Industries (Coffee Roasting and Grinding)
Industrial Supervisor, Prison Industries (Concrete Construction)
Industrial Supervisor, Prison Industries (Crop Farm)
Industrial Supervisor, Prison Industries (Dairy)
Industrial Supervisor, Prison Industries (Detergent Plant)
Industrial Supervisor, Prison Industries (Egg Production)
Industrial Supervisor, Prison Industries (Electronic Components)
Industrial Supervisor, Prison Industries (Fabric Products)
Industrial Supervisor, Prison Industries (Farm Equipment Maintenance)
Industrial Supervisor, Prison Industries (Fiberglass Products)
Industrial Supervisor, Prison Industries (Furniture Refurbishing)
Industrial Supervisor, Prison Industries (Knitting Mill)
Industrial Supervisor, Prison Industries (Laundry)
Industrial Supervisor, Prison Industries (Mailing Machine Operations)
Industrial Supervisor, Prison Industries (Maintenance and Repair)
Industrial Supervisor, Prison Industries (Mattress and Bedding)
Industrial Supervisor, Prison Industries (Meatcutting/Processing)
Industrial Supervisor, Prison Industries (Metal Fabrication)
Industrial Supervisor, Prison Industries (Micrographics)
Industrial Supervisor, Prison Industries (Optical Products)
Industrial Supervisor, Prison Industries (Paper Products)
Industrial Supervisor, Prison Industries (Poultry Abattoir)
Industrial Supervisor, Prison Industries (Poultry Production)
Industrial Supervisor, Prison Industries (Printing)
Industrial Supervisor, Prison Industries (Sausage Making/Cured Meats)
Industrial Supervisor, Prison Industries (Sewing Machine Repair)
Industrial Supervisor, Prison Industries (Shoe Manufacturing)

Industrial Supervisor, Prison Industries
(Shoes and Boots, Lasting to Packing)
Industrial Supervisor, Prison Industries (Swine Abattoir)
Industrial Supervisor, Prison Industries (Swine Production)
Industrial Supervisor, Prison Industries (Telemarketing)
Industrial Supervisor, Prison Industries
(Textile Mill/Finishing)
Industrial Supervisor, Prison Industries
(Textile Mill/Spinning and Weaving)
Industrial Supervisor, Prison Industries (Tobacco Processing)
Industrial Supervisor, Prison Industries (Tool and Die)
Industrial Supervisor, Prison Industries (Upholstery)
Industrial Supervisor, Prison Industries
(Vehicle Reconditioning and Servicing)
Industrial Supervisor, Prison Industries (Wood Products)
Industrial Therapist
Information Officer I (Specialist)
Information Officer I (Supervisor)
Information Officer II
Information Program Specialist I, II & III (Various Programs)
Information Program Specialist II
(Information and Referral)
Information Program Specialist II (Microsystems)
Information Program Specialist III (Library Automation)
Information Program Specialist III (Literacy)
Information Program Specialist III (Community Organization)
Information Systems Supervisor,
California Postsecondary Education Commission
Inheritance and Gift Tax Examiner I & II
Insect Biosystematist
Inspector, Board of Pharmacy
Inspector I & II, Department of Consumer Affairs
Inspector of Automotive Equipment
Inspector, Department of Motor Vehicles
Inspector, Office of California State Police
Institution Artist/Facilitator
Institution Firefighter (Part Time)
Institutional Personnel Officer, Department of Corrections
Instructional Counselor, Diagnostic Schools
Instructional Counselor, School for the Blind
Instructional Counselor, School for the Deaf
Instructor of School Bus Driver Trainers
Instrument Technician I, II & III, Air Quality
Insurance Claims Specialist
Insurance Examiner
Insurance Investigator
Insurance Officer
Insurance Policy Officer
Insurance Rate Analyst
Insurance Rate Specialist
Insurance Trainee
Interagency Messenger
Investigation Specialist I & II, Franchise Tax Board
Investigative Auditor, Alcoholic Beverage Control
Investigator Assistant
Investigator I & II, Fair Political Practices Commission
Investigator, Structural Pest Control Board

Investment Officer I & II, Retirement Systems
Investment Officer, California Housing Finance Agency
Investment Operations Manager

J

Jackhammer Operator
Janitor
Janitor, Correctional Facility
Janitor, Limited Service
Janitor Supervisor I, II & III
Janitor Supervisor I, II & III, Correctional Facility
Jewish Chaplain
Jewish Chaplain, Intermittent
Job Agent
Junior Architectural Assistant
Junior Aviation Consultant
Junior Chemical Testing Engineer
Junior Chemist
Junior Civil Engineer
Junior Civil Engineer (Hispanic)
Junior Construction Inspector
Junior Engineering Technician
Junior Estimator of Building Construction
Junior Forester
Junior Health Physicist
Junior Industrial Hygienist
Junior Inspector of Automotive Equipment
Junior Landscape Architect
Junior Leasing Officer
Junior Microbiologist I & II
Junior Property Agent
Junior Property Appraiser
Junior Public Health Biologist
Junior Right of Way Agent
Junior Safety Engineer
Junior Small Business Officer
Junior Space Planner
Junior Staff Analyst (General)
Junior Utilities Engineer

K

Key Accounts Specialist, California State Lottery
Key Data Operator
Key Data Supervisor I, II, III & IV

L

Labor Compliance Officer, Division of Highways
Labor Relations Analyst
Labor Relations Coordinator
Labor Relations Counsel I, II & III
Labor Relations Manager
Labor Relations Specialist I & II
Labor Standards Investigator
Labor Supervisor

Labor Supervisor (Casual Employment)
Laboratory Assistant
Laboratory Technician, (Chemical Analysis)
Laboratory Technician, (Criminalistics)
Laboratory Technician II, (Animal Pathology)
Laboratory Testing Supervisor, Office of the State Fire Marshall
Laborer
Laborer, Correctional Facility
Laborer (Female)
Laborer, Building Trades (Casual Employment)
Land and Water Use Analyst
Land Survey Technician
Land Surveyor Supervisor
Land Title Searcher
Landscape Technician
Landscape Technician II
Language, Speech and Hearing Specialist
Latent Print Analyst I & II
Latent Print Supervisor
Launderer
Launderer, Correctional Facility
Launderer Assistant
Laundry Supervisor I & II
Laundry Supervisor I & II, Correctional Facility
Laundry Worker
Laundry Worker, Correctional Facility
Laundry Worker Assistant
Law Enforcement Consultant I & II, Commission on Peace Officer Standards and Training
Law Indexer
Law Librarian
Lead Automobile Mechanic
Lead Automobile Mechanic, Correctional Facility
Lead Groundskeeper
Lead Groundskeeper, Correctional Facility
Lead Groundskeeper, Correctional Facility (Female)
Lead Heavy Equipment Bodyworker/ Painter
Lead Heavy Equipment Electrician
Lead Motorcycle Mechanic
Lead Security Guard
Lead Senior Structural Engineer
Lead Snow Gauger
Lead Structural Steel Painter
Lead Transportation Officer, Youth Authority
Legal Analyst
Legal Assistant
Legal Counsel
Legal Counsel (Hispanic)
Legal Documents Examiner
Legal Office Administrator I & II
Legal Secretary
Legal Support Supervisor I & II
Legislative and Information Coordinator, Commission on Teacher Credentialing (CEA)
Legislative and Public Affairs Coordinator, California Community Colleges
Legislative Assistant, California Housing Finance Agency

Legislative Clerk I & II
Legislative Coordinator, Department of Education
Legislative Coordinator, Commission on the Status of Women
Legislative Coordinator, Department of Corrections
Legislative Coordinator, Department of Housing and Community Development
Legislative Coordinator, Department of Real Estate
Legislative Coordinator, Fair Political Practices Commission
Legislative Coordinator, Secretary of State's Office
Legislative Corrections Specialist
Letter Press Operator
Librarian
Librarian, Correctional Facility
Library Technical Assistant I & II
License Inspector (Seasonal)
Licensed Vocational Nurse
Licensed Vocational Nurse (Hispanic)
Licensing Officer, Alcoholic Beverage Control
Licensing Program Analyst I & II
Licensing Program Manager
Licensing Program Supervisor
Licensing/Registration Examiner, Department of Motor Vehicles
Lieutenant, Fish and Game Patrol Boat
Lieutenant, Office of California State Police
Lieutenant, State Fair Police
Lifeguard
Lifeguard I & II (Seasonal)
Lifeguard Supervisor I, II & III
Light Power Shovel Operator
Limited Examination and Appointment Program Candidate (Identified Class)
Linotype Operator
Lithographic Negative Assembler
Lithographic Plate Maker
Livestock Inspector
Locksmith I & II
Locksmith I, Correctional Facility
Locksmith I, (Female)
Locksmith I, Correctional Facility (Female)
Lottery Agent
Lottery Application Data Systems Manager
Lumber Mill Operator

M

Machine Operations Coordinator, Officeof Support Services
Machinist
Machinist, Correctional Facility
Machinist and Instrument Maker
Mailing Machines Operator
Mailing Machines Operator I & II
Mailing Machines Supervisor I & II
Mailing Machines Trainee
Maintenance Aid (Seasonal)
Maintenance and Operations Supervisor I & II, District Fairs
Maintenance and Service Occupational Trainee

Maintenance Mechanic
Maintenance Mechanic, Correctional Facility
Maintenance Mechanic, Correctional Facility (Female)
Maintenance Mechanic (Female)
Maintenance Worker, District Fairs (Female)
Maintenance Worker, Department of the
California Highway Patrol
Maintenance Worker, Department of the
California Highway Patrol (Female)
Maintenance Worker, District Fairs
Maintenance Worker, Tunnels and Tubes
Maintenance Worker, Tunnels and Tubes (Female)
Management Services Assistant
Management Services Technician
Manager, Administrative Programs,
California Horse Racing Board
Manager I, II, III, IV & V, Department of Motor Vehicles
Manager I, II, III & IV, State Compensation Insurance Fund
Manager, Motor Carrier Safety Program,
California Highway Patrol
Manager of Education Programs, California
Museum of Science and Industry
Manager of Exhibit Services
Manager of Program Services, Veterans
Home and Medical Center
Manager of Support Services, Veterans
Home and Medical Center
Manager Right of Way Program, District 07
Manager Trainee, Department of Motor Vehicles
Manager, Transportation Services,
California Highway Patrol
Manager, California Educational Loan
Program, Student Aid Commission
Manager, Commodity Processing Program
Manager, Cooperative Development Program
Manager, Disabled Access Compliance Unit,
Office of State Architect
Manager, Division of Measurement Standards
Manager, Electronic Data Processing Acquisition
Manager, Event Coordination Unit
Manager, Grand National Shows, 1-A District
Agricultural Association
Manager, Rapid Transit Systems Section,
Public Utilities Commission
Manager, Standards and Technologies
Programs, California Waste Management Board
Manager, Telecommunications Maintenance
Marine Biologist
Marine Resources Supervisor
Marine Terminal Safety Coordinator
Marine Terminal Safety Inspector
Maritime Vocational Instructor I, II & III
Market Data Compiler
Marketing Analyst I & II, California State Lottery
Marketing Specialist
Marketing Specialist, California Museum
of Science and Industry

Marketing Specialist, California State Lottery
Mason, Correctional Facility (Female)
Mason, Correctional Facility
Mason I & II
Master, Fisheries Vessel
Mate, Fish and Game Vessel
Materials and Research Engineering Associate (Specialist)
Materials and Research Engineering Associate (Supervisor)
Materials and Stores Supervisor I & II
Materials and Stores Supervisor I & II, Correctional Facility
Materials Manager, Prison Industries
Measurement Standards Specialist I, II & III
Meat and Food Inspector
Mechanic's Helper
Mechanic's Helper (Female)
Mechanical and Technical Occupational Trainee
Mechanical Construction Inspector
Mechanical Construction Supervisor I & II
Mechanical Drafting Technician
Mechanical Engineer
Mechanical Engineering Technician I, II & III
Mechanical Estimator I, II & III
Mechanical Project Inspector (Various Sites)
Medfly Project Assistant I, II & III
Medi-Cal Field Office Administrator I & II
Medi-Cal Technician I & II
Medi-Cal Technician III (Specialist)
Medi-Cal Technician III (Supervisory)
Media Director, Fair Political Pracitices Commission
Medical Consultant, Department of Rehabilitation
Medical Consultant I & II, Department of Health Services
Medical Consultant I (Hispanic), Department of Health Services
Medical Consultant, State Board of Medical Quality Assurance
Medical Director, Chief Deputy (CEA)
Medical Director, Division on Industrial Accidents (CEA)
Medical Director, Employment Development Department (CEA)
Medical Director, State Hospital
Medical Officer, State Compensation Insurance Fund (CEA)
Medical Officer, State Personnel Board (CEA)
Medical Program Consultant, Department of Health Services
Medical Record Consultant
Medical Record Director
Medical Resident (Various Specialties)
Medical Stenographer
Medical Supply Technician
Medical Technical Assistant
Medical Technical Assistant, Correctional Facility
Medical Technical Assistant, Correctional Facility (Hispanic)
Medical Transcriber
Mental Health Human Resources Specialist II
Mental Health Nurse I & II
Mental Health Program Administrator
Mental Health Program Specialist I, II, III & IV
Microfilm Technician I & II
Migrant Education Administrator II
Military Department Equipment Operator
Milk Production Cost Analyst I & II

Mill and Cabinet Supervisor
Mill and Cabinet Worker
Mineral and Land Audit Program Manager
Mineral and Land Auditor Specialist II, III & IV
Mineral Resources Engineering Technician I, II & III
Mining and Petroleum Engineer
Mobile Equipment Superintendent
Mobilehome Registration Manager
Mobilehome Registration Specialist
Mobilehome Registration Supervisor I, II & III
Mobility Evaluation Specialist
Molding Press Operator
Mortgage Investment Officer
Mortgage Investment Specialist I & II
Mortgage Loan Accountant
Mortgage Loan Accounting Administrator
Mortgage Loan Accounting Officer
Mortgage Loan Accounting Supervisor
Motion Picture Assistant
Motion Picture Operator
Motion Picture Production Analyst
Motion Picture Specialist
Motor Carrier Specialist I, II & III, California Highway Patrol
Motor Vehicle Assistant
Motor Vehicle Field Representative
Motor Vehcile Program Supervisor I &II
Motor Vehicle Technician
Motor Vessel Engineer
Motorcycle Mechanic
Museum Curator I, II & III
Museum Custodian
Museum Electrician
Museum Guard
Museum Security Officer
Museum Technician
Music Therapist
Muslim Chaplain
Muslim Chaplain (Intermittent)

N

Neuropathology Technologist
New Program Consultant
Nurse Evaluator I, II, III & IV, Health Services
Nurse Instructor
Nurse Practitioner
Nurse Anesthetist
Nusing Consultant (Office of Prevention)
Nusing Consultant I, II & III
Nursing Consultant, Program Review
Unit, Department of Health Services
Nursing Coordinator
Nursing Education Consultant
Nursing Education Director, Veterans Home
Nursing Treatment Specialist
Nutrition Education and Training Assistant
Nutrition Education and Training Consultant (Nonsupervisory)

Nutrition Education and Training Consultant (Supervisory)

O

Occupational Technician (Accounting)
Occupational Technician (General)
Occupational Therapist
Occupational Therapy Assistant
Occupational Therapy Consultant
Oceanographer
Office Assistant (General)
Office Assistant (Typing)
Office Assistant I & II (General)
Office Assistant I & II (Typing)
Office Assistant II (Cashiering)
Office Building Manager I, II, III & IV
Office Machine Service Technician
Office Machine Service Technician (Electronic)
Office Machine Service Technician Trainee
Office Manager I & II, California Energy Commission
Office Occupations Clerk
Office Occupations Trainee
Office of Program Review Consultant (Medical), State Hospitals
Office of Program Review Consultant, State Hospitals
Office Services Manager I & II
Office Services Supervisor I (Cashiering)
Office Services Supervisor I (Filing)
Office Services Supervisor I (Typing)
Office Services Supervisor I, II & III (General)
Office Technician (Cashiering)
Office Technician (Typing)
Office Technician (General)
Offset Press Assistant
Offset Process Camera Operator
Oil and Gas Technician I, II & III
Operations Research Specialist I, II & III
Operations Security Officer
Operator, Tunnels and Tubes
Operator, Tunnels and Tubes, (Female)
Optometrist

P

Painter Apprentice
Painter I & II
Painter I (Female)
Painter I & II, Correctional Facility
Painter I & II, Correctional Facility Female
Painter Supervisor
Painter Supervisor, Correctional Facility
Park Aid (Seasonal)
Park and Recreation Specialist
Park Interpretive Specialist (Seasonal)
Park Landscape Maintenance Technician
Park Maintenance Assistant
Park Maintenance Chief I & II
Park Maintenance Supervisor

Park Maintenance Worker I & II
Park Regional Maintenance Specialist
Park Safety and Enforcement Specialist
Parking Operations Supervisor
Parole Administrator I & II, Adult Parole
Parole Agent I & III, Adult Parole
Parole Agent I & III, Youth Authority
Parole Agent II, Adult Parole (Supervisor)
Parole Agent II, Adult Parole (Specialist)
Parole Agent II, Youth Authority (Supervisor)
Parole Agent II, Youth Authority (Specialist)
Parole Services Assistant I & II
Parts Operations Manager
Pathologist
Pathology Assistant
Patient Benefit and Insurance Officer I, III, IV & V
Patient Benefit and Insurance Officer II (Specialist)
Patient Benefit and InsuranceOfficer II (Supervisor)
Payroll Auditor, Division of Labor Standards Enforcement
Payroll Officer, State Controller's Office
Payroll Services Manager, Employment
Development Department
Payroll Services Specialist I, II & III
Payroll Services Technician
Personnel Assistant I, II, III & IV
Personnel Selection Consultant I & II
Personnel Technician I
Personnel Technician II (Specialist)
Personnel Technician II (Supervisor)
Pest Control Technician
Pest Management Specialist
Pest Management Specialist III & IV
Pesticide Evaluation Toxicologist
Pesticide Review Scientist
Pesticide Use Specialist
Petroleum Drilling Engineer
Petroleum Geologist
Petroleum Laboratory Specialist
Petroleum Production Engineer
Petroleum Production Inspector I, II & III
Petroleum Products Chemist I, II & III
Petroleum Reservoir Engineer, State Lands Division
Pharmaceutical Consultant I & II, Department
of Health Services
Pharmicist I & II
Pharmacology Specialist
Pharmacy Assistant
Pharmacy Services Manager
Photo-Electronics Specialist, Department of Justice
Photocomposition Keyboard Operator
Photocomposition Machine Operator
Photocompositor
Photogrammertrist I & II
Photographer
Physical Testing and Evaluation Specialist
Physical Testing Engineering Technician
Physical Therapist I & II

Physical Therapist License Applicant
Physical Therapy Assistant
Physical Therapy Assistant Applicant
Physical Therapy Consultant
Physician and Surgeon
Physician and Surgeon Intermittent
Pianist
Planner
Planner I, II & III, Energy Facility Siting
Plans and Program Advisor, Solid Waste\Management Board
Plant Ecologist
Plant Pathologist (Diagnostician)
Plant Pathologist (Field)
Plant Quarantine Inspector
Plant Quarantine Officer
Plant Quarantine Supervisor I & II
Platform Scales Operator
Plumber Apprentice
Plumber I & II
Plumber I (Female)
Plumber I & II, Correctional Facility
Plumber I & II, Correctional Facility (Female)
Plumber Supervisor
Plumber Supervisor, Correctional Facility
Podiatric Consultant
Podiatrist
Political Reform Consultant I & II, Fair
Political Practices Commission
Polygraph Examiner
Polygraph Examiner, Department of Youth Authority
Polygraphy Examiner Supervisor
Pool Lifeguard
Pool Lifeguard (Seasonal)
Postsecondary Education Administrator I & II
Postsecondary Education Specialist I, II & III
Postsecondary Education Specialist, Health Sciences
Pre-Licensed Psychiatric Technician
Pre-Licensed Psychiatric Technician, Forensic Facility
Pre-Registered Clinical Dietitian
Pre-Registered Nurse
Precision Electronics Specialist
Presiding Administrative Law Judge, Unemployment Insurance Appeals Board
Presiding Conciliator, Department of Industrial Relations
Presiding Workers' Compensation Judge
Principal Architect
Principal Architect, Health Facilities
Principal Bridge Engineer
Principal Business Taxes Compliance Supervisor
Principal Buyer
Principal CalTrans Administrator
Principal Claim Auditor
Principal Construction Engineer, Water Resources
Principal Construction Engineer, Department of Corrections
Principal Deputy Legislative Counsel I & II
Principal Driver Improvement Analyst
Principal Electric Utilities Engineer

Principal Engineer, Water Resources
Principal Geologist
Principal Hydraulic Engineer
Principal Investment Officer, Retirement Systems
Principal Landscape Architect
Principal Librarian
Principal Mechanical and Electrical Engineer, Hydraulic Structures
Principal Planner, Comprehensive Health Program
Principal Power Operations and Maintenance Engineer
Principal Program Budget Analyst I, II &III
Principal Property Appraiser
Principal Public Utility Financial Examiner
Principal Right of Way Agent
Principal Safety Engineer (Construction)
Principal Safety Engineer (Electrical)
Principal Safety Engineer (Elevators)
Principal Safety Engineer (Industrial)
Principal Safety Engineer (Mineral Industries Mining and Tunneling)
Principal Safety Engineer (Pressure Vessels)
Principal Safety Engineer (Staff Services)
Principal Staff Biologist
Principal State Meteorologist
Principal Structural Engineer
Principal Tax Auditor, Board of Equalization
Principal Transportation Division, Public Utilities Commission
Principal Transportation Engineer, CalTrans
Principal Transportation Planner
Principal Water Resource Control Engineer
Printer, State Compensation Insurance Fund
Printing Art Planner
Printing Assistant, State Compensation Insurance Fund
Printing Materials Supervisor
Printing Mechanical Superintendent
Printing Operations Assistant
Printing Operations Planner
Printing Operations Supervisor, State Compensation Insurance Fund
Printing Plant Machinist
Printing Plant Superintendent
Printing Process and Operations Planner
Printing Process and Operations Supervisor
Printing Process Planner
Printing Production Supervisor
Printing Supervisor, State Compensation Insurance Fund
Printing Trades Assistant I & II
Printing Trades Specialist I, II & III (General)
Printing Trades Specialist I (Finishing)
Printing Trades Specialist I (Photocopy)
Printing Trades Specialist Trainee
Printing Trades Supervisor I & II (General)
Prison Canteen Manager I & II
Prison Industries Engineer
Processing Fruit and Vegetable Inspector I, II, III & IV (Seasonal)
Processing Fruit and Vegetable Inspector III & IV (Permanent Intermittent)

Procurement and Services Officer I & II
Product Engineering Technician, Prison Industries
Production Manager I & III, Prison Industries
Production Manager II, Prison Industries (Agriculture)
Production Manager II, Prison Industries (Food Products)
Production Manager II, Prison Industries (General)
Production Manager II, Prison Industries (Laundry)
Production Manager II, Prison Industries (Metal Products)
Production Manager II, Prison Industries (Printing)
Production Manager II, Prison Industries (Records Management)
Production Manager II, Prison Industries (Textile Products)
Production Manager II, Prison Industries (Transportation/Distribution)
Production Manager II, Prison Industries (Wood Products)
Program Administrator, Correctional Institution
Program Administrator I & II, Department of Rehabilitation
Program Administrator I, II & III (Hospital Operations)
Program Administrator, Correctional School (Managerial)
Program Administrator, Correctional School (Supervisory)
Program Administrator, Division of Fairs and Expositions
Program Administrator, Office Machine Repair Service
Program and Project Supervisor, Public Utilities Commission
Program Assistant, Developmental Disabilities Programs
Program Assistant, Medical
Program Assistant, Mental Disabilities Programs
Program Coordinator, Sexual Assault Victim Services Program
Program Director, Developmental Disabilities Programs
Program Director, Medical
Program Director, Mental Disabilities Programs
Program Director, General Medical and Surgical Program
Program Manager Blind Programs, Department of Rehabilitation
Program Manager I & II, Bureau of Automotive Repair
Program Manager, Bureau of Repair Service

Classifications Requiring a Bachelor's Degree

Aging Programs Analyst I
Alcohol and Drug Program Analyst I
Assistant Information Systems Analyst
Business Taxes Representative
Corporations Investigator
Deputy Commissioner I, Dept. of Real Estate
Deputy Registrar of Contractors I
Disability Evaluation Analyst
Disability Insurance Program Representative
Editorial Technician
Employment Program Representative
Field Examiner I, ALRB
Health Facilities Evaluator Trainee
Industrial Relations Representative
Insurance Investigator
Junior Aviation Consultant
Junior Staff Analyst
Law Indexer
Manager Trainee, DMV
Public Utilities Regulatory Analyst
Recycling Specialist I
Research Analyst (General)
Right of Way Agent
Staff Services Analyst (General)
Veterans Claims Representative I
Vocational Rehabilitation Trainee
Workers' Compensation Insurance Representative
Youth Counselor

Program Manager, California Museum
of Afro-American History and Culture
Program Manager, Deaf Program, Department
of Rehabilitation
Program Manager, Printing Services
Program Manager, Projects, Contracts and Services
Program Manager, Public Utilities Commission
Program Manager, Sexual Assault and Abuse Programs
Program Manager, Student Aid Commission
Program Manager, Transportation Services (Managerial)
Program Manager, Transportation Services(Supervisory)
Program Manager, Victim/Witness Assistance Program
Program Representative I, II & III, Bureau of Automotive Repair
Program Specialist, Agricultural Chemicals
Program Specialist I, II & III, Franchise Tax Board
Program Specialist, Spray Residue and Agricultural Pest Control
Program Specialist, Feed, Fertilizer and Livestock Drugs
Program Supervisor, Fruit and Vegetable Quality Control
Program SupervisorI & II, Student Aid Commission
Program Supervisor, Department of Rehabilitation
Program Supervisor, Division of Measurement Standards
Program Technician I, II & III (Alcoholic Beverage Control)
Program Technician I & II (Automotive Repair Services)
Program Technician I, II & III (Business Taxes)
Program Technician I & II(California Children's Services)
Program Technician I, II & III (California
Youth Authority, Records)
Program Technician I & II (Contractors' Licensing)
Program Technician I & II (Corporate Filing and Services)
Program Technician I (Corporations Licensing)
Program Technician I, II & III (Corrections Records)
Program Technician I, II & III (Criminal Records)
Program Technician I (Horse Racing Licensing)
Program Technician I, II & III (Medi-Cal Recovery)
Program Technician I & II (Mobilehomes)
Program Technician I & II (Notary Public
Program Technician I (Personnel Services)
Program Technician I & II (Pesticide Enforcement)
Program Technician I, II & III (Political Reform)
Program Technician I, II & III (Property Taxes)
Program Technician I, II & III (Public Utilities Regulation)
Program Technician I, II & III (Real Estate Licensing)
Program Technician I (Real Estate Subdivisions)
Program Technician I, II & III (Retirement Systems)
Program Technician I (Student Aid Commission)
Program Technician I & II (Traffic Records)
Program Technician I &III (Uniform Commercial Code)
Program Technician I, II & III (Veterans Affairs)
Program Technician I (Vital Statistics)
Program Technician II (Community Care Licensing)
Program Technician II (Corporations Licensing)
Program Technician II (Deferred Compensation)
Program Technician II (Disability Evaluation)
Program Technician II (Employer Status)
Program Technician II & III (Emploment Tax Services)
Program Technician II & III (Health Facilities Construction)
Program Technician II (Inheritance and Gift Tax)

Program Technician II (Insurance Licensing)
Program Technician III (Taxpayer Services)
Program Technician Trainee (General)
Program Technician Trainee (Mobilehomes)
Program Water and Power Dispatcher
Program/Regional Manager I & II, Office of Emergency Services
Programmer Apprentice
Programmer I & II
Programmer I (Hispanic)
Project Director I, II & III
Promotional Specialist, Prison Industries
Proofreader
Property Controller I & II
Property Inspector (Specialist)
Protestant Chaplain
Protestant Chaplain Intermittent
Psychiatric Nursing Education Director
Psychiatric Social Worker
Psychiatric Social Worker, Health Facility
Psychiatric Social Worker, Health Facility (Hispanic)
Psychiatric Technician
Psychiatric Technician, Forensic Facility
Psychiatric Technician Apprentice
Psychiatric Technician Instructor
Psychiatric Technician Student
Psychiatric Technician Trainee
Psychiatric Technician Training Candidate
Psychoacoustician
Psychologist (Clinical)
Psychologist (Counseling)
Psychologist (Educational)
Psychologist (Experimental)
Psychologist (Health Facility-Clinical)
Psychologist (Health Facility-Counseling)
Psychologist (Health Facility-Educational)
Psychologist (Health Facility-Experimental)
Psychologist (Health Facility-Social)
Psychology Associate
Psychology Internship Director
Psychometrist
Public Employment Relations Counsel I & II
Public Employment Relations Counsel III (Specialist)
Public Health Assistant I & II
Public Health Chemist I & II
Public Health Chemist III (Specialist)
Public Health Chemist III (Supervisor)
Public Health Laboratory Technician I,Chemical Analysis
Public Health Laboratory Technician I, Microbiology
Public Health Medical Administrator I
Public Health Medical Administrator II (CEA)
Public Health Medical Officer II & III
Public Health Medical Officer III, Epidemiology
Public Health Medical Officer III, Maternal and Child Health
Public Health Medical Officer III, Radiologic Health
Public Health Microbiologist I, II & III
Public Health Microbiologist II & III, Virology
Public Health Nurse I, II, III & IV

Public Health Nurse I (Hispanic)
Public Health Nutrition Consultant I & II
Public Health Nutrition Consultant III (Specialist)
Public Health Nutrition Consultant III (Supervisory)
Public Health Social Work Consultant I, II & III
Public Health Veterinarian
Public Liaison Specialist, State Energy
Resources Conservation and Development Commission
Public Utilities Counsel I, II, III & IV,Public Utilties Commission
Public Utilities Regulatory Program Specialist I, II & III (Economics)
Public Utilities Regulatory Program Specialist I, II & III (Finance)
Public Utilities Regulatory Program Specialist I, II & III (Policy)
Public Utility Financial Examiner II, III & IV
Publications Consultant, Department of Education
Publications Specialist, Department of Justice
Publications Supervisor, Division of Mines and Geology
Purchasing Manager
Purchasing Specifications Analyst

Q

Quality Assurance Manager, Prison Industries
Quality Control Specialist I & II
Questioned Documents Examiner I & II
Questioned Documents Supervisor

R

Race Track Maintenance Supervisor
Racing License Technician I & II
Radiation Protection Specialist I & II
Radio Officer
Radiological Instrument Technician, Office of Emergency Services
Radiological Officer, Office of Emergency Services
Railroad Consultant I, II, III & IV
Railroad Restoration Specialist
Re-Education Program Specialist I & II
Reading Specialist, Remedial and Development Education Programs, Youth Authority
Real Estate Counsel I & II
Real Estate Counsel III (Specialist)
Real Estate Counsel III (Supervisor)
Real Estate Examination Technician
Real Estate License Examiner I & II
Real Estate Manager I, II, III & IV
Reciprocity Officer, State Controller's Office
Records Management Analyst I
Records Management Analyst II (Specialist)
Records Management Analyst II (Supervisor)
Records Manager I & II
Recreation and Wildlife Resources Advisor
Recreation Therapist
Recruitment Manager, State Personnel Board
Recycling Program Manager I & II

Recycling Specialist I & II
Recycling Specialist III (Supervisory)
Recycling Specialist III (Technical)
Regional Administrative Officer I, II & III, Resources Agency
Regional Administrative Technician
Regional Administrator, Milk and Dairy Foods Control Branch
Regional Brand Supervisor
Regional Compliance Officer, Health Facilities Construction
Regional Construction and Maintenance Superintendent, Department of Motor Vehicles
Regional Coordinator, Department of Food and Agriculture
Regional Coordinator, Western States Information Network
Regional Director, Agricultural Labor Relations Board
Regional Director II, Agricultural Labor Relations Board
Regional Director, Public Employment Relations Board
Regional Interpretative Specialist
Regional Manager, California State Lottery
Regional Manager, Corporations Investgations Program
Regional Manager, Division of Occupational Safety and Health
Regional Medical Coordinator
Regional Patrol Chief, Department of Fish and Game
Registered Nurse I, II & III
Registered Nurse I & II (Hispanic)
Registrar of Charitable Trusts
Registrar of Interpretive Collections
Resgistration Specialist, Agricultural Chemicals
Rehabilitation Therapist, State Hospitals (Art)
Rehabilitation Therapist, State Hospitals (Dance)
Rehabilitation Therapist, State Hospitals (Music)
Rehabilitation Therapist, State Hospitals (Occupational)
Rehabilitation Therapist, State Hospitals (Recreation)
Reinsurance Specialist
Rental Agent
Rentals and Operations Officer, 1-A District Agricultural Association
Research Analyst I & II (Economics)
Research Analyst I & II (Social/Behavioral)
Research Analyst I & II (General)
Research Analyst I &II (Demography)
Research Assistant I, II, III, IV & V (Various Studies)
Research Chemist
Research Clinical Chemist
Research Manager I & II (Demography)
Research Manager I & II (Economics)
Research Manager I & II (General)
Research Manager I, II & III (Social/Behavioral)
Research Microbiologist
Research Program Specialist I & II
Research Program Specialist I (Demography)
Research Program Specialist I & II (Economics)
Research Program Specialist I & II (Health)
Research Program Specialist I (Market Research)
Research Program Specialist I& II (Mental Health)
Research Program Specialist I (Range Management/Wildlife Ecology)
Research Program Specialist I (Urban Economics)
Research Program Specialist I & II (Social/Behavioral)

Research Program Specialist I (Remote Sensing/Watershed)
Research Program Specialist II (Occupational Health Pharmacology/Toxicology)
Research Program Specialist II (Soil Erosion)
Research Program Specialist II (Resource Economical Operations Research)
Research Program Specialist II (Soil Vegetation)
Research Program Specialist II (Transportation Economics)
Research Radiochemist
Research Scientist I, II, III & IV (Chronic Diseases Epidemiology)
Research Scientist I, II, III & IV (Enviromental Epidemiology)
Research Scientist I, II, III & IV (Hazard Evaluation System and Information Service)
Research Scientist I, II, III & IV (Immunology and Epidemiology of Designated Viral Diseases)
Research Scientist I, II, III & IV (Infectious Diseases Epidemiology)
Research Scientist I, II, III & IV (Population Laboratory for Epidemiologic Studies)
Research Scientist I, II, III & IV (Public Health Aerosol Physics)
Research Scientist I, II, III & IV (Public Health Atmospheric Chemistry)
Research Scientist I, II, III & IV (Public Health Diagnostic Microbiology)
Research Scientist I, II, III & IV (Public Health Environmental Biochemistry)
Research Scientist I, II , III & IV (Public Health Environmental Virology)
Research Scientist I, II, III & IV (Public Health Geochemical Electron Microscopy)
Research Scientist I, II , III & IV (Public Health Microbial Physiology)
Research Scientist I, II, III & IV (Public Health Molecular Virology)
Research Scientist I, II , III & IV (Public Health Viral Electron Microscopy)
Research Scientist I, II, III & IV (Risk Reduction Epidemiology)
Research Scientist I, II, III & IV (Veterinary Medicine in the Study of the Care,Breeding, Utilization and Diseases of Laboratory Animals)
Research Specialist I, II, III, IV & V (Various Studies)
Research Writer
Residential Care Unit Leader
Resource Specialist, Special Education
Resources Agency Management Trainee
Respiratory Care Practitioner
Restoration and Maintenance Supervisor, Historic Railroads
Restoration Architect
Restoration Supervisor I & II
Restoration Work Specialist
Restoration Work Specialist (Female)
Restoration Worker
Restoration Worker (Female)
Retail Marketing Manager, California State Lottery
Retirement Program Specialist I

Retirement Program Specialist II (Supervisor)
Retirement Program Specialist II (Technical)
Right of Way Agent
Rural Loan Packaging Coordinator I, II, III & IV
Rural Loan Packaging Coordinato Trainee

S

Safety and Security Manager, California Exposition and State Fair
Safety Coordinator, Department of Conservation
Safety Engineering Technician
Sales Manager, Prison Industries
Sales Order Supervisor
Sales Representative, Prison Industries
Sanitarian I, II, III & IV
Sanitary Engineer
Sanitary Engineering Associate
Sanitary Engineering Technician
Sanitary Engineering Technician Trainee
Savings and Loan Examiner
Savings and Loan Examiner IV (Specialist)
Savings and Loan Examiner IV (Supervisor)
School Approvals Administrator I
School Approvals Assistant II
School Approvals Consultant
School Bus Driver
School Facilities Program Administrator I, II & III
School Facilities Program Analyst I & II
School Health Education Assistant I & II
School Health Education Consultant
School Psychologist
School Pupil Transportation Safety Coordinator
Seamer
Seamer, Correctional Facility
Seasonal Clerk
Secretary
Section Chief, Hazardous Waste Management Programs
Securities Trader, Public Employees Retirement System
Security Guard
Security Officer I & II
Security Officer I & II, Department of Justice
Seed Botanist
Seismic Safety Planning Specialist
Seismological Instrument Aid
Seismological Instrument Technician I, II & III
Self-Help Sponsor (Part Time)
Senior Account Clerk
Senior Accounting Officer (Specialist)
Senior Accounting Officer (Supervisor)
Senior Actuarial Statistician
Senior Administrative Analyst, Accounting Systems
Senior Adoptions Case Worker
Senior Agricultural Biologist
Senior Agricultural Economist
Senior Air Operations Officer
Senior Air Pollution Specialist

Senior Air Resources Engineer
Senior Air Sanitation Engineer
Senior Appellate Law Judge, Unemployment
Insurance Appeals Board (CEA)
Senior Apprenticeship Consultant
Senior Architect
Senior Architect, Health Facilities
Senior Architectural Project Analyst
Senior Arson and Bomb Investigator
Senior Assistant Attorney General
Senior Assistant Attorney General, Legislative Affairs Unit
Senior Assistant Attorney General, Special Projects Section
Senior Assistant Attorney General, Special Prosecutions Unit
Senior Automotive Equipment Standards Engineer
Senior Aviation Consultant
Senior Board Counsel, Agricultural Labor Relations Board
Senior Boating Administrator
Senior Boundary Determination Officer (Specialist)
Senior Boundary Determination Officer (Supervisory)
Senior Brand Inspector
Senior Bridge Engineer
Senior Casualty Actuary
Senior Certification Officer
Senior Chemical Testing Engineer
Senior Civil Engineer
Senior Claims Specialist, Victims of Crime Program
Senior Clinical Laboratory Technologist
Senior Commission Counsel (Specialist),
Fair Political Practices Commission
Senior Commission Counsel (Supervisor),
Fair Political Practices Commission
Senior Computer Equipment Technician
Senior Computer Operator
Senior Consultant, Guaranteed Student Loan Program, Student
Aid Commission
Senior Control System Engineer
Senior Coordinator (Radiological), Office
of Emergency Services
Senior Coordinator (Communications),
Office of Emergency Services
Senior Coordinator (Fire Services), Office
of Emergency Services
Senior Coordinator (Law Enforcement),
Office of Emergency Services
Senior Corporations Counsel (Specialist)
Senior Corrosion Engineer
Senior Cost Estimator, Water Resources
Senior Criminalist
Senior Data Processing Analyst (Specialist)
Senior Data Processing Analyst (Supervisor)
Senior Data Processing Technician
Senior Delineator
Senior Deputy State Public Defender
Senior Design Officer, California Housing Finance Agency
Senior Development Specialist
Senior Development Specialist (Industrial)

Senior Development Specialist
(Small Business Development)
Senior Economic Entomologist (Specialist)
Senior Economic Entomologist (Supervisor)
Senior Egg and Poultry Quality Control Inspector
Senior Electric Utilities Engineer
Senior Electrical Engineer
Senior Electrical Engineer, Hydraulic Structures
Senior Electrical Engineer, CalTrans (Specialist)
Senior Electrical Engineer, CalTrans (Supervisor)
Senior Electrical Mechanical Testing Engineer
Senior Electronic Data Processing Acquisition Specialist
(Supervisory)
Senior Electronic Data Processing Acquisition Specialist
(Technical)
Senior Electronics Engineer
Senior Emergency Management Coordinator,
Office of Emergency Services
Senior Emergency Operations Planner,
Office of Emergency Services
Senior Engineer, Districts Securities Commission
Senior Engineer, Water Resources
Senior Engineer, San Francisco Bay
Conservation and Development Commission
Senior Engineering Geologist
Senior Engineering Registration Examiner
Senior Environmental Hazards Scientist (Specialist)
Senior Environmental Hazards Scientist (Supervisor)
Senior Environmental Planner
Senior Equipment Engineer
Senior Equipment Parts Worker
Senior Estimator of Building Construction
Senior Estimator, California Housing Finance Agency
Senior Field Representative, Bureau of
Electronic and Appliance Repair
Senior Fish Pathologist
Senior Food and Drug Investigator
Senior Forest Property Appraiser
Senior Foundation Driller
Senior Geological Drafting Technician
Senior Geologist (Specialist)
Senior Geologist (Supervisor)
Senior Graphic Artist
Senior Group Supervisor
Senior Hazardous Materials Specialist (Supervisor)
Senior Hazardous Materials Specialist (Technical)
Senior Health Care Service Plan Analyst
Senior Health Physicist
Senior Hearing Reporter, Public Utilities Commission
Senior Highway Electrical Engineer
Senior Highway Outdoor Advertising Inspector
Senior Housing Construction Inspector,
California Housing Finance Agency
Senior Hydraulic Engineer
Senior Hydroelectric Plant Operator
Senior Industrial Hygiene Specialist,
State Compensation Insurance Fund

Senior Industrial Hygienist
Senior Insect Biosystematist (Specialist)
Senior Insect Biosystematist (Supervisor)
Senior Inspector of Automotive Equipment
Senior Insurance Examiner (Specialist)
Senior Insurance Examiner (Supervisor)
Senior Insurance Investigator
Senior Insurance Policy Officer
Senior Insurance Rate Analyst
Senior Investigator, Structural Pest Control Board
Senior Laboratory Assistant
Senior Land Agent (Specialist)
Senior Land Agent (Supervisor)
Senior Land and Water Use Analyst
Senior Land Surveyor
Senior Landscape Architect
Senior Law Enforcement Consultant,
Commission on Peace Officer Standards and Training
Senior Law Indexer
Senior Legal Stenographer
Senior Legislative Clerk
Senior Librarian (Specialist)
Senior Librarian (Supervisor)
Senior Librarian, Correctional Facility
Senior Life Actuary
Senior Livestock Inspector (Specialist)
Senior Livestock Inspector (Supervisor)
Senior Maintenance Worker, District Fairs
Senior Management Auditor
Senior Marine Biologist
Senior Marketing Specialist
Senior Materials Research Engineer
Senior Mechanical Engineer
Senior Mechanical Engineer, Hydraulic Structures
Senior Mechanical Engineer, CalTrans (Specialist)
Senior Mechanical Engineer, CalTrans (Supervisor)
Senior Medical Coordinator (Pesticide Use
and Worker Health and Safety)
Senior Medical Stenographer
Senior Medical Technical Assistant
Senior Medical Transcriber
Senior Meteorologist, Air Sanitation
Senior Meteorologist, Water Resources
Senior Microfilm Technician
Senior Mineral Resources Engineer
Senior Mining Engineer
Senior Motor Vehicle Pollution Control Engineer
Senior Occupational Therapist
Senior Oil and Gas Engineer (Specialist)
Senior Oil and Gas Engineer (Supervisor)
Senior Park Aid (Seasonal)
Senior Park and Recreation Specialist
Senior Pesticide Evaluation Scientist (Biology)
Senior Pesticide Evaluation Scientist (Chemistry)
Senior Pesticide Evaluation Scientist (Entomology)
Senior Pesticide Evaluation Scientist (Microbiolgy)
Senior Pesticide Evaluation Scientist (Plant Physiology)

Senior Pesticide Use Specialist
Senior Petroleum and Mining Appraisal Engineer
Senior Photo-Electronic Specialist, Department of Justice
Senior Photographer
Senior Pipeline Safety Engineer
Senior Planner (Specialist)
Senior Planner (Supervisor)
Senior Plant Hematologist (Specialist)
Senior Plant Hematologist (Supervisor)
Senior Plant Pathologist (Field)
Senior Plant Pathologist, Diagnostician (Specialist)
Senior Plant Pathologist, Diagnostician (Supervisor)
Senior Plant Taxo?omist
Senior Power Operations and Maintenance Engineer
Senior Precision Electronics Specialist
Senior Printing Trades Specialist (General)
Senior Procurement Engineer
Senior Program Review Analyst
Senior Programmer Analyst (Specialist)
Senior Programmer Analyst (Supervisor)
Senior Property Agent
Senior Property Appraiser
Senior Property Auditor-Appraiser
Senior Psychiatric Technician
Senior Psychiatric Technician, Forensic Facility
Senior Psychiatrist
Senior Psychologist
Senior Psychologist, Health Facility
Senior Public Health Biologist
Senior Radiological Instrument Technician,
Office of Emergency Services
Senior Rapid Transit Computer Control Systems Specialist
Senior Rapid Transit Control Systems Engineer
Senior Restoration Architect
Senior Right of Way Agent
Senior Safety Engineer (Construction)
Senior Safety Engineer (Electrical)
Senior Safety Engineer (Elevators)
Senior Safety Engineer (Industrial)
Senior Safety Engineer (Mining and Tunneling)
Senior Safety Engineer (Pressure Vessels)
Senior Sanitary Engineer
Senior Seed Botanist
Senior Seismologist
Senior Small Business Officer
Senior Special Agent, Department of Corrections
Senior Special Investigator
Senior Specification Writer, Hydraulic Structures
Senior Staff Counsel (Specialist)
Senior Staff Counsel (Supervisor)
Senior State Park Resource Ecologist
Senior Stenographer
Senior Stenographer, Legal
Senior Structural Engineer
Senior Structural Engineer, Emergency
Senior Subsidence Engineer, State Lands Division
Senior Survey Interviewer

Senior Tax Area Delineator
Senior Telecommunications Technician
Senior Telephone Operator
Senior Tourism Specialist
Senior Transportation Engineer
Senior Transportation Engineer, CalTrans
Senior Transportation Operations
Supervisor, Public Utilities Commission
Senior Transportation Planner
Senior Transportation Rate Expert
Senior Transportation Representative
Senior Typist, Legal
Senior Utilities Engineer
Senior Vocational Rehabilitation Counselor
Senior Warden/Pilot, Department of Fish and Game
Senior Waste Management Engineer
Senior Waste Management Specialist (Supervisory)
Senior Water and Power Dispatcher
Senior Water Quality Biologist
Senior Water Quality Engineer
Senior Water Resource Control Engineer
Senior Word Processing Technician
Senior X-Ray Technician
Senior Youth Counselor
Sergeant, State Fair Police
Service Assistant (DMV Operations)
Service Assistant (Duplicating)
Service Assistant (Equipment Parts Operator)
Service Assistant (Food)
Service Assistant (Hospital)
Service Assistant (Janitor)
Service Assistant (Key Data Operations)
Service Assistant (Laboratory)
Service Assistant (Laundry)
Service Assistant (Maintenance and Operations)
Service Assistant (Maintenance)
Service Assistant (Toll Collection)
Service Assistant, Automotive
Service Assistant, EDP Operations
Service Assistant, Engineering
Service Assistant, Warehouse and Stores
Sheet Metal Worker
Sheetfed Offset Press Operator I, II & III
Shoemaker
Shoemaker, Correctional Facility
Siskiyou Ranger Unit Chief
Skilled Laborer
Skilled Laborer, Correctional Facility
Skilled Laborer (Female)
Skilled Trades Apprentice, Casual Employment
Skilled Trades Apprentice, Casual Employment (Asbestos Worker Mechanic)
Skilled Trades Apprentice, Casual Employment (Blacksmith)
Skilled Trades Apprentice, Casual Employment (Carpenter)
Skilled Trades Apprentice, Casual Employment (Carpet/Soft Tile Settler/Resilient Floor Covering Installer)

Skilled Trades Apprentice, Casual Employment (Cement Finisher)
Skilled Trades Apprentice, Casual Employment (Construction Equipment)
Skilled Trades Apprentice, Casual Employment (Electrician)
Skilled Trades Apprentice, Casual Employment (Fusion Welder)
Skilled Trades Apprentice, Casual Employment (Glazier)
Skilled Trades Apprentice, Casual Employment (Hodcarrier)
Skilled Trades Apprentice, Casual Employment (Lather
Skilled Trades Apprentice, Casual Employment (Mason)
Skilled Trades Apprentice, Casual Employment (Metal Trades)
Skilled Trades Apprentice, Casual Employment (Millwright)
Skilled Trades Apprentice, Casual Employment (Operating Engineer)
Skilled Trades Apprentice, Casual Employment (Painter)
Skilled Trades Apprentice, Casual Employment (Plasterer)
Skilled Trades Apprentice, Casual Employment (Plumber)
Skilled Trades Apprentice, Casual Employment (Reinforcing Steel)
Skilled Trades Apprentice, Casual Employment (Roofer)
Skilled Trades Apprentice, Casual Employment (Sheet Metal)
Skilled Trades Apprentice, Casual Employment (Shipwright)
Skilled Trades Apprentice, Casual Employment (Steamfitter)
Skilled Trades Apprentice, Casual Employment (Structural Steel)
Skilled Trades Apprentice, Casual Employment (Tile Setter)
Skilled Trades Apprentice, Casual Employment (Welder)
Skilled Trades Journeyperson, Casual Employment
Skilled Trades Journeyperson, Casual Employment (Air Compressor Operator)
Skilled Trades Journeyperson, Casual Employment (Asbestos Worker Mechanic)
Skilled Trades Journeyperson, Casual Employment (Auto Mechanic)
Skilled Trades Journeyperson, Casual Employment (Blacksmith)
Skilled Trades Journeyperson, Casual Employment (Carpenter)
Skilled Trades Journeyperson, Casual Employment (Carpet/Soft Tile Setter/Resilient Floor Covering Installer)
Skilled Trades Journeyperson, Casual Employment (Cement Finisher)
Skilled Trades Journeyperson, Casual Employment (Construction Equipment)
Skilled Trades Journeyperson, Casual Employment (Electrician)
Skilled Trades Journeyperson, Casual Employment (Fence Erector)
Skilled Trades Journeyperson, Casual Employment (Fusion Welder)
Skilled Trades Journeyperson, Casual Employment (Glazier)
Skilled Trades Journeyperson, Casual Employment (Gunite Technician)
Skilled Trades Journeyperson, Casual Employment (Hodcarrier)
Skilled Trades Journeyperson, Casual Employment (Instrument Mechanic)
Skilled Trades Journeyperson, Casual Employment (Laborer)
Skilled Trades Journeyperson, Casual Employment (Lather)
Skilled Trades Journeyperson, Casual Employment (Lumber Mill)

Skilled Trades Journeyperson, Casual Employment (Mason)
Skilled Trades Journeyperson, Casual Employment (Metal Trades)
Skilled Trades Journeyperson, Casual Employment (Millwright)
Skilled Trades Journeyperson, Casual Employment (Operating Engineer)
Skilled Trades Journeyperson, Casual Employment (Painter)
Skilled Trades Journeyperson, Casual Employment (Plasterer)
Skilled Trades Journeyperson, Casual Employment (Plumber)
Skilled Trades Journeyperson, Casual Employment (Reinforcing Steel)
Skilled Trades Journeyperson, Casual Employment (Roofer)
Skilled Trades Journeyperson, Casual Employment (Service and Repair Mechanic Class III)
Skilled Trades Journeyperson, Casual Employment (Sheet Metal)
Skilled Trades Journeyperson, Casual Employment (Shipwright)
Skilled Trades Journeyperson, Casual Employment (Steamfitter)
Skilled Trades Journeyperson, Casual Employment (Steel Rolling Door)
Skilled Trades Journeyperson, Casual Employment (Structural Steel)
Skilled Trades Journeyperson, Casual Employment (Tile Setter Helpers)
Skilled Trades Journeyperson, Casual Employment (Tile Setter)
Skilled Trades Journeyperson, Casual Employment (Welder)
Skilled Trades Journeyperson, Casual Employment (Wood Caulker, Historic Ships)
Skilled Trades Supervisor, Casual Employment
Skilled Trades Supervisor, Casual Employment (Asbestos Worker Mechanic)
Skilled Trades Supervisor, Casual Employment (Blacksmith)
Skilled Trades Supervisor, Casual Employment (Carpenter)
Skilled Trades Supervisor, Casual Employment (Carpet/Soft Tile Setter/Resilient Floor Covering Installer)
Skilled Trades Supervisor, Casual Employment (Cement Finisher)
Skilled Trades Supervisor, Casual Employment (Construction Equipment)
Skilled Trades Supervisor, Casual Employment (Electrician)
Skilled Trades Supervisor, Casual Employment (Fence Erector)
Skilled Trades Supervisor, Casual Employment (Glazier)
Skilled Trades Supervisor, Casual Employment (Hodcarrier)
Skilled Trades Supervisor, Casual Employment (Laborer)
Skilled Trades Supervisor, Casual Employment (Lather)
Skilled Trades Supervisor, Casual Employment (Mason)
Skilled Trades Supervisor, Casual Employment (Metal Trades)
Skilled Trades Supervisor, Casual Employment (Millwright)
Skilled Trades Supervisor, Casual Employment (Operating Engineer)
Skilled Trades Supervisor, Casual Employment (Painter)
Skilled Trades Supervisor, Casual Employment (Plasterer)
Skilled Trades Supervisor, Casual Employment (Plumber)
Skilled Trades Supervisor, Casual Employment (Reinforcing Steel)
Skilled Trades Supervisor, Casual Employment (Roofer)
Skilled Trades Supervisor, Casual Employment (Sheet Metal)

Skilled Trades Supervisor, Casual Employment (Shipwright)
Skilled Trades Supervisor, Casual Employment (Steamfitter)
Skilled Trades Supervisor, Casual Employment (Structural Steel)
Skilled Trades Supervisor, Casual Employment (Tile Setter)
Skilled Trades Supervisor, Casual Employment (Welder)
Slide Tape Production Technician
Small Business Assistant I & II
Snow Gauger
Social Service Administrator I & II
Social Service Administrator III (CEA)
Social Service Aid
Social Service Assistant I & II, Mental Health
Social Service Consultant I, II & III
Social Work Associate
Solar Energy Program Specialist I, II & III
Special Advisor for Inheritance Taxes, State Controller's Office
Special Advisor To a Commissioner, State Energy Resources Conservation and Development Commission
Special Agent, Department of Corrections
Special Agent Supervisor, Department of Justice
Special Agent-In-Charge, Department of Justice
Special Agent, Department of Justice
Special Assistant Attorney General, Policy, Planning and Legislation (CEA)
Special Assistant Attorney General, Special Counsel (CEA)
Special Assistant Permits and Regulations
Special Assistant to the Director, Department of the Youth Authority
Special Assistant, Department of Food and Agriculture (General)
Special Assistant, Department of Food and Agriculture (Marketing Services)
Special Assistant, Department of Food and Agriculture (Measurement Standards)
Special Assistant, Department of Food and Agriculture (Pest Management)
Special Assistant, Department of Food and Agriculture (Plant Industry)
Special Consultant
Special Education Administrator I & II
Special Education Assistant I & II
Special Education Consultant
Special Investigator I
Special Representative, Department of Veterans Affairs
Specialist II, Railroad Restoration and Maintenance Project (Metal Fabrication)
Specialist in Academic Planning and Development, California Community Colleges
Specialist in Agricultural Education. California Community Colleges
Specialist in Business Education, California Community Colleges
Specialist in Child Abuse Prevention
Specialist in Criminal Justice Education, California Community Colleges
Specialist in Employment and Certification, California Community Colleges

Specialist in Facilities Planning and Utilization, California Community Colleges
Specialist in Fiscal Planning and Administration, California Community Colleges
Specialist in General Vocational Education, California Community Colleges
Specialist in Health Occupations, California Community Colleges
Specialist in Homemaking Education, California Community Colleges
Specialist in Industrial Education, California Community Colleges
Specialist in Information Systems and Analysis, California Community Colleges
Specialist in Public Service Occupations, California Community Colleges
Specialist in Student Service Planning andDevelopment, California Community Colleges
Specialist, California Educational Loan, Program, Student Aid Commission
Specialty Press Operator
Specification Writer I & II
Spectroscopist
Speech Pathologist Aide
Speech Pathologist I & II
Speech Pathologist License Applicant
Staff Administrative Analyst, Accounting Systems
Staff Air Pollution Specialist
Staff Chemical Engineer, Department of Water Resources
Staff Counsel
Staff Counsel (Hispanic)
Staff Data Processing Analyst (Specialist)
Staff Data Processing Analyst (Supervisor)
Staff Electronic Data Processing Acquisition Specialist
Staff Electronics and Instrumentation Engineer
Staff Finance Budget Analyst
Staff Governmental Program Analyst
Staff Health Care Service Plan Analyst
Staff Investment Analyst, California Housing Finance Agency
Staff Leasing Officer
Staff Management Auditor
Staff Park and Recreation Specialist
Staff Program Review Analyst
Staff Programmer Analyst (Specialist)
Staff Programmer Analyst (Supervisor)
Staff Psychiatrist
Staff Psychologist, Clinical
Staff Psychologist, Counseling
Staff Risk Manager
Staff Services Analyst (General)
Staff Services Analyst, Fair Political Practices Commission
Staff Services Management Auditor
Staff Services Management Auditor (Hispanic)
Staff Services Manager I & III
Staff Services Manager II (Managerial)
Staff Services Manager II (Supervisory)
Staff Space Planner

Staff Supervisor, Bureau of Milk Pooling
Staff Tax Auditor, Board of Equalization
Staff Toxicologist
Staff Toxicologist (Hispanic)
Staff Vocational Education Analyst, California Advisory Council
Staff Wildlife Pathologist
Standards and Quality Control Manager
Standards Compliance Coordinator
State Archeologist I, II & III
State Facilities Manager I & II
State Fair Activity Supervisor
State Fair Police Officer
State Fair Police Officer (Seasonal)
State Fair Worker, Casual Employment (Various)
State Financial Examiner II & III
State Fire Marshal Trainee
State Forest Ranger I, II, III & IV
State Geologist (CEA)
State Historian I, II & III
State Intergroup Relations Coordinator
State Long Term Care Ombudsman
State Oil and Gas Supervisor (CEA)
State Park Cadet (Lifeguard)
State Park Cadet (Ranger)
State Park Equipment Operator
State Park Interpreter Assistant (Permanent Intermittent)
State Park Interpreter I, II & III
State Park Naturalist I & II
State Park Ranger (Intermittent)
State Park Ranger I, II, III & IV
State Park Superintendent I, II, III & IV
State Park Wildlife Ecologist
State Parks Land Officer
State Police Officer
State Police Officer Cadet (Female)
State Police Officer Cadet (Male)
State Security Officer
State Traffic Captain
State Traffic Lieutenant
State Traffic Officer
State Traffic Officer Cadet (Female)
State Traffic Officer Cadet (Male)
State Traffic Sergeant
Stationary Engineer
Stationary Engineer, Correctional Facility
Stationary Engineer, Correctional Facility (Female)
Stationary Engineer (Female)
Stationary Engineer Apprentice
Stationary Engineer Apprentice, Four Year
Program, Correctional Facility
Stationary Engineer Apprentice, Four Year Program
Statistical Clerk
Statistical Consultant, Employment Development Department
Statistical Methods Analyst I, II & III
Steamfitter
Steamfitter, Correctional Facility
Steamfitter Supervisor, Correctional Facility

Stenographer
Stock Clerk
Structural Drafting Technician I, II & III
Structural Engineering Associate
Structural Pest Control Board Specialist
Structural Steel Inspector (Nondestructive Testing)
Structural Steel Painter
Structural Steel Painter (Female)
Structural Steel Painter Apprentice
Structural Steel Painter Apprentice (Female)
Structural Steel Painter Superintendent
Structural Steel Painter Supervisor
Structural Steel Welder
Student Affairs Assistant, California Maritime Academy
Student Affairs Officer I, II & III, California Maritime Academy
Student Aide
Student Assistant
Student Assistant, Engineering and Architectural Sciences
Student Engineering Aid
Student Financial Needs Analyst I &II, Student Aid Commission
Substitute Teacher Intermittent
Superintendent, California School for the Blind
Superintendent, California School for the Deaf
Superintendent, Diagnostic School for Neurologically Handicapped Children
Superintendent III, Department of Corrections (CEA)
Supervising Account Clerk I & II
Supervising Actuarial Statistician
Supervising Administrative Analyst, Accounting Systems
Supervising Air Pollution Research Specialist
Supervising Air Pollution Specialist
Supervising Air Resources Engineer
Supervising Architect
Supervising Architect, Health Facilities
Supervising Architectural Advisor, Bureau of School Planning
Supervising Auditor I & II, State Controller's Office
Supervising Auditor I & II, Department of Real Estate
Supervising Auditor I & II, Milk Marketing
Supervising Automotive Equipment Standards Engineer
Supervising Aviation Consultant
Supervising Bank Examiner
Supervising Bank Examiner, Electronic Data Processing
Supervising Book Repairer
Supervising Boundary Determination Officer
Supervising Bridge Engineer
Supervising Casework Specialist I & II, Youth Authority
Supervising Casualty Actuary
Supervising Certification Officer
Supervising Chemist, Bureau of Home Furnishings
Supervising Child Nutrition Consultant
Supervising Civil Engineer, Resources Agency
Supervising Claim Auditor
Supervising Claim Auditor, Welfare Programs
Supervising Clinical Laboratory Technologist

Supervising Communicable Disease Representative
Supervising Construction Engineer, Water Resources
Supervising Construction Engineer, Department of Corrections
Supervising Control System Engineer
Supervising Cook I & II
Supervising Cook I & II, Correctional Facility
Supervising Corporation Examiner
Supervising Corporations Investigator
Supervising Cosmetology Examiner
Supervising Counsel, Legal Program, Department of Corporations
Supervising Deputy State Public Defender
Supervising Design Officer, California Housing Finance Agency
Supervising Egg and Poultry Quality Control Inspector
Supervising Electric Utilties Engineer
Supervising Electrical Engineer
Supervising Electrical Engineer, Hydraulic Structures
Supervising Engineer, Civil Section, Office of Architecture and Construction
Supervising Engineer, Equipment and Materials Section
Supervising Engineer, Water Resources
Supervising Engineering Geologist
Supervising Engineering Geologist, CalTrans
Supervising Environmental Planner
Supervising Equipment Engineer
Supervising Estimator of Building Construction
Supervising Estimator, California Housing Finance Agency
Supervising Field Representative, School Administration
Supervising Food and Drug Investigator
Supervising Geologist
Supervising Governmental Auditor I & II
Supervising Groundskeeper I & II
Supervising Groundskeeper I & II, Correctional Facility
Supervising Hazardous Materials Specialist
Supervising Health Physicist
Supervising Hearing Reporter
Supervising Hearing Transcriber/Typist, Public Utilties Commission
Supervising Highway Electrical Engineer
Supervising Housekeeper I & II
Supervising Housing Construction and Rehabilitation Specialist
Supervising Hydraulic Engineer
Supervising Industrial Hygienist
Supervising Inheritance and Gift Tax Examiner I & II
Supervising Inspector, Board of Pharmacy
Supervising Insurance Examiner
Supervising Insurance Investigator
Supervising Insurance Policy Officer
Supervising Insurance Rate Analyst
Supervising Investigator, Fair Political Practices Commission
Supervising Laboratory Assistant I & II
Supervising Land Agent (Managerial)
Supervising Land Agent (Supervisory)
Supervising Land and Water Use Analyst

Supervising Land Surveyor
Supervising Landscape Architect
Supervising Law Indexer
Supervising Legal Stenographer I
Supervising Librarian
Supervising Librarian, Correctional Facility
Supervising Life Actuary
Supervising Lottery Agent
Supervising Management Auditor
Supervising Materials and Research Engineer
Supervising Heat Inspector
Supervising Mechanical and Electrical Engineer, CalTrans
Supervising Mechanical Engineer
Supervising Mechnical Engineer, Hydraulic Structures
Supervising Microfilm Technician
Supervising Milk Production Cost Analyst
Supervising Mineral Resources Engineer
Supervising Motor Vehicle Pollution Control Engineer
Supervising Motor Vehicle Representative
Supervising Museum Security Officer
Supervising Nurse II & III
Supervising Nursing Education Consultant
Supervising Oil and Gas Engineer
Supervising Park Interpretive Specialist (Seasonal)
Supervising Personnel Selection Consultant
Supervising Pesticide Use Specialist
Supervising Photographer, Department of Transportation
Supervising Power Operation and Maintenance Engineer
Supervising Program Review Analyst
Supervising Program Technician I, II & III, (Alcoholic Beverage Control)
Supervising Program Technician I, II & III, (Business Taxes)
Supervising Program Technician I, II & III, (California Youth Authority, Records)
Supervising Program Technician I, II & III, (Contractors' Licensing)
Supervising Program Technician I, II & III, (Corporate Filing and Services)
Supervising Program Technician I, II & III, (Corporations Licensing)
Supervising Program Technician I, II & III, (Corrections Records)
Supervising Program Technician I, II & III, (Mobilehomes)
Supervising Program Technician I, II & III, (Notary Public)
Supervising Program Technician I, II & III, (Personnel Services)
Supervising Program Technician I, II & III, (Real Estate Licensing)
Supervising Program Technician I, II & III, (Retirement System)
Supervising Program Technician I, II & III, (Student Aid Commission)
Supervising Program Technician I, II & III, (Traffic Records)
Supervising Program Technician I, II & III, (Veterans Affairs)
Supervising Program Technician I, II & III, (Vital Statistics)
Supervising Property Agent
Supervising Prorate Tax Auditor

Supervising Psychiatric Nurse
Supervising Psychiatric Social Worker I & II
Supervising Psychiatric Social Worker I, (Mental Health)
Supervising Public Health Biologist
Supervising Racing License Technician
Supervising Right of Way Agent
Supervising Sanitary Engineer
Supervising Savings and Loan Examiner
Supervising Special Investigator, Alcoholic Beverage Control
Supervising Special Investigator I & II
Supervising State Financial Examiner I, II & III
Supervising State Park Resource Ecologist
Supervising Stenographer I
Supervising Structural Engineer
Supervising Tax Auditor I, II & III Board of Equalization
Supervising Tax Auditor I, Employment Development Department
Supervising Telecommunications Engineer
Supervising Telecommunications Technician
Supervising Telephone Operator
Supervising Transportation Engineer, Public Utilties Commission
Supervising Transportation Engineer, CalTrans
Supervising Transportation Officer, Youth Authority
Supervising Transportatation Planner
Supervising Transportation Rate Expert
Supervising Transportation Representative
Supervising Waste Management Engineer
Supervising Waste Management Specialist
Supervising Water Resource Control Engineer (Managerial)
Supervising Water Resource Control Engineer (Supervisory)
Supervising Worker's Compensation Consultant
Supervisor, Chemical Testing Section, Hydraulic Laboratory
Supervisor, Local Government Budgets and Reports
Supervisor of Academic Instruction, Correctional Facility
Supervisor of Building Trades
Supervisor of Building Trades, Correctional Facility
Supervisor of Commercial Diver Training
Supervisor of Compensatory Education Program
Supervisor of Conciliation, Department of Industrial Relations (CEA)
Supervisor of Correctional Education Programs
Supervisor of Drafting Services
Supervisor of Environmental Sanitation, Veterans Home and Medical Center
Supervisor of Equipment and Materials Inspection, Hydraulic Structures
Supervisor of Exhibit Installation
Supervisor of Exhibit Preparation
Supervisor of Guides, Historical Monument
Supervisor of Photography
Supervisor of Printing and Planning Services
Supervisor of Regional Fish Hatcheries
Supervisor of Registration, Agricultural Chemicals
Supervisor of Technical Publications
Supervisor of Tool and Instrument Shop
Supervisor of Vocational Instruction

Supervisor, Operations and Safety Section,
Public Utilties Commission
Supervisor, Public Liability Claims
Supervisor, Tax Area Services
Supervisor, Tax/Deeded Land, State Controller's Office
Supervisor, California Educational Loan
Program, Student Aid Commission
Supervisor, Sheltered Workshop
Supervisor, Tax Return Audit Bureau
Supervisor, Tunnels and Tubes
Supervisor, Waste Water Treatment
Training Center
Supply Operations Manager
Support Services Assistant (General)
Support Services Assistant (Interpreter)
Supportive Equipment Adapter
Supportive Equipment Adapter Trainee
Surgical Nurse I & II
Surplus Property Coordinator
Surplus Property Officer
Survey Interviewer
Systems Software Specialist I, II & III (Supervisory)
Systems Software Specialist I, II & III Technical)

T

Tabulating Machine Operator
Tabulating Operations Supervisor I
Tahoe Conservancy Program Analyst I & II
Tahoe Conservancy Program Manager
Tax Administrator I, II & III, Employment Developmen
Department
Tax Area Delineator
Tax Auditor II, Board of Equalization
Tax Auditor II, III & IV, Employment Development Department
Tax Auditor II & III, Franchise Tax Board
Tax Auditor, Board of Equalization
Tax Compliance Representative I & II
Tax Compliance Representative III (Supervision)
Tax Compliance Representative III (Technical)
Tax Compliance Supervisor
Tax Compliance Supervisor II
Tax Program Specialist I, II & III
Tax Service Specialist
Tax Technician, Franchise Tax Board
Teacher, Correctional Facility (Emotionally/Learning
Handicapped)
Teacher, Correctional Facility (Hearing Impaired)
Teacher, Correctional Facility (Industrial Arts)
Teacher, Correctional Facility (Speech Development and
Correction)
Teacher, Correctional Facility (Arts and Crafts)
Teacher, Correctional Facility (Business Education)
Teacher, Correctional Facilit (Elementary Education)
Teacher, Correctional Facility (High School Education)
Teacher, Correctional Facility (Home Economics)
Teacher, Correctional Facility (Librarian)

Teacher, Correctional Facility (Music)
Teacher, Correctional Facility (Recreation and Physical Education)
Teacher, (Businees Education)
Teacher, (Emotionally Handicapped)
Teacher, (High School Education)
Teacher, (Home Economics)
Teacher, (Librarian)
Teacher, (Mentally Retarded Children)
Teacher, (Recreation and Physical Education)
Teacher, (Speech Development and Correction)
Teacher, (Orientation and Mobility for the Blind)
Teacher, Orientation Center for the Blind (Typing and Braille)
Teacher Preparation Administrator I, Examinations and Research
Teacher Preparation Administrator I, Program Evaluation and Research
Teacher, Department of Health, (Mentally Retarded Children)
Teacher, State Hospital (Adult Education)
Teacher, State Hospital (Arts and Crafts)
Teacher, State Hospital (Communication Handicapped)
Teacher, State Hospital (Elementary Education)
Teacher, State Hospital (High School Education)
Teacher, State Hospital (Home Economics)
Teacher, State Hospital (Music)
Teacher, State Hospital (Physically Handicapped)
Teacher, State Hospital (Recreation and Physical Education)
Teacher, State Hospital (Speech Development and Correction)
Teacher, State Hospital (Learning Handicapped, Developmentally Disabled)
Teacher, State Hospital (Learning Handicapped, Mentally Disabled)
Teacher, State Hospital (Severely Handicapped, Mentally)
Teacher, State Hospital (Severely Handicapped, Developmentally Disabled)
Teaching Assistant
Technical Assistant I & II, Fair Political Practices Commission
Telecommunications Systems Manager II (Managerial)
Telecommunications Assistant
Telecommunications Specialist
Telecommunications Systems Analyst I & II
Telecommunications Systems Manager I (Specialist)
Telecommunications Systems Manager I (Supervisor)
Telecommunications Systems Manager II (Supervisor)
Telecommunications Technician
Telecommunications Technician Trainee
Telemarketing Representative I & II
Telemarketing Representative Supervisor
Telephone Operator
Telephone Operator, Switchboard for the Blind
Teletypewriter Operator
Television Assistant
Television Specialist
Temporary Clerk
Test Validation and Development Specialist I & II
Textbook Consultant
Textile Chemist I & II

Textile Technician I & II
Title Specialist I, II & III
Toll Captain
Toll Collector
Toll Lieutenant
Toll Sergeant
Toll Services Manager
Totalisator Systems Manager
Totalisator Systems Examiner
Tractor Operator/Laborer
Trading Specialist
Traffic Analyst
Traffic Manager
Training Coordinator, San Marcos Training Center
Training Officer I, II & III
Translator
Transportation Analyst
Transportation Coordinator, Special Schools
Transportation Engineering Technician
Transportation Officer, Youth Authority
Transportation Planner
Transportation Rate Clerk
Transportation/Legislative Advisor to a Commissioner, Public Utilities Commission
Treasury Guard/Clerk
Treasury Program Manager I, II & III
Treasury Teller
Treasury Vault Officer
Treatment Team Supervisor
Tree Maintenance Leadworker
Tree Maintenance Supervisor
Tree Maintenance Worker
Tree Maintenance Worker (Female)
Truck Driver
Truck Driver (Female)
Truck Driver, Correctional Facility
Truck Driver, Correctional Facility (Female)

U

Unit Supervisor
Upholsterer
Utility Shops Specialist, Correctional Facility
Utility Shops Supervisor
Utility Shops Supervisor, Correctional Facility

V

Vector Control Assistant I
Vehicle Pollution Advisor, Air Resources Board
Veterans Claims Representative I, II & III
Veterans Educational Representative
Veterinary Medical Officer (Animal Health)
Veterinary Medical Officer (Meat Inspection)
Veterinary Medical Officer III & IV (Animal Health)
Veterinary Medical Officer III & IV (Meat Inspection)
Vocational Education Administrator I & II

Vocational Education Assistant I & II
Vocational Education Consultant
Vocational Education Gender Equity Consultant
Vocational Instructor (Auto Body and Fender Repair)
Vocational Instructor (Garment Making)
Vocational Instructor (Stockkeeping and Warehousing)
Vocational Instructor (Upholstering)
Vocational Education Supervisor, Correctional Program
Vocational Instructor, Correctional Facility(Airframe Mechanics)
Vocational Instructor, Correctional Facility (Animal Husbandry)
Vocational Instructor, Correctional Facility (Auto Body and Fender Repair)
Vocational Instructor, Correctional Facility (Auto Mechanics)
Vocational Instructor, Correctional Facility (Baking)
Vocational Instructor, Correctional Facility (Barbershop Practices)
Vocational Instructor, Correctional Facility (Book Binders)
Vocational Instructor, Correctional Facility (Building Maintenance)
Vocational Instructor, Correctional Facility (Carpentry)
Vocational Instructor, Correctional Facility (Commercial Driver Training)
Vocational Instructor, Correctional Facility (Computer and Related Technologies)
Vocational Instructor, Correctional Facility (Cosmetology)
Vocational Instructor, Correctional Facility (Culinary Arts)
Vocational Instructor, Correctional Facility (Diesel Mechanic)
Vocational Instructor, Correctional Facility (Dog Grooming and Handling)
Vocational Instructor, Correctional Facility (Dry Cleaning Work)
Vocational Instructor, Correctional Facility (Drywall Installer/Taper)
Vocational Instructor, Correctional Facility (Electrical Work)
Vocational Instructor, Correctional Facility (Farming, Diversified Crops)
Vocational Instructor, Correctional Facility (Fiberglass Technology)
Vocational Instructor, Correctional Facility (Floor Cover Layer)
Vocational Instructor, Correctional Facility (Furniture Refinishing)
Vocational Instructor, Correctional Facility (Garment Making)
Vocational Instructor, Correctional Facility (Glazier)
Vocational Instructor, Correctional Facility (Horse Trainer)
Vocational Instructor, Correctional Facility (Insulation Installer, Building and Pipe)
Vocational Instructor, Correctional Facility (Machine Shop/Automotive)
Vocational Instructor, Correctional Facility (Machine Shop Practices)
Vocational Instructor, Correctional Facility (Masonry)
Vocational Instructor, Correctional Facility (Meat Cutting)
Vocational Instructor, Correctional Facility (Mechanical Driving)
Vocational Instructor, Correctional Facility (Mill and Cabinet Work)
Vocational Instructor, Correctional Facility (Office Machine Repair)

Vocational Instructor, Correctional Facility (Office Services and Related Technologies)
Vocational Instructor, Correctional Facility (Painting)
Vocational Instructor, Correctional Facility (Plastering)
Vocational Instructor, Correctional Facility (Plumbing)
Vocational Instructor, Correctional Facility (Power Plant Mechanics)
Vocational Instructor, Correctional Facility (Printing Graphic Arts)
Vocational Instructor, Correctional Facility (Radiologic Technology)
Vocational Instructor, Correctional Facility (Refrigeration and Air Conditioning Repair)
Vocational Instructor, Correctional Facility (Roofer)
Vocational Instructor, Correctional Facility (Sewing Machine Repair)
Vocational Instructor, Correctional Facility (Small Engine Repair)
Vocational Instructor, Correctional Facility (Solar Energy/Alternate Energy)
Vocational Instructor, Correctional Facility (Stockkeeping and Warehousing)
Vocational Instructor, Correctional Facility (Sheet Metal Work)
Vocational Instructor, Correctional Facility (Shoemaking)
Vocational Instructor, Correctional Facility (Silk Screen)
Vocational Instructor, Correctional Facility (Vocational Nursing)
Vocational Instructor, Correctional Facility (Welding)
Vocational Psychologist
Vocational Rehabilitation Assistant
Vocational Rehabilitation Counselor
Vocational Rehabilitation Counselor (Blind)
Vocational Rehabilitation Trainee
Vocational Testing and Counseling Specialist, Correctional Program
Volunteer Services Program Manager, Youth Authority
Volunteer State Service Intern

W

Warden/Pilot, Department of Fish and Game
Warehouse Manager I & II
Warehouse Manager I & II, Correctional Facility
Warehouse Operations Manager
Warehouse Worker
Warehouse Worker, Correctional Facility
Warning Controller, Office of Emergency Services
Waste Management Engineer
Waste Management Engineer (Hispanic)
Waste Management Specialist
Water and Power Dispatcher
Water and Sewage Plant Supervisor
Water and Sewage Plant Supervisor, Correctional Facility
Water Quality Biologist
Water Reclamation Sludge Specialist
Water Resource Control Engineer
Water Resources Engineering Associate (Specialist)
Water Resources Engineering Associate (Supervisor)

Water Resources Technician I & II
Water Services Supervisor
Webfed Offset Press Operator I, II & III
Welfare Fraud Prevention Coordinator
Wildlife Biologist
Wildlife Habitat Assistant
Wildlife Habitat Supervisor I & II
Wildlife Management Supervisor
Window Cleaner
Window Cleaner Supervisor
Wood Caulker, Historic Ships (Casual Employment)
Word Processing Technician
Workers' Compensation Assistant
Workers' Compensation Consultant
Workers' Compensation Insurance Representaive I, II & III
Workers' Compensation Insurance Supervisor I & II
Workers' Compensation Insurance Technician
Workers' Compensation Judge
Workers' Compensation Manager
Workers' Compensation Rehabilitation Consultant

X

X-Ray Technician

Y

Youth Aide
Youth Authority Administrator, Community and Staff Services
Youth Authority Administrator, Rehabilitation Services
Youth Authority Teacher
Youth Counselor
Youthful Offender Parole Board Representive

The State Civil Service Examination Process

How to Find Out About Upcoming Exams

The State Personnel Board (SPB) is the most reliable resource for finding out about upcoming state civil service examinations, since all upcoming examinations must be reported to the SPB.

The SPB will even have information about open examinations administered and processed by individual departments. (These are, in my opinion, not widely publicized by the departments.)

The headquarters SPB Office is located, in Sacramento, at:

801 Capitol Mall
Sacramento, CA 95814
916-322-2530

There is also an office in Los Angeles located at:

107 South Broadway, Room 1021
Los Angeles, CA 90012
231-620-2770

These offices post upcoming state civil service examination announcements for the public to view, and, at your request, SPB staff will provide you with copies of any posted examination announcement along with the state application form.

If you live near either of these offices, it's a good idea to visit the public bulletin boards at least once a week, to stay informed of all the upcoming examinations you may qualify for. Friday is the best day to visit the offices because SPB staff change the announcements and add new announcements each Friday.

Jobseekers in San Francisco can visit public bulletin boards at the Department of Employment Development (EDD) located at:

745 Franklin Street
San Francisco, California
(415)-557-8651

Although the SPB no longer has an office in San Francisco, the EDD staff will provide copies of exam announcements and state applications. You must, however, contact the Sacramento or the Los Angeles SPB office if you have any questions about the examinations.

The SPB also provides 24 hour recordings of upcoming civil service examination, for those of you who are unable to visit the SPB offices. The recordings, like the bulletin boards, are changed every Friday. For specific career fields, call the number designated:

In the Sacramento area:

Clerical and General	916-323-3475
Health and Related classes	916-323-3473
Law Enforcement and Social Services	916-323-3472
Legal, Professional and Technical	916-323-3471
Trades and Labor classes	916-323-3474
TDD (For the hearing impaired)	916-323-7490

In the Los Angeles area:

Clerical, Domestic and Janitorial	213-620-4210
General Testing	213-620-4175
Health and Related classes	213-620-4192
Legal, Professional and Technical	213-620-4199
TDD (For the hearing impaired)	213-620-3242

In the San Diego Area:

General Testing	619-236-9238

Clerical, Domestic and Janitorial	619-692-8891
Professional and Technical	619-292-7334
Health and Related Classes	619-236-9239

In the San Francisco Bay area:

Clerical	415-557-0310
Health and Related classes	415-557-9359
Law Enforcement and Social Services	415-557-9358
Legal, Professional and Technical	415-557-9357
Trades and Labor classes	415-557-9350
TDD (For the hearing impaired)	415-557-8691

Understanding the Examination Announcement

The *examination announcement* is an invaluable source of information to you as a jobseeker. It's really your potential employer's tool for establishing what's expected of you if you come to work in a particular classification. Therefore, as soon as you spot an examination you'd like to take, get a copy of the examination announcement as well as a copy of the specification. Study the announcement carefully to make sure you meet the minimum qualifications and keep it for handy reference until the examination process has been completed. Announcements are usually color coded according to the category of eligible applicants.

1. **White**-open/nonpromotional: this is the most desirable examination announcement for the first time state civil service job seeker. Anyone can apply and the examination is given for positions throughout the state of California. You do not need to be a state employee to take these examinations.

2. **Pink**-promotional: Examinations that are printed on pink paper may only be taken by state civil service employees. If the examination is a departmental promotional, only employees of that department may take the examination.

3. **Green**-open/nonpromotional spot: Again, anyone can apply, however, the examination is being given for one or more specific geographic locations or "spots."

4. **Blue**-Limited Examination and Appointment Program (LEAP): Although you do not have to be a state employee to apply, in order to be eligible to take the examination, you must be certified by the State Department of Rehabilitation as having a disability.

Interpreting the Examination Announcement

Figure 2

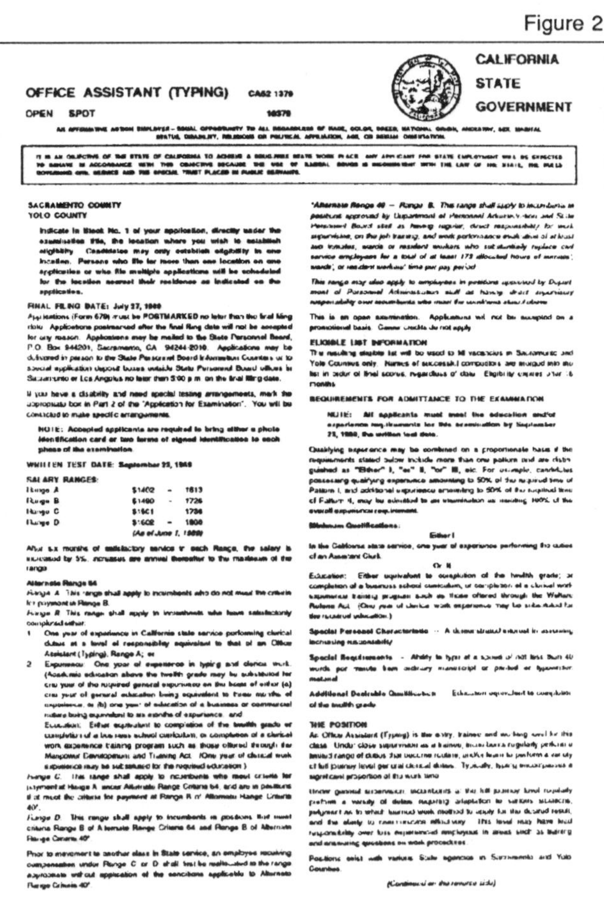

CALIFORNIA STATE GOVERNMENT

OFFICE ASSISTANT (TYPING) CA62 1379

OPEN SPOT 10379

AN AFFIRMATIVE ACTION EMPLOYER – EQUAL OPPORTUNITY TO ALL REGARDLESS OF RACE, COLOR, CREED, NATIONAL ORIGIN, ANCESTRY, SEX, MARITAL STATUS, DISABILITY, RELIGIOUS OR POLITICAL AFFILIATION, AGE, OR SEXUAL ORIENTATION.

IT IS AN OBJECTIVE OF THE STATE OF CALIFORNIA TO ACHIEVE A DRUG-FREE STATE WORK PLACE. ANY APPLICANT FOR STATE EMPLOYMENT WILL BE EXPECTED TO BEHAVE IN ACCORDANCE WITH THIS OBJECTIVE BECAUSE THE USE OF ILLEGAL DRUGS IS INCONSISTENT WITH THE LAW OF THE STATE, THE RULES GOVERNING CIVIL SERVICE AND THE SPECIAL TRUST PLACED IN PUBLIC SERVANTS.

SACRAMENTO COUNTY
YOLO COUNTY

Indicate in Block No. 1 of your application, directly under the examination title, the location where you wish to establish eligibility. Candidates may only establish eligibility in one location. Persons who file for more than one location on one application or who file multiple applications will be scheduled for the location nearest their residence as indicated on the application.

FINAL FILING DATE: July 27, 1989
Applications (Form 678) must be POSTMARKED no later than the final filing date. Applications postmarked after the final filing date will not be accepted for any reason. Applications may be mailed to the State Personnel Board, P.O. Box 944201, Sacramento, CA 94244-2010. Applications may be delivered in person to the State Personnel Board Information Counters or to special application deposit boxes outside State Personnel Board offices in Sacramento or Los Angeles no later than 5:00 p.m. on the final filing date.

If you have a disability and need special testing arrangements, mark the appropriate box in Part 2 of the "Application for Examination". You will be contacted to make specific arrangements.

NOTE: Accepted applicants are required to bring either a photo identification card or two forms of signed identification to each phase of the examination.

WRITTEN TEST DATE: September 23, 1989

SALARY RANGES:

Range A	$1402	-	1613
Range B	$1490	-	1726
Range C	$1561	-	1786
Range D	$1602	-	1806

(As of June 1, 1989)

After six months of satisfactory service in each Range, the salary is increased by 5%. Increases are annual thereafter to the maximum of the range.

Alternate Range 64
Range A. This range shall apply to incumbents who do not meet the criteria for payment in Range B.
Range B. This range shall apply to incumbents who have satisfactorily completed either:
1. One year of experience in California state service performing clerical duties at a level of responsibility equivalent to that of an Office Assistant (Typing), Range A; or
2. Experience: One year of experience in typing and clerical work. (Academic education above the twelfth grade may be substituted for one year of the required general experience on the basis of either (a) one year of general education being equivalent to three months of experience, or (b) one year of education of a business or commercial nature being equivalent to six months of experience. and
Education: Either equivalent to completion of the twelfth grade or completion of a business school curriculum, or completion of a clerical work experience training program such as those offered through the Manpower Development and Training Act. (One year of clerical work experience may be substituted for the required education.)

Range C. This range shall apply to incumbents who meet criteria for payment at Range A under Alternate Range Criteria 64, and are in positions that meet the criteria for payment at Range B of Alternate Range Criteria 40*.
Range D. This range shall apply to incumbents in positions that meet criteria Range B of Alternate Range Criteria 64 and Range B of Alternate Range Criteria 40*.

Prior to movement to another class in State service, an employee receiving compensation under Range C or D shall first be reallocated to the range appropriate without application of the conditions applicable to Alternate Range Criteria 40*.

**Alternate Range 40 – Range B. This range shall apply to incumbents in positions approved by Department of Personnel Administration and State Personnel Board staff as having regular, direct responsibility for work supervision, on the job training, and work performance evaluation of at least two inmates, wards or resident workers who substantially replace civil service employees for a total of at least 173 allocated hours of inmates', wards', or resident workers' time per pay period.*

This range may also apply to employees in positions approved by Department of Personnel Administration staff as having direct supervisory responsibility over incumbents who meet the conditions stated above.

This is an open examination. Applications will not be accepted on a promotional basis. Career credits do not apply.

ELIGIBLE LIST INFORMATION
The resulting eligible list will be used to fill vacancies in Sacramento and Yolo Counties only. Names of successful competitors are merged into the list in order of final scores, regardless of date. Eligibility expires after 18 months.

REQUIREMENTS FOR ADMITTANCE TO THE EXAMINATION

NOTE: All applicants must meet the education and/or experience requirements for this examination by September 23, 1989, the written test date.

Qualifying experience may be combined on a proportionate basis if the requirements stated below include more than one pattern and are distinguished as "Either" I, "or" II, "or" III, etc. For example, candidates possessing qualifying experience amounting to 50% of the required time of Pattern I, and additional experience amounting to 50% of the required time of Pattern II, may be admitted to an examination as meeting 100% of the overall experience requirement.

Minimum Qualifications:

Either I

In the California state service, one year of experience performing the duties of an Assistant Clerk.

Or II

Education: Either equivalent to completion of the twelfth grade; or completion of a business school curriculum, or completion of a clerical work experience training program such as those offered through the Welfare Reform Act. (One year of clerical work experience may be substituted for the required education.)

Special Personal Characteristics -- A demonstrated interest in assuming increasing responsibility.

Special Requirements - Ability to type at a speed of not less than 40 words per minute from ordinary manuscript or printed or typewritten material.

Additional Desirable Qualifications -- Education equivalent to completion of the twelfth grade.

THE POSITION
An Office Assistant (Typing) is the entry, trainee and working level for this class. Under close supervision as a trainee, incumbents regularly perform a limited range of duties that become routine, and/or learn to perform a variety of full journey level general clerical duties. Typically, typing encompasses a significant proportion of the work time.

Under general supervision, incumbents at the full journey level regularly perform a variety of duties requiring adaptation to various situations, judgment as to which learned work method to apply for the desired result, and the ability to make decisions effectively. This level may have lead responsibility over less experienced employees in areas such as training and answering questions on work procedures.

Positions exist with various State agencies in Sacramento and Yolo Counties.

(Continued on the reverse side)

All examination announcements follow the same basic format, but let's take a closer look at one of the "foot in the door" examination announcements—the Office Assistant—to see what the various terms mean.

The examination title usually appears in the upper left hand corner, and just below it, in smaller print is information on the category of eligible applicants for the examination. An examination may be given on a promotional-only (for state employees) basis, a combined open and promotional basis or an open, non-promotional basis.

This Office Assistant examination announcement (which is printed on green paper) is an open "spot" examination. The announcement will spec-

Figure 3

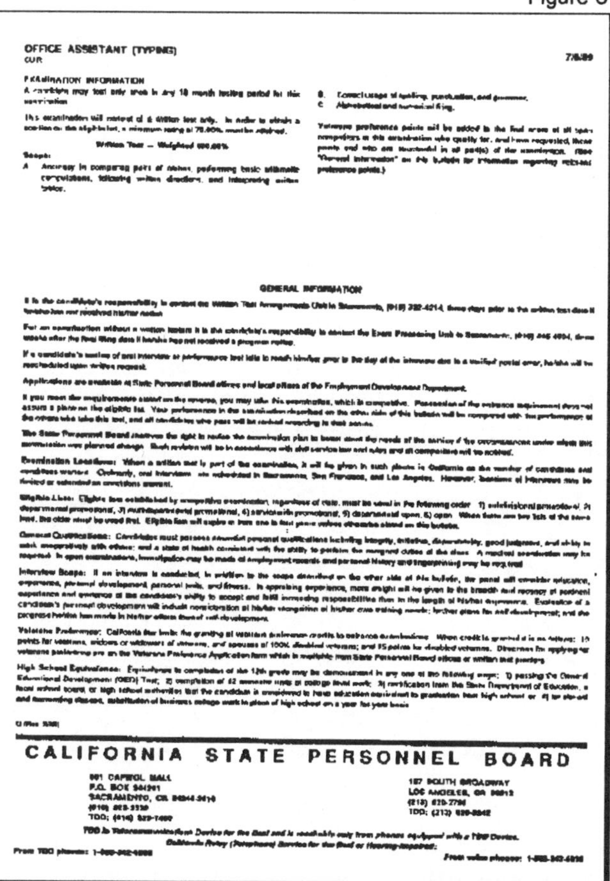

OFFICE ASSISTANT (TYPING)

EXAMINATION INFORMATION

GENERAL INFORMATION

CALIFORNIA STATE PERSONNEL BOARD

ify in which county or counties the State anticipates available positions for this class. In this case, the counties are Sacramento and Yolo.

The **Final Filing Date** is usually next (see figure 4 on page 118). This is the most important information on the announcement. Think of it as your deadline. If you don't meet this deadline, you can't take this examination, and there is no way of knowing when it will be offered again.

Figure 4

SACRAMENTO COUNTY
YOLO COUNTY

Indicate in Block No. 1 of your application, directly under the examination title, the location where you wish to establish eligibility. Candidates may only establish eligibility in one location. Persons who file for more than one location on one application or who file multiple applications will be scheduled for the location nearest their residence as indicated on the application.

FINAL FILING DATE: July 27, 1989

Applications (Form 678) must be POSTMARKED no later than the final filing date. Applications postmarked after the final filing date will not be accepted for any reason. Applications may be mailed to the State Personnel Board, P.O. Box 944201, Sacramento, CA 94244-2010. Applications may be delivered in person to the State Personnel Board Information Counters or to special application deposit boxes outside State Personnel Board offices in Sacramento or Los Angeles no later than 5:00 p.m. on the final filing date.

If you have a disability and need special testing arrangements, mark the appropriate box in Part 2 of the "Application for Examination". You will be contacted to make specific arrangements.

NOTE: Accepted applicants are required to bring either a photo identification card or two forms of signed identification to each phase of the examination.

Just below the Final Filing Date is the address to which you must mail your application. The address is not the same on all examination announcements, especially on the departmental examination announcements. Occasionally an announcement will state that applications must be filed in person on a certain day, between specified hours, at a particular location, and to be eligible to apply for such an examination, you must adhere to the application filing requirements.

Somewhere on the left hand side there will be information regarding the type of examination that will be given. While our sample examination announcement indicates that it will be a written examination, the other formats are oral interview only or a combination of a written and oral examination. Written examinations are given in a wide variety of locations throughout the state, whereas oral examinations are usually given only in large metropolitan areas.

In addition, within this examination process, the SPB or other examining department may investigate your character, personality, education and experiences and may test your intelligence capacity, technical knowledge, manual skill or physical fitness.

If the examination for which you are applying has a written portion, the announcement will include the anticipated written test date as our sample indicates. If your examination has an interview portion, the announcement will include a statement that indicates when interviews can be anticipated, such as, "It is anticipated that interviews will be held in November 1990."

The anticipated date is the testing department's notice to applicants to alert them when they should plan to be available. If the testing department meets this date and you are unavailable at the time scheduled for your interview, it is unlikely that you will be rescheduled.

Salary Ranges. This section identifies the range of monthly salary bases for persons employed in the particular classification. The Office Assistant (Typing) has four salary ranges, Range A-D, with various criteria for determining which range applies to an applicant.

Figure 5

SALARY RANGES:

Range A	$1402	–	1613
Range B	$1490	–	1726
Range C	$1501	–	1736
Range D	$1602	–	1860
	(As of June 1, 1989)		

After six months of satisfactory service in each Range, the salary is increased by 5%; increases are annual thereafter to the maximum of the range.

Eligible List Information. Specifies the period of time for which successful examination applicants can apply for jobs based on the results of this examination. This section also provides information on the location of anticipated vacancies for the classification.

Figure 6

ELIGIBLE LIST INFORMATION

The resulting eligible list will be used to fill vacancies in Sacramento and Yolo Counties only. Names of successful competitors are merged into the list in order of final scores, regardless of date. Eligibility expires after 18 months

Requirements for Admittance to the Examination. To qualify for an examination, you must meet the minimum qualifications as stated on the announcement. Anyone who meets the minimum qualifications for a state position is eligible, regardless of age, to take a civil service examination given for that position. In state service, all experience requirements are full-time equivalents whether stated or not. If you have qualifying experience that is part time, it will be accepted and prorated, but the total amount must equal or exceed the minimum number of months or years of experience required to be admitted to the examination. For the Office Assistant (Typing), there are two "Patterns."

Under Pattern I, if you have one year experience performing the duties of an Assistant Clerk in California state service, you qualify to compete in this examination. Under Pattern II, if you have completed the 12th grade or completed business school or have one year of clerical experience, you qualify to take the examination.

Figure 7

REQUIREMENTS FOR ADMITTANCE TO THE EXAMINATION

NOTE: All applicants must meet the education and/or experience requirements for this examination by September 23, 1989, the written test date.

Qualifying experience may be combined on a proportionate basis if the requirements stated below include more than one pattern and are distinguished as "Either" I, "or" II, "or" III, etc. For example, candidates possessing qualifying experience amounting to 50% of the required time of Pattern I, and additional experience amounting to 50% of the required time of Pattern II, may be admitted to an examination as meeting 100% of the overall experience requirement.

Minimum Qualifications:

Either I

In the California state service, one year of experience performing the duties of an Assistant Clerk.

Or II

Education: Either equivalent to completion of the twelfth grade; or completion of a business school curriculum, or completion of a clerical work experience training program such as those offered through the Welfare Reform Act. (One year of clerical work experience may be substituted for the required education.)

Special Personal Characteristic -- A demonstrated interest in assuming increasing responsibility

Special Requirements - Ability to type at a speed of not less than 40 words per minute from ordinary manuscript or printed or typewritten material

Additional Desirable Qualification Education equivalent to completion of the twelfth grade

If you have 50% of the experience required under Pattern I and 50% of the experience required under Pattern II, you qualify to take the examination. The more qualifying patterns there are for an examination, the better your opportunity to qualify. For example, if an examination announcement has four patterns, and you possess 25% of the experience required under each pattern, you qualify to compete in the examination. All that matters is that your experience within each of the different patterns totals 100% when added all together. You should also include any volunteer experience if you believe it will help you qualify.

Special Requirements. Includes abilities you must possess prior to appointment to the classification. "Special Personal Characteristics" and "Additional Desirable Qualifications" are required or desired by the employer. These factors are <u>not</u> required for applicants to establish your eligibility to compete in the examination, however, these factors become competitive rating items that are applied in the examination itself.

The Position. Describes, in general terms, the duties of a person working in the classification. This section also includes information on actual and anticipated vacancies if they exist.

Figure 8

THE POSITION

An Office Assistant (Typing) is the entry, trainee and working level for this class. Under close supervision as a trainee, incumbents regularly perform a limited range of duties that become routine, and/or learn to perform a variety of full journey level general clerical duties. Typically, typing encompasses a significant proportion of the work time.

Under general supervision, incumbents at the full journey level regularly perform a variety of duties requiring adaptation to various situations, judgment as to which learned work method to apply for the desired result, and the ability to communicate effectively. This level may have lead responsibility over less experienced employees in areas such as training and answering questions on work procedures.

Positions exist with various State agencies in Sacramento and Yolo Counties.

(Continued on the reverse side)

Examination Information. Explains the type of examination for which you are applying. If the examination is a written test, like the Office Assistant (Typing), this section lets you know the written test is counted 100% toward your placement on the employment list. The "scope" of the written test provides a general overview of the types of questions that will be asked on your written examination.

Figure 9

EXAMINATION INFORMATION

A candidate may test only once in any 18 month testing period for this examination.

This examination will consist of a written test only. In order to obtain a position on the eligible list, a minimum rating of 70.00% must be attained.

Written Test – Weighted 100.00%

Scope:

A. Accuracy in comparing pairs of names, performing basic arithmetic computations, following written directions, and interpreting written tables.

B. Correct usage of spelling, punctuation, and grammar.

C. Alphabetical and numerical filing.

Veterans preference points will be added to the final score of all ope competitors in this examination who qualify for, and have requested, ther points and who are successful in all part(s) of the examination. (Sc "General Information" on this bulletin for information regarding veterar preference points.)

Examinations which include an interview have a section which, like the written section, explains what percentage of your score will be based on the oral interview in determining your score. The "scope" of the interview is divided into two sections: "Knowledge of:" and "Ability to:." These items provide a more in-depth overview of procedures, policies and practices you must know in order to score well on your interview.

Lastly, information on *career credits* and *veterans preference points* is located in this section. If you request career credits on your application, and have permanent civil service status as a state employee, you will have three points added to the final score of your examination if you get a passing score.

Veterans Preference Credits are awarded in most open examinations requiring less than college graduation and two years experience. Veterans, widows and widowers of veterans are entitled to additional credits in the scoring of their civil service examinations as follows:

1. Disabled veteran, 15 points
2. All other veterans, widows or widowers of veterans and the spouses of 100% disabled veterans, 10 points.

If you can qualify for either of these preferences, by all means indicate this on your application.

The **General Information** section on the back of the announcement should not be overlooked. Although the language is pretty standard on all announcements, the information is important because it: (a) tells you what your responsibilities are as applicants; (b) provides certain discretion to the testing department to make changes to the examination while in progress; and (c) provides additional general information about the examination that should be of interest to you and the other applicants.

State law permits the SPB to refuse to examine or, after examination, refuse to certify anyone who falls under any of the following categories:

1. Lacks any of the requirements established by the SPB for the examination or position.
2. Has, at the time of the examination, permanent status in an equal or higher class than the examination for which he or she applies.
3. Is physically or mentally so disabled as to be rendered unfit to perform the duties of the position to which he or she seeks appointment.
4. Is excessively addicted to alcohol.
5. Is excessively addicted to controlled substances.
6. Has been convicted of a felony or of a misdemeanor involving moral turpitude.
7. Has been guilty of disgraceful conduct.
8. Has been dismissed from any position for whatever reason, which would be a reason for dismissal from state service.
9. Has resigned from any position not in good standing or in order to avoid dismissal.
10. Has intentionally attempted to deceive in his or her application, examination or in securing eligibility.
11. Has waived appointment three times from the same employment list.
12. Has failed to reply within a reasonable time to communications concerning his or her availability for employment.
13. Has requested that his or her name be withheld from certification.
14. Is found to be unsuited or not qualified for employment.

How to Apply for Your Examination

All applications for state civil service examinations must be submitted on form STD 678, called "Application for Examination." These applications are available at the SPB offices in Sacramento and Los Angeles, and at local offices of EDD. (See listing beginning on Page 182 to see if there is an EDD office in your city).

The information requested on the detachable left-hand panel is purely voluntary; you don't have to fill it out. You can detach the stub and throw it away. If you choose to complete the panel, you should know that this information will not be used in a discriminatory manner in your examination and selection process.

Figure 10

2317036

2317036

PLEASE PRINT OR TYPE

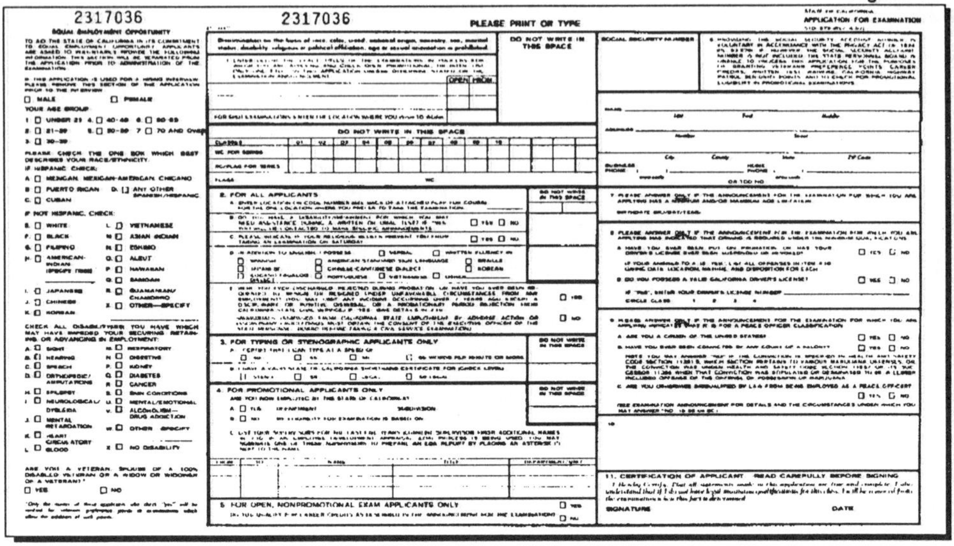

This Equal Employment Opportunity information will be used for one or more of the following purposes: (1) Research to determine the fairness of the examination selection process; (2) To provide for corrective action when adversities arise; (3) To evaluate the state's affirmative action programs; or (4) To prevent discrimination in the random certification process.

To complete the application, follow these steps with the corresponding number on the application.

1. Neatly print or type the exact examination title as shown on the examination announcement; mark an "X" in the open box.

2A. Choose one of the 58 two-digit codes for county location from the reverse side of the application and print it here.

2B. Mark yes or no. If you mark "yes," SPB staff will contact you to make arrangements to accommodate your needs.

2C. Mark yes or no.

2D. Check here if you are bilingual; check all that apply. If none, leave blank.

2E. Answer this question truthfully. If yes, briefly explain in section #10.

3A. Typing and Stenographer applicants, check the appropriate box.

3B. Check the appropriate box. If none, leave blank.

Figure 11

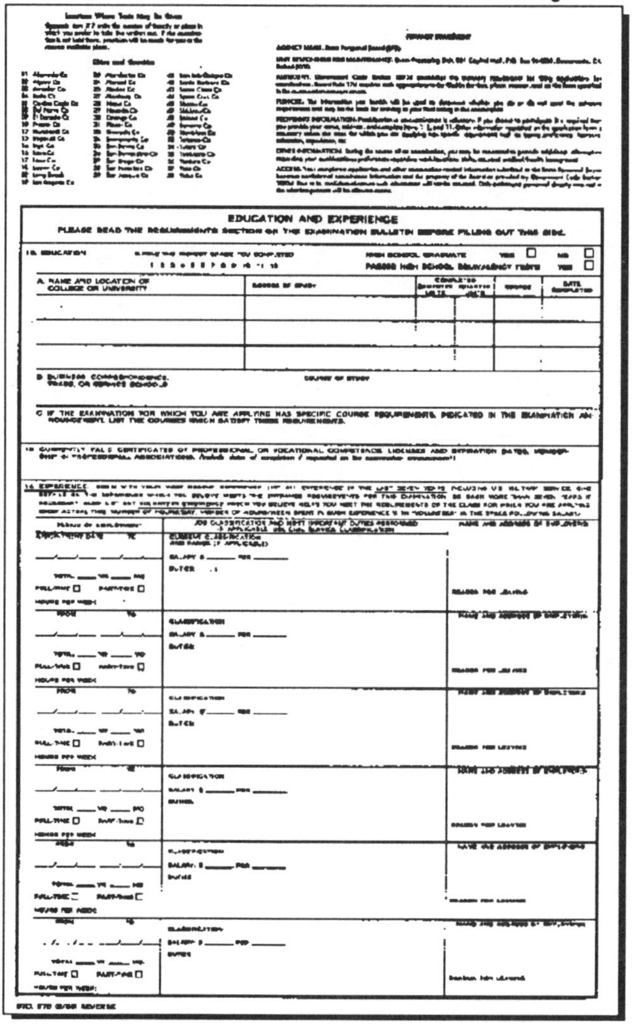

EDUCATION AND EXPERIENCE

PLEASE READ THE REQUIREMENTS SECTION ON THE EXAMINATION BULLETIN BEFORE FILLING OUT THIS SIDE.

4. This section is for current state employees who are applying for a promotional examination. If you are not a promotional applicant, leave blank.
5. This is for current state employees and former state employees who have attained permanent civil service status. If you have not, check "no."
6. You should print your Social Security number here. (It's not mandatory, but it is recommended because the SPB cannot process veteran's preference points or career credits, among other things, without your Social Security number.) Then complete

your name, address and telephone numbers.

7. Don't answer unless the examination announcement requests you age.
8. Don't answer unless the examination announcement includes driving as a minimum qualification.
9. Don't answer unless the examination you are applying for is a peace officer classification such as State Police Officer, or Correctional Officer. (See list of peace officer classifications in the Appendix).
10. Please see #2E.
11. Sign your application and date it.

12A-C. Complete these sections detailing your educational background.

13. Include all licenses, certificates and memberships if any. If none, write "none."
14. This section may be most important in determining whether you qualify to compete in this examination. Make sure you include all dates; fill in the "total" blanks; check whether full time or part time; and most importantly, indicate the number of hours you worked per week in each job. (If you did volunteer work or worked overtime, by all means, include it, because it may help you to qualify for the examination.) Be brief but accurate when describing your duties. Be truthful in your reasons for leaving.

Once you've completed your application, make a photocopy for your records. Review the examination announcement again to determine where and how your application must be submitted.

If the examination announcement states that the application must be filed in person on a certain day or days, **do not mail it**. If you mail it, it will be rejected. If the examination announcement does not require you to file your application in person, make sure you mail it or drop it off at least one day (but preferably 3-5 days) before the final filing date.

Applications for open examinations that are not postmarked or date stamped by the testing department on or before the final filing date, will be rejected. The only exceptions to this general rule are if your applications was: (1) Delayed because of a verifyable error on the part of SPB or other state agency; (2) Delayed due to a documented error by the U.S. Postal Service; or (3) Submitted by mistake to the wrong state agency but was postmarked by the Post Office or date stamped by the agency before the final filing date.

Applications for civil service examinations remain on file for at least two years. Applications for examinations in progress become the property of the State of California and are not returned to the applicants. Once you file an application for examination, you will usually be notified whether you've been accepted within four to six weeks after the final filing date.

If, however, the examination for which you applied has a written portion, and you have not received your acceptance letter five days before the announced written test date, call the department conducting the examination and inquire about the status of your application. The telephone number should be located on the back of the examination announcement.

Once your application has been reviewed, if the department notifies you that you've been denied admittance into the examination, and you believe you meet the minimum qualifications, contact the examining department immediately and discuss your qualifications with the examination analyst. The telephone number should be on your notification letter. This is the time to elaborate on any aspects of your experience that you may not have stated fully on your application, or to discuss any qualifying experience that you may have omitted on the application. After talking to the analyst, you may be asked to submit additional documentation to prove your eligibility. If so, send in your information as soon as possible.

If you are accepted, your acceptance letter will be similar to the sample acceptance letter for a Qualifications Appraisal Interview shown in Figure #12 on the next page. Important: If you move during the examination process or while you are on

Figure 12

CA STATE DEPARTMENT OF JUSTICE
TESTING & SELECTION OFFICE
P.O. BOX 944255
SACRAMENTO, CALIFORNIA 94244-2550
(916) 324-5039
JANUARY 19, 1990

NOTICE OF QUALIFICATIONS APPRAISAL INTERVIEW

SMITH, JOHN A
1234 MAIN STREET
SACRAMENTO, CA 95814

YOUR IDENTIFICATION NUMBER IS: 1234567

EXAMINATION TITLE(S): SECURITY OFFICER I, DOJ

AS PART OF YOUR EXAMINATION(S) NAMED ABOVE, AN APPOINTMENT HAS BEEN MADE FOR YOUR QUALIFICATIONS APPRAISAL PANEL INTERVIEW. PRESENT THIS NOTICE AT THE TIME AND PLACE INDICATED BELOW:

DATE: FEBRUARY 4, 1990
TIME: 10:50 AM
LOCATION: DEPARTMENT OF JUSTICE
4949 BROADWAY, ROOM 200
SACRAMENTO, CA

NOTE: YOU ARE REQUIRED TO BRING A PICTURE IDENTIFICATION CARD OR TWO FORMS OF SIGNED IDENTIFICATION WITH YOU TO THE INTERVIEW. PLEASE NOTIFY US AT (916) 324-5039 IF YOU WILL NOT KEEP THIS APPOINTMENT. FAILURE TO APPEAR FOR THIS INTERVIEW AT THE TIME AND PLACE INDICATED ABOVE WILL RESULT IN YOUR ELIMINATION FROM THIS EXAMINATION. INTERVIEWS WILL NOT BE RESCHEDULED.

IF YOU HAVE ANY QUESTIONS, PLEASE CONTACT THE EXAMINATION ANALYST AT (916) 324-5039.

SUSAN JONES
EXAMINATION ANALYST
TESTING AND SELECTION OFFICE

any employment list, notify the appropriate department as soon as possible. You don't want to miss any potentially job-related correspondence.

Preparing for Your Examination

Whether your examination is a written test or an oral interview or a combination of both, there is no way to prepare 100% for the examination. There is no way for you to know in advance what questions you will be asked on the written or the oral test. Especially on the written test, either you know the subject area or you don't. But you've carefully analyzed your qualifications before you applied for this examination so you're already comfortable with the subject matter.

Now what you need to do is prepare to the best of your ability, by reviewing general subject areas. You already have a copy of the examination announcement, now you need to get a copy of the specification for the classification. Call the SPB office in Sacramento at 916-322-2530 or the Los Angeles office at 213-620-2770 to request a copy of the specification, and SPB staff will mail it to you at no cost.

Review the section in the specification that describes the typical duties of a person working in the classification. Compare these duties with those in your current job or your past positions. If you notice a number of general similarities, that is a plus and you'll need to mention these similarities in your Qualifications Appraisal Interview. The interview panel may not ask you a direct question pertaining to your experience as it relates to the position, so you'll need to tactfully volunteer the information. You might add it on to the response of another question. Or, at the end of your interview when the panel asks you if there is anything else you would like to add, you might mention it.

In the "scope" section of the examination announcement, review the criteria under "Knowledge of." The interview and the written test will be structured to measure your knowledge in the areas specified in this category. If you are rusty in any of these areas, go to your local library and read through books, manuals, etc. on the subject to refresh your memory.

Also study the "Ability to" criteria. In your interview, the panel will evaluate your experiences, your education, your personal characteristics, for example, as they relate to your ability to perform typical duties of a person in the prospective classification. However, members of the panel can only ask questions that pertain to areas that are identified in the "scope" section.

The actual length of the written tests and interviews varies from classification to classification. Your notice for the written examination will indicate how much time you will be alotted, and it's usually not more than two to three hours. The majority of oral interviews vary in length from about 10 minutes to about 20 minutes.

Your Written Examination

Make sure you get plenty of rest the night before the examination. Bring your notification letter and your identification—a driver's license or some other form of indentification that has your picture on it— and try to arrive at least five to ten minutes early.

Before entering the examination, SPB staff will check your identification. You'll need identification to get into the examination. Make sure it's your identification you're using since it is a misdemeanor to use a false ID in connection with entering any examination. Once you have been cleared to enter the examination, the SPB staff will then explain the structure and rules of the examination. All state civil service written examinations are prepared so that the identity of the applicant is concealed from the SPB staff who are scoring it.

During the examination, SPB staff cannot give you any information that might help you or any other applicant to answer an examination question. They can, however, make the necessary general explanations to the whole group taking the written examination. If you have a question while you're taking your examination, by all means, ask one of the SPB staff persons. If they are unable to answer it for whatever reason, they will let you know. If they can respond to your question, and it is information the other applicants may want to know, they will probably make an announcement to the entire group.

Communication among the applicants during the examination is not allowed. It is against the law (a misdemeanor) for anyone to give information to an applicant for the purpose of either improving or hurting the score of any applicant. Any applicant caught cheating will have their examination voided and may be restricted from competing in any other future civil service examination.

Some applicants may complete the examination before others. Remember, this is not a track meet. You will be given plenty of time to complete the exam. If you finish before the time is up, go back over your test and review your answers. Be sure to check whether you have skipped a question. If by chance you did, that will completely throw off your coded answers for all the questions that follow.

Your Oral Interview

If your examination consists of a Qualifications Appraisal Interview, you should do your best to be prepared. The oral interviews make most people very nervous. Make sure you are dressed in neat, clean and appropriate clothing for your particular classification.

The Qualifications Appraisal Interview panel, or the group of people who will be conducting your interview, will be composed of two to three persons (occasionally more) who are familiar with state service. There will be one representative from the SPB, who will chair the panel, and one to two people who are familiar with the job requirements of the classification for which you are applying. When you show up for your interview, you will be told the names and positions of all the panel members.

The panel will review your education, experience and personal qualifications as they relate to the minimum qualifications for the classification, and as they relate to the comparable qualifications of the other applicants. When the panel reviews your education and experience, they will take into consideration the quality, length and importance of your education and experience, and to what extent your total education and work histories have prepared you to work in the classification.

During the interview, all applicants will be asked the same questions to determine the most and least qualified applicants and determine an overall score. The questions are developed based on the "Knowledges and Abilities" section on the examination announcement.

It may comfort you to know that the panel members' assessment of your qualifications will not be determined by your answer to any single question. Their scores will be based on your overall training, experience and/or personal fitness for the classification for which you are applying.

Try not to be nervous. Don't give simple "yes" or "no" answers to questions; elaborate, if you can, and incorporate real life situtations and experiences into your responses. If you don't know the answer to a question, don't guess; be truthful and say that you are not familiar with that subject area. When the interview is completed, thank the panel for their time.

In scoring your interview, each member of the panel will rate you with a percentage. The ratings of each of the panel members are averaged to come up with your final score. If you have scored 70% or more, you pass.

You can be given a failing overall test score, however, even if your average score is 70% or more, when the majority of the panel members score you below 70%. For instance, if your interview panel consists of three members and two members rate you at 65%, and one member rates you at 90%, your overall score would be 73%, but because the majority of the panel members rated you below 70%, you have failed the examination.

Scoring Your Examination

Your final examination score is the rating assigned by the panel members as the result of your total presentation. In all open, nonpromotional examinations, there is a limited range of scores which can be assigned. For nonmanagerial examinations, there are nine passing scores; and for managerial or special cases, there are six passing scores.

As soon as the scoring of your examination has been completed and the employment list established, you will be notified in writing of the results. Usually it takes about four to six weeks after your examination date to receive your score.

If you are successful in the examination, your "Notice of Examination Results" letter will detail your final score, your ranking on the employment

Figure 13

STATE OF CALIFORNIA - STATE PERSONNEL BOARD 88362
801 CAPITOL MALL, P.O. BOX 944201
SACRAMENTO, CALIFORNIA 94244-2010

NOTICE OF EXAMINATION RESULTS TEL. (916) 322-2530
TDD FOR HEARING IMPAIRED ONLY (916) 323-7490

SMITH, JOHN A
1234 MAIN STREET
SACRAMENTO, CA 95814

YOUR IDENTIFICATION
NUMBER IS: 1234567

EXAMINATION TITLE(S):
ASSISTANT INFORMATION OFFICER 87654

EXAMINATION DATE: 03/10/90

CONGRATULATIONS ON YOUR SUCCESS IN THE EXAMINATION NAMED ABOVE. YOU HAVE BEEN PLACED ON THE ELIGIBLE LIST. THE NUMBER SHOWN BELOW FOR 'RANK IN EXAM' IS YOUR RANK AMONG COMPETITORS QUALIFYING IN THE EXAMINATION. THIS NOTICE SHOULD BE KEPT FOR THE LENGTH OF YOUR ELIGIBILITY ON THIS EMPLOYMENT LIST.

FINAL SCORE	RANK	TYPE LIST	LIST DATE
91%	3	OPEN	05/12/90

NOTE: THE ENCLOSED BROCHURE HAS ADDITIONAL INFORMATION REGARDING HOW THIS EMPLOYMENT LIST WILL BE USED IN MAKING APPOINTMENTS AND AN EXPLANATION OF ABBREVIATIONS USED IN THIS NOTICE. THE EMPLOYMENT LIST FOR THIS EXAMINATION WILL BE AVAILABLE FOR VIEWING IN STATE PERSONNEL BOARD OFFICES FOR 60 DAYS. PLEASE CALL YOUR LOCAL STATE PERSONNEL BOARD OFFICE TO CONFIRM WHEN THE LIST FOR THIS EXAMINATION WILL BE AVAILABLE FOR INSPECTION. INFORMATION ON INDIVIDUAL RANK OR VACANCIES IS NOT PROVIDED, HOWEVER THE STATE PERSONNEL BOARD REPORT 1015 WHICH LISTS CLASSES USED BY EACH STATE AGENCY IS ALSO AVAILABLE FOR VIEWING AT SPB INFORMATION COUNTERS.

list, the type of list and the list date as indicated in Figure 13.

The *Employment List* is any list of persons who were successful in an examination and are eligible for certification to a specific classification. Employment lists in open examinations are usually established by ranking the successful candidates in order of numerical score.

Your initial ranking on the employment list as shown on your results notification letter may vary from day to day because of various factors. For example, job appointments are made from the list; eligible persons may decide to become inactive (or temporarily removed from the list for whatever reason); inactive persons may return to active status; or someone may change their location choice. In some instances, the employment list on which your name appears may be preceded by a list from an earlier examination.

These are just a few of the circumstances which could alter your rank on the employment list. You will remain eligible for state employment in this classification as long as the employment list is in existence. The duration of the list is indicated on the examination announcement. As candidates are removed from the list for any of the reasons above, you will move up or down on the list accordingly.

What if You Have Failed?

If you have failed your examination, keep in mind that there are usually more applicants than there are vacant positions and that the purpose of the interview is to help select the best qualified of all the persons who compete. Therefore, a disqualifying or failing score does not necessarily mean that you could not do the job, rather, it probably means that you were not as competitive as the other applicants for this particular examination.

Failing in one examination does not decrease your chances for future examinations—even in the same category. Actually, the practical experience you have gained in this examination will be very useful for future examinations in which you compete.

If you feel you were scored unfairly in your examination for whatever reason, you have the right to appeal. The appeal procedures vary depending on whether it was a written examination or an oral examination.

Written Examination: Your examination papers are open to inspection by you and if applicable, your attorney. All written examinations are prepared so that the identity of the applicant is concealed from the SPB staff who are scoring it. You must submit a written request to the State Personnel Board within 60 days after you receive your examination results. The address to mail your request is:

State Personnel Board
Examination Appeals Section
801 Capitol Mall
Sacramento, CA 95814

Under the supervision of an SPB staff member, you are authorized to compare your answer sheet(s) with the scoring key to determine whether your answers have been scored correctly.

Copying questions or answers contained in the written examination, erasing or altering the markings on the papers, or any mutilation is not allowed. If it is evident that you or your attorney have done any of these things, you could be forbidden to compete in future examinations or declared ineligible for State employment or both.

If, after you review your examination papers, you decide to appeal, you may do so, in writing, on the grounds of fraud or clerical error in scoring the examination. Remember, you must file your appeal within 60 days after the date you received your examination results.

The examination will not be scored until all the disputed items have been reviewed and, if necessary, corrections in the scoring key are made or the disputed items are eliminated.

Oral Examination: The first step in deciding whether you want to appeal is to request from the SPB the reasons for your disqualification. Send your request to the attention of:

State Personnel Board
Examination Appeals Section
801 Capitol Mall
Sacramento, CA 95814

In the oral examination situation, if you decide to appeal, you must do so, within 30 days after you receive your examination results. Your appeal must be in writing and state the facts, information or circumstances upon which your appeal is based. Indicate the type of examination which you are appealing, its title and a statement upon which the appeal is based. By law, your appeal must be based on one or more of the following:

1. Failure to follow prescribed rating standard;
2. Erroneous interpretation of the minimum qualifications prescribed for the class;
3. Fraud;
4. Discrimination;
5. Other improper acts or circumstances.

A convenient hearing date will be scheduled and you will be officially informed of its time and date approximately one week before the hearing is to be held.

The best preparation for your appeal is to make an outline that will assist you at the hearing in covering the major points of your appeal. Depending upon the nature of the examination problem, your appeal should cover at least:

1. The reasons for disqualification. Make sure your appeal covers all of the issues raised by the original interview panel.
2. Any written support of you, including letters of recommendation from supervisors or others should be presented to the appeals panel.

Your appeal will be heard by SPB staff. It will last about 15 minutes, with approximately 10 minutes devoted to the presentation of your case. Hearings are casual and much less formal than the examination itself. Just relax and present the facts in your own words along with any documentation you have prepared. You might want to rehearse in front of a mirror several times the night before.

In considering your appeal, the Board will decide on one of the following solutions:

1. Sustain your original rating (or score);
2. Grant your appeal and give you a rating of 70% on education, experience and personal qualifications;

3. If it determines that your rating was the result of fraud or of discrimination, the Board will give you a passing rating that it deems appropriate, or cancel part or all of the interview ratings given by that panel, arrange for you and other affected competitors to be re-interviewed by a different panel, and withhold part or all of the employment list from certification until the re-examination is completed;
4. The Board may request the review of your rating either by the original or by a new interview panel. Once your score has been reviewed, the panel shall recommend that your rating be sustained or reversed. After this recommendation, the Board may sustain your rating, give you a rating of 70% or the revised rating recommended by the panel.

Applying for State Civil Service Jobs

Getting Started

Now that you're on a list of certified employables, you're ready to start applying for state jobs. When there is a job opening in state government, the hiring department requests a *certification* list from the State Personnel Board (SPB) for the class in which the job vacancy is being filled. Eligible candidates are contacted in order of their rank on the certification list—those with the highest scores are contacted first. It is important to note that a department **can** fill a job vacancy without having contacted every eligible person on the employment list. For this reason, it is not possible to predict when you might be contacted or selected.

When the *Rule of Three Ranks* is the basis of the certification, the hiring department may contact any or all of the eligible persons in the top three ranks. This rule applies to certification lists in classes designated as professional, scientific or administrative or for any employment list established by an "open" examination.

Under this rule, the names of all those persons whose scores, at the time of the certification, represent the three highest ranks, and who have indicated their willingness to accept employment under the specified conditions (job location, full time or part-time, etc.), are forwarded to the hiring departments as certified employment candidates.

Once you are contacted by a hiring department, it is your responsibility to respond, within a reasonable time, regarding your interest in the job. If you are contacted for a job interview and do not respond, or if you waive a job offer three times, your name will be permanently removed from the employment list.

If you request that your name be placed on inactive status, your name will be temporarily removed from the employment list until you request active reinstatement. During this period, you will not be contacted for potential employment.

Even if you are in the first three ranks (or "reachable") on the employment list, there is no guarantee that you'll be contacted by hiring departments to fill job vacancies. Don't sit around and wait to be contacted. Start applying for jobs **now!**

How do you begin your job vacancy search? How can you find out if there is a state department that has a job opening for the class in which you're eligible? There are three ways to conduct your job search.

24-Hour Job Hotlines

Some state departments operate 24-hour job vacancy hotlines. When you call one of these telephone numbers, you will get a recording which lists all of the current job vacancies for the department. The recording also usually indicates the deadline for submitting your job application.

The state departments that operate job hotlines and their telephone numbers are:

Air Resources Board	916-322-1920
	or 800-637-8910
Department of Conservation	916-327-2672
Department of Corrections	916-323-3040
Department of Education	916-323-6818
California State Lottery	916-322-0023
Department of Parks and Recreation	916-322-7392

Department of Transportation	916-323-5588
Water Resources Control Board	916-322-1166
Department of the Youth Authority	916-424-7066

As you see, only a few departments operate job lines, so in terms of diversifying your job search efforts, the job line method is probably the least effective. If you use this method, you should combine it with one or more of the other methods discussed here.

Capitol Weekly

The Capitol Weekly is a weekly newspaper published in Sacramento, which provides a wide variety of information on California state government, the Legislature and most importantly, state employment.

Each week, the Capitol Weekly lists job openings by individual state department. These listings include the classification title, a brief description of the job duties, the monthly salary, the deadline for applying and the name and telephone number of the contact person for job inquiries.

These listings are updated each week, and although not every single hiring department is included in the job vacancy listing, it does represent many departments, and lists job vacancies throughout California.

As a matter of fact, I found out about the job opening in my current state position by reading the Capitol Weekly job listing. Weekly subscriptions are available, by mail, at $59 per year. As someone searching for a state job vacancy, you will find this weekly publication to be an excellent resource.

Departmental Personnel Offices

Lastly, probably the best possible resource in your job search will be the personnel offices of individual state departments. At least once a month, you should contact each personnel office to find out (a) if their department has any job openings in the class for which you are eligible and (b) if they anticipate any openings in the future.

A listing of all the state departments, along with the address and telephone number of the personnel offices is in Chapter 7. This listing also includes, for each department, the names of cities statewide in which field or branch offices are located.

When you call these offices, be polite, cordial and businesslike. Always give your name and get the name of the person you speak with. You can write the person's name down next to his/her telephone number in the listing in Chapter 7. Then, each time you call that personnel department, you can ask for the same person, and hopefully establish a good professional relationship with them.

Although this method can be tedious, it is the best way for you to keep yourself informed about potential job openings for which you can apply. **You must be consistent**. In your search, you cannot call half the offices one month and the call the other half two months later. If you approach your job search in this manner, it simply won't work for you. Call all the departments on your list, each month.

You've Found the Job You Want! Now What?

When you discover a job opening for which you can apply, contact the personnel office for the department and request that they send you a copy of the *opportunity bulletin*. The opportunity bulletin usually describes the duties of the person who will be filling the vacant position, and the desirable qualifications all candidates should possess. It also identifies a contact person and telephone number as well as a mailing address to send your application (see Figure 14).

The opportunity bulletin also explains the conditions of employment: full time, part-time, Limited Term, Permanent Intermittent, and working hours. The conditions of "full time" and "part-time" permanent positions are pretty much self explanatory.

Limited Term positions are filled to meet the temporary staffing needs of a department, and in most cases, cannot exceed two years. None of the time you work in any limited term position may be counted toward qualifying for permanent civil service status. As a limited term employee, you can be dismissed for cause from your position at any time prior to the expiration of your term, the only requirement is that the department inform you of the reason, in writing, on or before your last day. As a limited term employee, you have no appeal from your dismissal. As a general rule, however, the causes for dismissal, by law, include failure to demonstrate merit, efficiency, fitness, and moral responsibility.

Permanent intermittent employees work a minimum of four hours per day, earning vacation and sick leave credits based on the number of hours worked. As an intermittent employee, you may be dismissed if you fail to report to work on three occasions, except for illness or some other reason which your department approves.

Figure 14

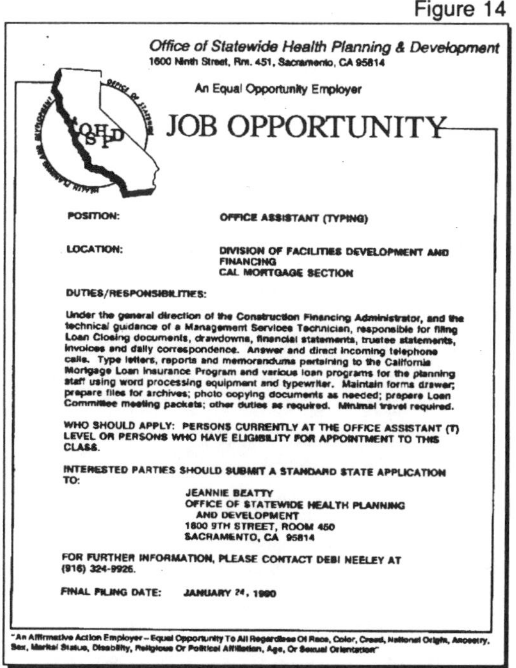

Office of Statewide Health Planning & Development
1600 Ninth Street, Rm. 451, Sacramento, CA 95814

An Equal Opportunity Employer

JOB OPPORTUNITY

POSITION: OFFICE ASSISTANT (TYPING)

LOCATION: DIVISION OF FACILITIES DEVELOPMENT AND FINANCING
CAL MORTGAGE SECTION

DUTIES/RESPONSIBILITIES:

Under the general direction of the Construction Financing Administrator, and the technical guidance of a Management Services Technician, responsible for filing Loan Closing documents, drawdowns, financial statements, trustee statements, invoices and daily correspondence. Answer and direct incoming telephone calls. Type letters, reports and memorandums pertaining to the California Mortgage Loan Insurance Program and various loan programs for the planning staff using word processing equipment and typewriter. Maintain forms drawer; prepare files for archives; photo copying documents as needed; prepare Loan Committee meeting packets; other duties as required. Minimal travel required.

WHO SHOULD APPLY: PERSONS CURRENTLY AT THE OFFICE ASSISTANT (T) LEVEL OR PERSONS WHO HAVE ELIGIBILITY FOR APPOINTMENT TO THIS CLASS.

INTERESTED PARTIES SHOULD SUBMIT A STANDARD STATE APPLICATION TO:

JEANNIE BEATTY
OFFICE OF STATEWIDE HEALTH PLANNING
AND DEVELOPMENT
1600 9TH STREET, ROOM 450
SACRAMENTO, CA 95814

FOR FURTHER INFORMATION, PLEASE CONTACT DEBI NEELEY AT (916) 324-9926.

FINAL FILING DATE: JANUARY 24, 1990

"An Affirmative Action Employer – Equal Opportunity To All Regardless Of Race, Color, Creed, National Origin, Ancestry, Sex, Marital Status, Disability, Religious Or Political Affiliation, Age, Or Sexual Orientation"

If an opportunity bulletin is unavailable or it's too close to the application deadline to request that one be sent in the mail, call the department's personnel office and ask for the analyst assigned to review and process applications for this vacant position, in order to get some background information on the position. You should ask the personnel analyst to read to you, over the telephone, the information on the opportunity bulletin or ask that it be faxed to a telefax number. (You don't have to have your own fax machine. Look in the yellow pages for companies that charge a nominal fee to use their fax to receive messages for you. Copying services are a good source.)

Preparing Your Job Application

Now that you either have a copy of the opportunity bulletin or are aware of the information contained within the bulletin, you need to prepare your application and/or resume.

If you are applying for a professional, technical, administrative or managerial job, in order to be competitive, you will need a resume to supplement your application. A resume is also needed in some clerical positions.

Not all applicants are scheduled for interviews. Departments often get 60, 80, or 100 applications for one vacant position. When this happens, all the applications are reviewed and only the most qualified applicants are scheduled for an interview. A complete application and/or an effective resume can get your foot in the door and lead to an interview.

Complete the State Application (STD 678) for all positions you apply for. You must either type it or print it neatly in blue or black ink. If you are going to include a resume with your application, it is not necessary to complete Section 14 on the state application. On the line just above the beginning of "14. Experience," neatly print or type the words: "Please see attached resume."

If you decide to include a resume with your application, you'll need to prepare the information. Consider your resume as a tool for marketing your unique qualifications, a commercial or an ad of yourself. The purpose of your "commercial" is to make yourself stand out among all the other applicants: you want to be called for an interview!

Your resume should be detailed enough to give a potential employer the information needed to assess your qualifications, but at the same time, it must be concise. Under no circumstances should your resume be more than two pages long, and preferably one page long. Three sample resumes are included at the end of this chapter. A typical outline for a resume includes:

Personal Data
Begin with your name, address and telephone number. Other personal information such as your marital status, age and dependents can appear at the end of your resume, but I don't recommend it. It detracts from your qualifications and experience and is non-job related information.

Employment Objective
This is not a must; in fact, it limits the type of job for which you can apply using this resume. But if you wish to use this heading, indicate here the type of job you are seeking.

Work History
You can organize this information in two ways. Choose the method that presents your work experience best.

The Job Description Method:
List each job separately, even if the jobs were within the same firm, starting with the most recent one and working backwards. For each job, list:

- Dates of Employment
- Name and address of employer and nature of the business
- Position(s) you held

Then describe your job showing
- Specific job duties; the tasks you performed, including any special assignments and use of special instruments or equipment;
- Scope of responsibility; your place in the organization, how many people you supervised, and in turn, the degree of supervision you received;

- Accomplishments; if possible, give concrete facts and figures.

The Function Description Method:
- List tasks you performed that are related to your current job objectives, specifically your field of specialization or types of work such as engineering, sales promotion or personnel management;
- Briefly describe the work you have done in each of these fields, without breaking it down by individual jobs.

Education

If this is your primary selling point, put it before your work history. List your formal education including:
- High school (this can be left out if you have a higher degree), college, graduate school and other courses or training;
- Dates of graduation or leaving school;
- Degrees or certificates received;
- Major and minor subjects and other courses related to your job goal;
- Scholarships, honors and awards;
- Extracurricular activities (only if you are a recent graduate and your activities pertain to your job goal).

Military Experience

List your military service experience if it is recent or if it pertains to your current job goal. Include:
- Branch and length of service;
- Major duties, including details of assignments related to the job you are seeking.

Miscellaneous

If it is appropriate to your field of work, include such information as:
- Knowledge of foreign languages
- Volunteer or leisure activities
- Special skills, such as typing, shorthand or computer experience
- Membership in professional organizations
- Articles published, inventions or patents.

References
Give the names, positions and addresses of at least three persons who have direct knowledge of your work competence. If you are a recent graduate, you can list teachers who are familiar with your school work. By all means, you should first get the permission from the persons you want to use as references before you send out your resume. You don't want anyone to be caught off guard by a telephone call from a potential employer who is trying to get more information about you.

Once your application, which now includes your resume, is completed to your satisfaction, submit it to the hiring department at the address indicated on the opportunity bulletin. Make sure you do so well before the application deadline.

The Interview

You want to arrive for your job interview as prepared and confident as possible. Although you can't anticipate the questions you'll be asked, you can go into the interview with some background information and general familiarity about the department, the division or unit you'd be working in, and the position itself.

Call the department to get copies of any published background information on the department: brochures, pamphlets, annual reports, etc.

It's also a good idea to talk to current employees at the department, preferably employees already working in the division or unit you're applying to, in order to get more in depth information about the department you'd like to work for. Call the personnel office and ask them to refer you to someone.

Or, you could review the listing of state departments and the summary of duties for each in Chapter 1. Your main objective here is to let your interviewers know that you have taken the time and made the effort to learn something about their department. This will impress them because it shows your interviewers that you've taken a sincere interest in the job and you're not even hired yet!

Under certain circumstances, the State of California has provisions for reimbursing the travel expenses of professional and technically trained job applicants who are called for job interviews. Before you can be reimbursed, the Department of Personnel Administration and the hiring department must certify that travel reimbursement is necessary in order to recruit qualified applicants.

I don't have personal knowledge of any cases where such travel reimbursement has been made, but you should at least inquire.

In almost all cases, the hiring department will send you a letter explaining why you did not get the job. If you were unsuccessful in this effort, don't be discouraged. It is a good idea to call the person with whom you interviewed to ask if he/she could offer you some constructive criticism about the areas you could improve upon before your next job interview.

If you were successful in your interview, the hiring department usually calls you, rather than send a letter, to offer you the job.

Figure 15

Jane Doe
2587 Bergett Avenue
Concord, CA 94521

EMPLOYMENT OBJECTIVE

Children's Librarian

EDUCATION

Hunter College, B.S., 1977. *Major*: Elementary education, *Minor*: Child psychology
Columbia University, master's degree, 1979, library science

EXPERIENCE

1977-80, Woodland Elementary School, 431 Alberta Lane, Walnut Creek, CA. Taught fifth grade. A major objective was to stimulate pupils to do more independent reading. To this end, prepared displays and organized field trips to nearby libraries in connection with annual book fair; assisted part-time librarian in reorganizing instructional materials center to make it easier to use and more inviting in appearance; took training course and for 2 years conducted a Junior Great Books course for pupils at Woodland.

1976-77 (part time during school year and full time during summer of 1977). Bowen Library, 2415 Olive Drive, Concord, CA. Library clerk. Located books for patrons and answered nonprofessional inquiries. Received, sorted, repaired and shelved books.

Summer, 1976. Mobile Manufacturing Company, 57 Clayton Road, Concord, CA. Clerk-typist. Acted as secretary to vice president while regular secretary was on vacation.

Summers, 1974 and 1975. Highpoint Camp, Highway 50, South Lake Tahoe, CA. Taught arts and crafts and supervised bunk of 10 and 11-year old girls.

SPECIAL SKILLS

Spanish: Good reading, writing, and speaking knowledge.
Operated various types of visual equipment.

REFERENCES

Dr. Margaret Martin, Professor of Library Science, Columbia Univeristy,
New York, N.Y. 10027

Mr. Wilbur Miller, Principal, Woodland Elementary School, 431 Alberta Lane,
Walnut Creek, CA 94525.

Mr. Walter Snyder, Chief Librarian, Bowen Library, 2415 Olive Drive,
Concord, CA 94521.

Function Description Format

Figure 16

Jane Doe
2587 Bergett Avenue
Concord, CA 94521

OBJECTIVE

Sales Executive

SALES PROMOTION

Devised and supervised sales promotion projects for large business firms and manufacturers, mostly in the electronics field. Originated newspaper, radio, and television advertising and coordinated sales promotion with public relations and sales management. Analyzed market potentials and developed new techniques to increase sales effectiveness and reduce sales costs. Developed sales training manuals.

As sales executive and promotion consultant handled a wide variety of accounts. Sales potentials in these firms varied from $100,000 to $5 million annually. Was successful in raising the volume of sales in many of these firms 25 percent within the first year.

SALES MANAGEMENT

Hired and supervised sales staff on a local area and national basis. Established branch offices throughout the United States and developed uniform systems of processing orders and sales records. Promoted new products as well as improving sales of existing ones. Developed sales training program. Developed a catalog system involving inventory control to facilitate movement of scarce stock between branches.

MARKET RESEARCH

Devised and supervised market research projects to determine sales potentials, as well as need for advertising. Wrote detailed reports and recommendations describing each step in distribution, areas for development, and plans for sales improvement.

SALES

Retail and wholesale,. Direct sales to consumer, jobber, and manufacturer. Hard goods, small metals and electrical appliances.

ORDER CLERK

Received, processed, and expedited orders. Trouble shooter. Set up order control system which was adopted for all branches.

FIRMS

1966-1982	B.B. Bowen Sales Development Co., San Francisco, California	Sales Executive
1955-1966	James Bresher Commercial and Industrial Sales Research Corp. Oakland, California	Sr. Sales Promotion Mgr
1950-1955	Dunnock Brothers Electronics Co., San Francisco, Calfiornia	Order Clerk, Salesworker

EDUCATION

University of California, B.S. 1950; *Major*: Business Administration.

Figure 17

Jane Doe
2587 Bergett Avenue
Concord, CA 94521

OBJECTIVE

Reporter, Copy Editor

EDUCATION

Sacramento State University, Sacramento, California. BA, cum laude, 1987. *Major:* Journalism, *Minor:* Psychology, other courses: Beginning and advanced photography.
Honors: Phi Kappa Phi
Extracurricular activities: Editor of college newspaper. Served earlier as copy editor and reporter.

EXPERIENCE

1986-87 school year. Correspondent in Sacramento for the Sacramento Union.

June - August 1986. Sacramento Union, Sacramento, California. Although working as a copy runner, I received a number of editorial assignments. Besides covering meetings and writing obituaries, I did a feature series with photographs on the county arts group. (Enclosed is a one-sheet photocopy showing clippings of stories I wrote for the Union.)

Summers 1984 and 1985. Wilder Dress Shop, 342 J Street, Sacramento, California. Sales Clerk.

REFERENCES

References and additional writing samples will be provided upon request.

What to Expect as a State Employee

Congratulations, you got the job! Welcome to California State Civil Service. The first thing you need to find out about is whether you are going to have to move. If you are required to change your place of residence as a result of you new job, you may be eligible for reimbursement from the state for your moving and relocation expenses.

If your new department determines that you are eligible for such reimbursement, the state will pay for:

1. Actual and necessary costs incurred due to the sale of your home;
2. Actual and necessary costs incurred in the settlement of an unexpired lease, up to one year;
3. The cost of moving your household effects;
4. Miscellaneous expenses.

How Do I Get Paid?

As a full time or part-time permanent employee, you will be paid once a month, for a monthly pay period which generally consists of 21 or 22 work days. Payday is usually the last day of the month or the first day of the next month. Intermittent employees are usually paid within 10 working days after the end of the pay period.

The salary range established for each class consists of a minimum rate and a maximum rate. The minimum of the range serves as the normal entrance rate for new employees in any position within that class and represents the lowest rate to be paid any employee who is considered qualified for appointment to a position. The maximum of the range represents the highest rate paid for the employees in the class. The maximum takes into consideration the level of difficulty of the duties and responsibilities of the class and the relation of the class to other classes.

If you come to this job with work experience that fits within the state Department of Personnel Administration (DPA) criteria for your classification, you may be eligible for a higher monthly starting salary based on *Alternate Ranges* scale.

For example, the Office Assistant (Typing) classification has four ranges (as of June 1, 1989):

Range A	$1402-1613
Range B	$1490-1726
Range C	$1501-1736
Range D	$1602-1860

New civil service employees in this class would generally start out at the first step in Range A or $1402 a month. But if you have either one year of clerical experience or two years of business or commercial education or four years of general education, you qualify to start out at the first step in Range B or $1490 a month.

The Alternate Range Criteria for each class is unique to that class and determined by DPA. Check with your personnel analyst when you start your new job, to determine whether you qualify for a higher starting salary based on the alternate range criteria.

Your Paycheck

As a state employee, you may authorize the State Controller to make monthly payroll deductions from your salary to pay for any of the following:

- Deposits into a bank account for services such as loans, checking or savings;
- Obligations to your credit union;
- Insurance premiums;
- U.S. Savings Bonds;
- Public transportation.

Many state employees elect to have their paychecks deposited to their checking or savings account to avoid the inevitable long lines on payday. For more information on how to do this, talk with your department's personnel officer.

Probation

When you start your new job, you will be on *probation* for either the first six, nine or 12 months. The length of your probation depends on your classification and whether you're full time, part time or intermittent.

During this probationary period, you will be assigned to a specific task or set of duties. Your

Figure 18

REPORT OF PERFORMANCE
FOR PROBATIONARY EMPLOYEE

QUALIFICATION FACTORS	RATINGS ARE INDICATED BY "X" MARKS			
	UNACCEPTABLE	IMPROVEMENT NEEDED	STANDARD	OUTSTANDING
1. SKILL				
2. KNOWLEDGE				
3. WORK HABITS				
4. RELATIONSHIPS WITH PEOPLE				
5. LEARNING ABILITY				
6.				
7. ABILITY AS SUPERVISOR				
8. ADMINISTRATIVE ABILITY				
9. FACTORS NOT LISTED ABOVE				
OVERALL RATING				

COMMENTS TO EMPLOYEE

DISTRIBUTION Copies: 1—Departmental File 2—Employee 3—Supervisor 4—Miscellaneous supervisor should provide you with a duty or position statement which describes your responsibilities and the standards for accomplishing them, if your supervisor does not provide you with this statement, ask for one.

During your probationary period, your supervisor is required to prepare at least three probation reports (like the one shown in Figure 18) covering your job performance, personal conduct and your ability to handle responsibility measured against the standards of your position. Your overall job performance will be reviewed with you and if there are any areas that need improvement, they will be specifically discussed with you.

If, on the other hand, you do meet the required level of performance by the end of your probationary period, you will pass probation and be granted permanent civil service status.

It is rare that a new employee is rejected on probation. This only occurs when a new employee is unsuccessful in learning a job and meeting performance standards during the probationary period. By law, reasons for such rejection must relate to the employee's qualifications or the employee's failure to demonstrate "merit, efficiency, fitness and moral responsibility." The employee's supervisor must give the employee a written notice detailing the effective date and reason for the rejection.

If you are rejected on probation you have the right to appeal your rejection, but you must do so, in writing, to the State Personnel Board (SPB) within 15 calendar days of the date the rejection is to become effective. The SPB will investigate the reason for your rejection. Sometimes the SPB will conduct this investigation by holding a hearing. Whether the investigation is performed with or without a hearing, once it's completed, the SPB has the following options:

1. Agree with the actions of your department;
2. Modify the actions of your department;
3. estore your name to the employment list from which you were certified; or

4. Restore you to the position from which you were rejected.

Travel

Many state jobs require travel on a regular basis either throughout the state or even out of state. Travel may be a significant part of your job or just a one-time event such as attending a training course or conference. Whatever the case may be, the state will provide reimbursement for your expenses.

Expenses eligible for reimbursement include such things as: airfare, rental car, hotel accommodations, business telephone calls, meals, mileage and personal expenses. In some cases you can request a cash advance on the expenses you expect to incur.

There are very specific rules and regulations regarding travel and reimbursement amounts. Since these rules change periodically, consult your supervisor for current expense limits, travel advances and reservation procedures when you're scheduled to travel.

Overtime

The rules of overtime in general are subject to Memorandums of Understanding (MOUs) and change occasionally. Different policies apply according to your collective bargaining agreements.

In my case, I work a lot of overtime in my current position, but when I think of a typical state position that requires overtime hours, I automatically think of a departmental budget office. State budget office are notorious for requiring a great deal of overtime.

Any time that I work in excess of your eight hour workday or my 40-hour workweek, with my supervisor's approval, is considered overtime by the state. My department pays me cash compensation at a rate of 1 $^1/_2$ times my regular hourly rate. (To compute the hourly rate, I divide my monthly salary by 173.33). Also, if I'd rather receive Compensating Time Off (CTO) for the overtime hours I worked, my department will provide me with 1 $^1/_2$

hours off for every one hour of overtime worked. This policy varies for employees in different collective bargaining units.

There are also provisions for reimbursement for other items such as meals and mileage when you work overtime; check with your supervisor to find out how overtime will be handled in your case. Remember: you must be authorized by your supervisor in advance to work overtime.

Employee Assistance Program (EAP)

The Employee Assistance Program (EAP) is a system cooperatively offered by management and labor for the prevention and/or reduction of an employee's problems as they relate to job performance. The EAP provides confidential counseling and referral service to employees, employees' families, and supervisors for dealing with medical or behavioral personnel problems.

The state recognizes that personal problems may hamper an employee's job performance, and provides the EAP to assist in such things as alcohol, nicotine, drug abuse and stress. Those are areas the State recognizes may adversely affect job performance but which are treatable conditions. Therefore, one of the methods the state employs to correct job performance problems is a referral to treatment for alcohol, nicotine, drug and stress-related problems such as marital, family, emotional, financial, medical, legal or other personal problems.

An employee undergoing such treatment may get approval from the supervisor to use accrued sick leave credits, CTO or vacation and holiday credits. Leave of absences without pay may also be used if all other leave is exhausted.

Records concerning an employee's referral and/or treatment are kept confidential. No manager, supervisor, department director or coordinator can disclose the nature of the employee's treatment or the reason for the employee's leave of absence.

Benefits

Medical

As a state employee, you may be eligible for health insurance to help you pay the cost of hospital and other medical bills incurred by you and your eligible dependents. Your eligibility is based upon your tenure and time base. To be eligible, for medical benefits, you must be in a permanent position or if you are in a limited term position, have an appointment which lasts for more than six months and be working at least half time.

The State will pay for part of your health plan premiums as soon as you enroll. The State contribution is a flat dollar amount per month depending on the number of enrolled dependents. There are a number of health plans available for you to choose from. You pay the difference between the cost of the plan and the State's contribution.

To join Foundation Health plan, for example, the monthly deduction is $6.19 for the employee and two dependents. The State matches this deduction with $322.00.

Dental

Dental insurance is available from one of several plans. Premiums under each plan are fully paid by the State for you and your eligible dependents. As a new employee, you must enroll in a dental plan within the first 60 days of employment or during the annual open enrollment period.

Vision Care

Vision insurance is available to all eligible employees and their dependents. Your monthly premium is fully paid by the State. You will be given a Vision Care booklet with your department's new employee orientation package.

Life Insurance

Group Term Life Insurance is available to management, supervisory, confidential and other nonrepresented employees. The State pays the premium for basic coverage. You must complete an enrollment form for the coverage to become effective. Supplemental coverage is available at the employee's expense.

Long Term Disability

Employee paid Long Term Disability Insurance is available to nonrepresented employees appointed to permanent positions and working half time or more. Eligible employees will receive an enrollment form and program information in the mail. The form must be completed and submitted to your personnel office by the expiration date.

Workers' Compensation

Workers' Compensation Insurance is a special kind of insurance which employers are required to provide to insure that workers who are injured on the job do not lose wages. It also guarantees that employees receive proper medical care to facilitate their return to work. Workers' compensation provides benefits to you or your survivors if you sustain a job-related injury, illness or accidental death. It also provides for cash awards, in some cases, if you are permanently disabled from your work related injury, whether or not you are able to return to work.

You are covered under workers' compensation insurance whenever and wherever you are rendering services for the State if the injury arises because of your employment. Notify your supervisor within 24 hours if you are injured on the job. Your supervisor will then report you injury to the State Compensation Insurance Fund (a state department that handles all workers' compensation claims for state employees).

As a state employee, you are entitled to receive your full salary for the first 22 days that you are unable to work due to your injury. From then on, you are entitled to receive 2/3 of your salary for up to one year while you are temporarily disabled, (this is called Industrial Disability Leave , see below).

Industrial Disability Leave

As a member of the Public Employees Retirement System (PERS), if you become temporarily disabled because of a work related injury you may be eligible to receive Industrial Disability Leave (IDL). Contact your department's personnel analyst for more information, should you require this.

FleXelect

You may be eligible to participate in FleXelect,

the State's blanket benefit program. This program permits you to establish reimbursement accounts to help pay for dependent care and out-of-pocket medical, vision and dental expenses from your pre-tax earnings. These accounts can reduce your taxable income thereby reducing your federal, state and social security taxes. Through the FleXelect program, you may choose to take cash under certain circumstances where you are covered by some other comprehensive group medical and/or dental insurance.

Public Employees' Retirement System (PERS)

Most full-time employees who are hired to work more than six months automatically become members of the State's retirement system—Public Employees' Retirement System (PERS) upon appointment. Employees with other types of appointments must meet certain criteria to become members of PERS.

PERS members are covered by Social Security (OASDI). If you retire from State service, you will be eligible to receive both PERS and Social Security benefits.

Deferred Compensation

Deferred compensation is a benefit which enables you to save money out of each paycheck to increase your financial independence at retirement. It also allows you to defer taxes on the amount you invest until it is withdrawn. This is a valuable benefit since both federal and state income taxes are reduced for each year that you defer income. Contributions are always made through payroll deductions.

Deferred Compensation is not an ordinary savings plan. The funds are only available to you when you separate from state service or when you retire. The only way you can withdraw any of these funds before that time is to prove a dire financial emergency which cannot be met through usual means.

The benefits you receive from deferred compensation have no effect on your PERS retirement plan or Social Security; they are over and above all your other benefits.

Leave Entitlements

Vacation

After six months of continuous service as a full-time state employee, you will earn five days of paid vacation. You cannot use your vacation until after you have worked six months. From then on, at the beginning of each new pay period, you will be credited with the vacation hours you earned for the previous pay period. You earn vacation credit as follows:

Length of Service	Vacation Allowance
1 month to 3 years	$^5/_6$ day per month
37 months to 10 years	1 $^1/_4$ days per month
121 months to 15 years	1 $^5/_{12}$ days per month
181 months to 24 years	1 $^7/_{12}$ days per month
289 months and over	1 $^2/_3$ days per month

Vacation can only be taken in full hour increments with your supervisor's prior approval. There may be times when your workload or other scheduled activities prevent you from taking vacation time.

Sick Leave

You are credited with sick leave on the first day of the month following the completion of each pay period. The number of sick leave hours you accrue depends on your time base and your collective bargaining unit agreement. You can start using your sick leave as soon as it has been earned.

Sick leave is a form of wage insurance that compensates employees during periods of absence due to personal injury or illness, or for the care of sick or injured family members.

Sick leave is defined as your necessary absence from work because of:

1. Illness or injury;
2. Exposure to a contagious disease;
3. Dental eye and other physical or medical examination or treatment by a licensed practioner;

4. Up to five days family leave per year to care for your sick or injured mother, father, husband, wife, son, daughter, brother or sister, or any person who lives in your immediate household (except servants or roommates);
5. The death of a person related to you by adoption, or by marriage or any person who lives in your immediate household (each such absence cannot exceed five days).

You are allowed reasonable time, normally two hours, for medical or dental appointments. Additional time may be allowed when justified and approved by your supervisor. Sick leave cannot be used for physical exams for life insurance policies, marriage licenses or other non-work related activities.

The number of sick leave hours you can accumulate are unlimited. Employees are expected to build up a substantial reserve of unused sick leave to protect them from loss of income if they ever suffer a lengthy illness or injury

Bereavement

If you are a full-time employee, you are entitled to bereavement leave with pay due to the death of your parent, step parent, spouse, child, grandchild, grandparent, brother, sister, mother-in-law, father-in-law, daughter-in-law, son-in-law, sister-in-law, brother-in-law, step child, adopted child or of any person who lives in your immediate household.

Such leave can be authorized for up to a total of three days per occurrence in a fiscal year. You should notify your supervisor as soon as possible, and if requested, provide substantiation to your supervisor to support your request.

If, as a result of your bereavement leave, you are required to travel over 400 miles one way, you can request up to two additional days off (deducted from your sick leave balance).

Personal Holiday

After you have completed six months as a full-time employee, you are eligible to receive a personal holiday. Personal holidays, considered a free vacation day, are credited to you on the first day of July and must be used anytime during the following 12 months. If you haven't used your personal holiday by June 30 of each year, you lose it.

Jury Duty

In general, if you are called for jury duty, you can serve with no loss of pay as long as you turn over to your department any of the fees you receive for jury duty. You do not have to turn over any payment you receive for travel expenses. Notify your supervisor when you are called for jury duty and for specific conditions concerning your work schedule.

Military Leave

You may qualify to take up to 30 calendar days with pay for military leave each year if you meet certain requirements. Check with your personnel department.

Exam Time Off

If you wish to participate in a state civil service exam, you will be granted reasonable time off, with pay, if your exam is scheduled during your normal working hours and you have given your supervisor reasonable notice (normally two working days).

Figure 19

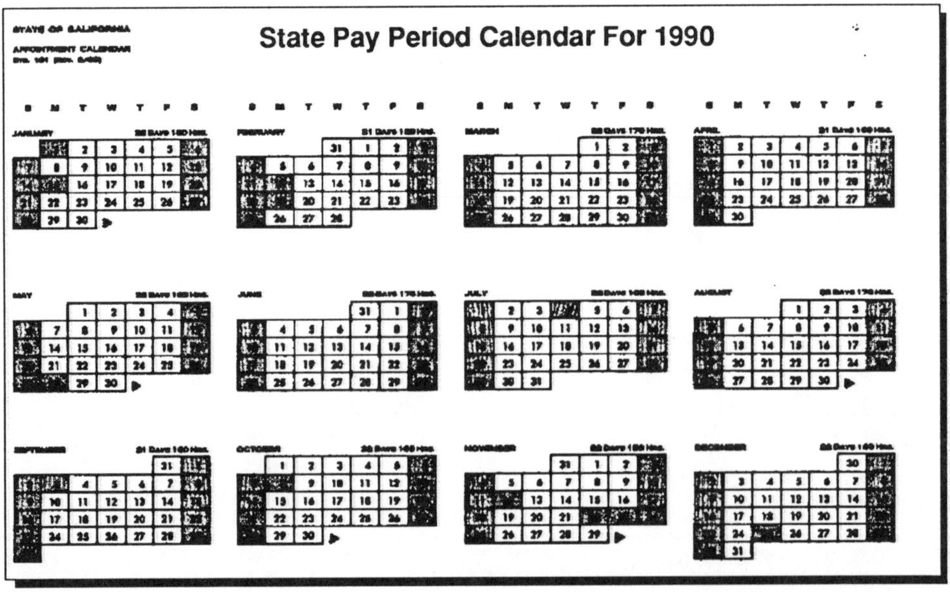

State Pay Period Calendar For 1990

You will also be given time off with pay to attend any state job interview for which you have been called as a result of your eligibility on any employment list.

State Holidays

You are entitled to receive pay for state holidays which are observed during the year, indicated by the shaded days on the state pay period calendar shown in Figure 19. They are:

New Year's Day
Martin Luther King, Jr. Day
Lincoln's Birthday
Washington's Birthday
Memorial Day
Independence Day
Labor Day
Columbus Day
Veteran's Day
Thanksgiving Day
Day after Thanksgiving
Christmas.

Usually every year, all state employees are given an extra four hours of paid time off which most use either on Christmas Eve or New Year's Eve. It's sort of a holiday present from the Governor.

Employees who are required to work on a holiday will be compensated in accordance with state regulations and collective bargaining agreements.

Pregnancy and Maternity Leave

The State believes that pregnant women must be treated the same as other employees (and job applicants) on the basis of their ability to work. Therefore a woman cannot be fired or refused a job or promotion on account of pregnancy. Also, pregnant women who are unable to work are allowed disability benefits, sick leave and health insurance just like employees who are unable to work for other medical reasons.

If you are a pregnant woman, State policy states that you can continue to work as long as your health, the health of your unborn fetus or your ability to adequately perform essential job duties in a safe manner are not adversely affected. Your department is obligated to arrange any reasonable modification of your job that will enable you to continue working.

You are also eligible for Nonindustrial Disability Insurance (NDI) when you suffer any injury or illness resulting form pregnancy, child birth, or related medical condition.

If you are a new parent, male or female, you are entitled to an unpaid leave of absence for up to a year to care for your newborn child. After your unpaid leave of absence, you are entitled to return to the same job classification, even though you may not be able to return to the exact same job you left.

Nonindustrial Disability

Nonindustrial Disability Insurance (NDI) is a wage continuation program that can provide you with some compensation if you are unable to work due to an injury or illness that is not job-related, including pregnancy and childbirth.

You are eligible to receive NDI payments equal to 60% of your full pay, but not more than $135 per week (before taxes). NDI benefits are paid monthly for up to 26 weeks for any one disability benefit period.

Reasonable Accommodation

"Reasonable accommodation" is an adjustment made to your job and/or your work environment if you are a qualified disabled person, to enable you to perform the essential duties of your position. It also includes any state department's efforts to remove artificial or real barriers which prevent or limit the employment of disabled persons. Methods for providing reasonable accommodation include:

1. Modifying work sites
2. Making facilities accessible
3. Adjusting work schedules
4. Restructuring jobs

5. Providing assistive devices
6. Adopting flexible leave policies

For more information, you should contact your department's Affirmative Action Coordinator.

Collective Bargaining Units

Collective bargaining agreements between employee organizations (unions) and the State define wages, hours and conditions of employment, such as overtime policy and benefits, affecting those employees who are assigned to one of 20 bargaining units. Each of these units is made up of employees performing similar or related duties with a community of interest in wages, hours and working conditions.

Employees designated managerial, supervisory, confidential, excluded and exempt are not covered by collective bargaining agreements. The Department of Personnel Administration is responsible for defining wages, hours and conditions of employment for these employees.

Each bargaining unit elects an employee orgainization which has exclusive rights to represent employees in that unit in bargaining with the State. All 20 bargaining units are listed below with a brief description of the classes of employees in each unit:

1 *Administrative, Financial and Staff Services* - 25,000 employeees performing administrative, fiscal and analytical functions such as accounting, planning, personnel, data processing, reasearch and analysis.

2 *Attorney and Hearing Officer* - 2,000 employees practicing law for the State or exercising quasi-judicial job duties within administrative hearings.

3 *Education* - 2,500 employees delivering educational or related services who are licensed by the Department of Education or hold advanced degrees.

4 *Office and Allied* - 35,000 employees providing vital support to the primary professional, technical or administrative objectives of each State department or agency.

5 *Highway Patrol* - 4,700 employees providing safe and lawful vehicular movement over highways.

6 *Corrections* - 14,000 employees providing custody, supervision and treatment of wards and inmates remanded to State custody.

7 *Protective Services & Public Safety* - 5,000 employees protecting State lands and buildings, furnishing emergency services, issuing licenses or permits, arresting individuals violating penal or administrative laws and protecting the public from fraudulent practices and schemes.

8 *Firefighter* - 3,200 employees fighting structural and forest fires.

9 *Professional Engineer* - 5,500 employees providing engineering, design, research, and related analytical information regarding structures, such as highways, bridges, dams and water treatment plants.

10 *Professional Scientific* - 1,600 employees engaged in scientific research, testing, design, and analysis in life, earth and evironmental sciences.

11 *Engineering & Scientific Technicians* - 2,600 employees utilizing scientific instruments and technology to gather and record data.

12. *Craft and Maintenance* - 9,700 employees operating and maintaining State equipment, facilities, buildings, grounds and roads.

13 *Stationary Engineer* - 600 employees maintaining and operating power generation facilities which heat, ventilate and air condition large office building and other State facilities.

14 *Printing Trades* - 800 employees preparing, composing and printing material for State agencies.

15 *Custodial and Services* - 5,700 employees providing custodial, food and laundry and other basic services to maintain a proper physical environment for State facilities.

16 *Physician, Dentist and Podiatrist* - 1,000 employees comprised of medical staff responsible for diagnosis, evaluation and treatment of patients within State institutions.

17 *Registered Nurse* - 2,300 employees involved in educational, preventive and treatment programs associated with State health care.

18 *Psychiatric Technician* - 7,700 employees providing psychiatric care for mentally ill and developmentally disabled patients in State-operated facilities.

19 *Health and Social Services/Professional* - 2,900 employees providing evaluation and assessment of client counseling and consultation or client follow-up service of a health, social or employment nature.

20 *Nonprofessional Medical and Social Services Support* - 1,800 employees providing direct and indirect health care and social service support to inmates and other recipients of State social service programs.

Mandatory Return or Reinstatement Rights

As a state employee with permanent civil service status, you may be reinstated without having to take an exam if you were separated from State service because of:

1. Resignation;
2. Service retirement;
3. Termination from a limited term, temporary, CEA or exempt appointment;
4. Accepting another civil service exempt appointment without a break in state service;
5. Absence without leave.

You have mandatory return rights and may request reinstatement to your former department or to another department. If you make you request to another department within 30 days after your resignation, before you can be reinstated, your former department must approve the reinstatement.

In addition to reinstatement to your former class, you may also request reinstatement to another class on the same, on a comparable, or a lower level. The department where you want to work will determine which classes are considered comparable for reinstatement purposes.

Also, you are eligible for reinstatement to your former position if you are terminated from a temporary or limited term appointment, or rejected during probation, or demoted from a managerial position. Reinstatement to your former positon is not automatic. You must initiate the request by writing to your former employer. Your written request must arrive at the department within 10 working days of your termination. However, if you've had a break in civil service, you are not eligible for reinstatement to your former job.

It is important to note that if you were separated for being absent without leave (AWOL), you must provide a satisfactory explanation of your separation to the hiring department. This is a permissive reinstatement, so your request may be granted or denied at the discretion of the hiring department.

Chapter 6:

Moving Up the State Career Ladder

The intent of this chapter is to give you a general familiarity with some of the methods you may consider in your efforts to promote within California State civil service. The State of California, as an employer, is an advocate and a believer in upward mobility. The methods I have detailed in this chapter are complex and multifaceted, and could be contained as the topic of a another entire book. If you have questions or concerns, please contact your departmental personnel analyst or the State Personnel Board at 916-322-2530.

Now that you're a state civil service employee, moving up the state career ladder should be your next major goal. As a state employee, with permanent civil service status, there are several ways to get to your next level:

1. Open examination
2. Promotional examination
3. Career Executive Assigment
4. Training and Development Assignment
5. Lateral Transfer

Take an "Open Examination"

Literally hundreds of "open" examinations are offered each year by state departments. Remember, this is how you got your first state job. Continue to seek out all "open" examination announcements and apply to take every one for which you're eligible to compete. The goal is to get on as many employment lists as possible. Even though you are currently employed, your ultimate goal is upward mobility until you reach your desired classification and the "perfect job."

As a state employee, when you compete in an open/nonpromotional examination, you are eligible to have three *career credit* points added to your final examination score.

Promotional Examination

Your department will be scheduling *promotional examinations* on a regular basis. As a permanent civil service employee, you are eligible to compete in any examination for which you meet the minimum qualifications.

If you are successful in your examination, and score within the first three ranks, you may apply for vacant positions within your department or any other state department that has a vacancy in that class. If you are interested in another state department, you can transfer your promotional list eligibility (or simply your score in the examination) to be merged with the existing list in another department. It's not a good idea to transfer your list eligibility out of your department unless you feel there is no chance for you to promote to that class in your current department.

Career Executive Assignments

A *Career Executive Assigment (CEA)* is a high administrative and policy influencing position within state service. Usually a person in this classification is primarily responsible for managing a major departmental function (such as Legislation, Budgets or Legal) or giving management advice to top-level administrators (see sample CEA announcement in Figure 20).

As a permanent employee in any class, from Assistant Clerk to Accounting Analyst, you can apply to compete in any CEA examination statewide for which you meet the minimum qualifications.

Figure 20

CAREER EXECUTIVE ASSIGNMENT

CALIFORNIA STATE GOVERNMENT - AN AFFIRMATIVE ACTION EMPLOYER

EQUAL OPPORTUNITY TO ALL REGARDLESS OF RACE, COLOR, CREED, NATIONAL ORIGIN, ANCESTRY, SEX, MARITAL STATUS, DISABILITY, RELIGIOUS OR POLITICAL AFFILIATION, AGE OR SEXUAL ORIENTATION.

DEPARTMENT DEPARTMENT OF CONSERVATION

POSITION TITLE Deputy Division Chief, Division of Recycling, CEA I

FINAL FILE DATE November 9, 1989

POSITION DESCRIPTION

Under the general direction of the Division Chief (CEA III), Division of Recycling, the incumbent will assist in the planning, organizing, staffing and directing the statewide program for the recycling of aluminum, glass, plastic and non-aluminum beverage containers. The incumbent will advise and assist in the development, evaluation and implementation of the Division's programs, policies, regulations and procedures. The incumbent acts in the absence of the Division Chief; represents the Division at meetings, workshops, hearings and other regulatory proceedings and provides liaison to the Governor's Office, Legislature and others on programmatic issues.

EXAMINATION INFORMATION

1. The examination process will consist of an application screening process by a departmental evaluation committee. The committee will screen the applications on the basis of background and good management potential, as well as the following DESIRABLE QUALIFICATIONS:

   Extensive knowledge of methods of planning, organizing, directing, and controlling major programs; knowledge of the California Beverage Container Recycling and Litter Abatement Act, the Division of Recycling's program areas and the recycling industry; knowledge of the state civil service grant and contract procedures and processes; knowledge of the State's budgetary process; fundamentals of economics and political science; ability to implement statewide administrative policies and evaluate program changes and accomplishments.

Training and Development

Another way to move up the career ladder even though you don't currently possess the skill necessary to test into the next promotion level is to accept a *training and development* assignment.

Training and development assignments, or T & Ds, permit you to learn and perform the duties of a different classification while remaining in your current classification.

The training class must have substantially the same salary of your current class, and provide you with experience that differs from the duties that you currently perform.

Lateral Transfers

If the maximum monthly salary of your current class is less than two salary steps higher or lower, or the same as the maximum monthly salary of another class, you can apply for a position in that class without having to take an examination. This technique for upward mobility is called a *lateral transfer*.

To calculate one step higher, multiply your current maximum monthly salary by 1.05 (this will equal 5%). To calculate the second step, multiply your product by 1.05 again (for a total of two steps). Do not multiply your monthly salary by 10% because the product must be compounded.

If you accepted your current job just to "get your foot in the door," the lateral transfer is an excellent way to pursue employment in a class that's more suitable to your experience and career objectives.

Addresses of State Department Personnel Offices

Office of Administrative Law
555 Capitol Mall, Suite 1290
Sacramento, CA 95814
916-323-6225

Commission on Aging
1020 Ninth Street, Room 260
Sacramento, CA 95814
916-322-5630

Department of Aging
1600 K Street
Sacramento, CA 95814
916-445-2417

Agricultural Labor Relations Board
915 Capitol Mall
Sacramento, CA 95814
916-322-5945

Other Offices In: El Centro, Salinas, Santa Maria, Visalia

Air Resources Board
1102 Q Street
Sacramento, CA 95814
916-322-8209

Other Offices In: El Monte

Department of Alcohol and Drug Programs
111 Capitol Mall, Suite 450
Sacramento, CA 95814
916-323-1864

Alcoholic Beverage Control Appeals Board
1001 Sixth Street, Suite 401
Sacramento, CA 95814
916-445-4005

Department of Alcoholic Beverage Control
1901 Broadway
Sacramento, CA 95818
916-445-4898

Other Offices In: Bakersfield, El Monte, Eureka, Fresno, Inglewood, Long Beach, Los Angeles, Oakland, Rancho Mirage, Redding, Salinas, San Bernardino, San Diego, San Francisco, San Jose, San Luis Obispo, Santa Ana, Santa Barbara, Santa Rosa, Stockton, Van Nuys, Yuba City.

California Alternative Energy Source Financing Authority
915 Capitol Mall, Suite 280
Sacramento, CA 95814
916-445-9597

California Arts Council
1901 Broadway, Suite A
Sacramento, CA 95818
916-323-4165

California Auctioneer Commission
1130 K Street, Suite LL20
Sacramento, CA 95814
916-324-5894

Auditor General
660 J Street, Suite 300
Sacramento, CA 95814
916-445-0255

State Banking Department
111 Pine Street, Suite 1100
San Francisco, CA 94111-5613

Other Offices In: Los Angeles, Sacramento, San Diego

Department of Boating and Waterways
1629 S Street
Sacramento, CA 95814
916-445-5199

Commission on California State Government Organization and Economy
1303 J Street, Suite 270
Sacramento, CA 95814
916-445-2125

California State University
Office of the Chancellor
400 Golden Shore
Long Beach, CA 90802-4275
213-590-5751

Other Offices In: Sacramento, Washington, D.C.; Campuses: Arcata, Bakersfield, Carson, Chico, Fresno, Fullerton, Hayward, Long Beach, Los Angeles, Northridge, Pomona, Rohnert Park, Sacramento, San Bernardino, San Diego, San Francisco, San Jose, San Luis Obispo, Turlock

Office of California-Mexico Affairs
1400 Tenth Street
Sacramento, CA 95814
916-322-4811

Child Development Programs Advisory Committee
915 Capitol Mall, Suite 250
Sacramento, CA 95814
916-322-8181

Board of Chiropractic Examiners
921 11th Street, Suite 601
Sacramento, CA 95814
916-445-3244

California Coastal Commission
631 Howard Street
San Francisco, CA 94105
415-543-8555

Other Offices In: Long Beach, San Francisco, Santa Barbara, Santa Cruz

State Coastal Conservancy
1330 Broadway, Suite 1100
Oakland, CA 94612-2530
415-464-1015

Other Offices In: Sacramento

Colorado River Board of California
107 S. Broadway, Room 8103
Los Angeles, CA 90012
213-620-4480

Department of Commerce
1121 L Street, Suite 600
Sacramento, CA 95814
916-322-1269

Other Offices In: Hollywood, Los Angeles, San Diego, San Francisco

---

California Community Colleges,
1107 Ninth Street, Suite 500
Sacramento, CA 95814
916-445-7911

California Conservation Corps
1530 Capitol Avenue
Sacramento, CA 95814
916-322-9362

Other Offices In: Auburn, Camarillo, Chatsworth, Escondido, Klamath, Magalia, Montague, Patton, Pomona, Richmond, San Luis Obispo, San Pedro, Santa Clara, Stockton, Valencia, Weott,

---

Department of Conservation
1416 Ninth Street, Room 1347
Sacramento, CA 95814
916-322-7685

Other Offices In: Bakersfield, Coalinga, El Centro, Los Angeles, Long Beach, Pleasant Hill, Santa Maria, Santa Rosa, Ventura, Woodland

---

Department of Consumer Affairs
1020 N Street
Sacramento, CA 95814
916-445-4626

Other Offices In: Anaheim, Bakersfield, Cottonwood, Culver City, Downey, El Monte, Fresno, Hayward, Inglewood, Long Beach, Los Angeles, North Highlands, Oakland, Oceanside, Pacoima, Pleasant Hill, Pomona Riverside, San Bernardino, San Diego, San Francisco, San Gabriel Valley, San Jose, San Mateo, Santa Ana, Santa Rosa, Torrance, Upland, Van Nuys, Ventura, Woodland Hills

Board of Control
770 L Street, 8th Floor
Sacramento, CA 95814
916-445-1540

State Controller
300 Capitol Mall, Room 811
Sacramento, CA 95814
916-322-6203

Other Offices In: El Monte, Los Angeles

Department of Corporations
1107 Ninth Street, Suite 800
Sacramento, CA 95814
916-445-6351

Other Offices In: Los Angeles, San Diego, San Francisco

Board of Corrections
600 Bercut Drive
Sacramento, CA 95814
916-445-5073

Department of Corrections
630 K Street
Sacramento, CA 95814
916-445-1107

Other Offices In: Acton, Alhambra, Alturas, Anaheim, Angels Camp, Auburn, Avenal, Azusa, Bakersfield, Bella Vista, Bishop, Blythe, Chico, Chino, Citrus Heights, Compton, Concord, Corcoran, Corona, Crestline, El Cajon, El Centro, Elk Creek, Eureka, Fallbrook, Folsom, Ft. Bragg, Ft. Jones, Fresno, Gardena, Georgetown, Hayward, Hemet, Huntington Park, Indio, Inglewood, Ione, Jamestown, Klamath, Long Beach, Los Angeles, Lower Lake, Malibu, McCain Valley, Merced, Miramonte, Modesto, Norco, North Hollywood, Oakland, Ontario, Palmdale, Paskenta, Redding, Redway, Redwood City, Represa,

Richmond, Salinas, San Bernardino, San Diego, San Francisco, San Jose, San Luis Obispo, San Quentin, Santa Ana, Santa Fe Springs, Santa Rosa, Smith River, Soledad, Springville, Stockton, Suisun City, Susanville, Tehachapi, Tracy, Vacaville, Van Nuys, Ventura, Victorville, Visalia, Warner Springs, Weaverville, West Covina, Woodland

---

Office of Criminal Justice Planning
1130 K Street, Suite 300
Sacramento, CA 95814
916-324-9160

California Debt Advisory Commission
915 Capitol Mall, Suite 400
Sacramento, CA 95814
916-324-2585

California Debt Limit Allocation Committee
915 Capitol Mall, Suite 417
Sacramento, CA 95814
916-324-0310

Area Boards on Developmental Disabilities
1507 21st Street, Room 205
Sacramento, CA 95814
916-323-0750

Other Offices In: Fresno, Los Angeles, Modesto, Napa, Oakland, Red Bluff, Riverside, San Diego, San Jose, Santa Barbara, Tustin, Ukiah

---

State Council on Developmental Disabilities
1507 21st Street, Room 320
Sacramento, CA 95814
916-322-8481

Department of Developmental Services
1600 Ninth Street, Room 240
Sacramento, CA 95814
916-445-0147

Other Offices In: Camarillo, Costa Mesa, Pomona, Porterville, San Jose, Sonoma, Stockton

Department of Economic Opportunity
1600 Ninth Street, Room 340
Sacramento, CA 95814
916-322-2940

Department of Education
721 Capitol Mall
Sacramento, CA 95814
916-322-4050

Other Offices In: Chico, Fremont, Fresno, Los Angeles, Oakland, Pomona, Riverside, San Francisco, Vallejo, Washington, D.C.

Emergency Medical Services Authority
9800 South Sepulveda, Suite 820
Los Angeles, CA 90045
213-620-4161

Other Offices In: Sacramento

Office of Emergency Services
2800 Meadowview Road
Sacramento, CA 95832
916-427-4509

Other Offices In: Fresno, Los Angeles, Oakland, Ontario, Pleasant Hill, Redding, Riverside, San Luis Obispo

Employment Development Department
800 Capitol Mall
Sacramento, CA 95814
916-322-2424

Other Offices In: Alturas, Anaheim, Antioch, Auburn, Bakersfield, Barstow, Berkeley, Bishop, Blythe, Calexico, Campbell, Carson, Chico, Colusa, Compton, Concord, Corona, Crescent City, Culver City, Delano, Dinuba, Downey, El Cajon, El Centro, El Monte, Escondido, Eureka, Fairfield, Fontana, Fort Bragg, Fremont, Fresno, Fullerton, Garden Grove, Gilroy, Glendale, Grass Valley, Hanford, Hayward, Hemet, Hollister, Hollywood, Huron, Indio, Inglewood, King City, Laguna Hills, Lakeport, Lakewood, Lamont, Lancaster, Lemoore, Lodi, Lompoc, Long Beach, Los Angeles, Los Banos, Madera, Mammoth Lakes, Manteca, Marysville, Mendota, Merced, Modesto, Monterey, Mount Shasta, Napa, North Hollywood, Norwalk, Oakdale, Oakland, Oceanside, Ontario, Oroville, Oxnard, Palm Springs, Pasadena, Paso Robles, Petaluma, Placerville, Pleasant Hill, Pomona, Porterville, Quincy, Red Bluff, Redding, Redlands, Redondo Beach, Richmond, Ridgecrest, Riverside, Roseville, Salinas, San Bernardino, San Diego, San Fernando, San Francisco, Sanger, San Jose, San Luis Obispo, San Mateo, San Rafael, Santa Ana, Santa Barbara, Santa Cruz, Santa Maria, Santa Monica, Santa Rosa, Simi Valley, Sonora, South Gate, South Lake Tahoe, South San Francisco, Stockton, Sunnyvale, Susanville, Tahoe City, Toorance, Tracy, Turlock, Ukiah, Vallejo, Van Nuys, Ventura, Victorville, Visalia, Wasco, Watsonville, West Covina, Whittier, Woodland, Yreka, Yuba City, Yucca Valley

---

Energy Resources Conservation and Development Commission
1516 Ninth Street
Sacramento, CA 95814
916-324-3035

State Board of Equalization
1020 N Street
Sacramento, CA 95814
916-445-3048

Other Offices In: Arcadia, Arroyo Grande, Au-

burn, Chicago, IL, Chico, Crescent City, Culver City, Downey, El Centro, Eureka, Fresno, Hayward, Hollywood, Houston, TX, Marysville, Modesto, Nevada City, New York, NY, Oakland, Orange, Oroville, Palmdale, Placerville, Quincy, Rancho Mirage, Redding, Salinas, San Bernardino, San Diego, San Francisco, San Jose, San Marcos, San Mateo, San Rafael, Santa Barbara, Santa Cruz, Santa Rosa, South Lake Tahoe, Stockton, Susanville, Torrance, Van Nuys, Ukiah, Vallejo, Ventura, Woodland, Yreka

California Exposition and State Fair
1600 Exposition Blvd.
Sacramento, CA 95815
916-924-2041

Fair Employment and Housing Commission
1390 Market Street, Suite 410
San Francisco, CA 94102-5377
415-557-2828

Department of Fair Employment and Housing
2014 T Street, Suite 210
Sacramento, CA 95814
916-739-4635

Other Offices In: Bakersfield, Fresno, Los Angeles, Oakland, San Bernardino, San Diego, San Francisco, Santa Ana, Ventura

Fair Political Practices Commission
428 J Street, Suite 800
Sacramento, CA 95814
916-322-5660

Commission on State Finance
915 Capitol Mall, Suite 435
Sacramento, CA 95814
916-323-5202

Department of Finance
915 L Street
Sacramento, CA 95814
916-445-3368

Office of the State Fire Marshal
7171 Bowling Drive, Suite 600
Sacramento, CA 95823
916-427-4189

Department of Fish and Game
1416 Ninth Street
Sacramento, CA 95814
916-445-3188

Other Offices In: Eureka, Fort Bragg, Fresno, Long Beach, Menlo Park, Monterey, Morro Bay, Napa, Rancho Cordova, Redding, San Diego, Stockton

Department of Food and Agriculture
1220 N Street, Room 100
Sacramento, CA 95814
916-445-4033

Other Offices In: Alturas, Anaheim, Anderson, Angels Camp, Antioch, Auburn, Bakersfield, Banning, Benton, Berkeley, Bishop, Blythe, Calexico, Campbell, Castroville, Cedarville, Ceres, Chico, Chilcoot, City of Industry, Cloverdale, Coachello, Colusa, Corcoran, Costa Mesa, Cottonwood, Crescent City, Del Mar, Delano, Dinuba, Dixon, Dorris, Escondido, Eureka, Exeter, Fallbrook, Folsom, Foster City, Fresno, Goleta, Grass Valley, Hanford, Hemet, Hollister, Hornbrook, Imperial, Lakeport, Lancaster, Los Angeles, Madera, Manteca, Mariposa, Merced, Modesto, Monterey, Napa, Needles, Northridge, Norwalk, O'Brien, Oregon, Oakland, Orland, Oxnard, Paso Robles, Petaluma, Plymouth, Red Bluff, Redding, Ridgecrest, Riverside, Rosemead, Salinas, San Bernardino, San Francisco, San Ysidro, Santa Barbara, Santa Maria, Santa Paula, Smith River, Sonora, South San Fran-

cisco, Stockton, Tahoe Paradise, Topaz, Tulare, Tulelake, Turlock, Ukiah, Van Nuys, Ventura, Victorville, Vidal, Visalia, Watsonville, West Sacramento, Winterhaven, Woodland, Yermo, Yreka, Yuba City

---

Department of Forestry and Fire Protection
1416 Ninth Street, Room 1525
Sacramento, CA 95814
916-445-0217

Other Offices In: Davis Ranger Units in the Following Counties: Amador-El Dorado, Fresno-Kings, Humboldt-Del Norte, Lake-Napa, Madera-Mariposa, Medocino, Owens Valley, Riverside, San Benito-Monterey, San Bernardino, San Diego, San Luis Obispo, San Mateo-Santa Cruz, Santa Clara, Shasta-Trinity, Siskiyou, Sonoma, Tehama, Tulare, Tuolumne-Calaveras

---

Franchise Tax Board
9645 Butterfield Way
Sacramento, CA 95827
916-369-3603

Other Offices In: Bakersfield, Chicago, IL, El Monte, Fresno, Houston, TX, Long Beach, Los Angeles, Manhasset, NY, Manhattan, NY, Oakland, San Bernardino, San Diego, San Francisco, San Jose, Santa Ana, Santa Barbara, Santa Rosa, Stockton, Van Nuys, West Los Angeles

---

Department of General Services
915 Capitol Mall, Suite 590
Sacramento, CA 95814
916-445-8590

Other Offices In: Alturas, Auburn, Bakersfield, Barstow, Berkeley, Bishop, Blythe, Byron, Camino, Castaic, Crescent City, El Cajon, Escondido, Fairfield, Fortuna, Foster City, Fresno, Fullerton, Gardena, Hayward, Imperial, Indio, Long Beach, Los Angeles, Los Banos, Martinez, Marysville,

Merced, Mill Valley, Mojave, Nevada City, Newhall, North Highlands, Oakland, Orange, Oroville, Pearblossom, Pico Rivera, Quincy, Red Bluff, Redding, Salinas, St. Helena, San Andreas, San Bernardino, San Francisco, San Jose, San Luis Obispo, Santa Ana, Santa Clara, Santa Fe Springs, Santa Rosa, Stockton, Truckee, Ukiah, Van Nuys, Visalia, Yreka

---

Governor's Office
State Capitol
Sacramento, CA 95814
916-445-1697

Other Offices In: Los Angeles, San Francisco, Washington, D.C.

Hastings College of the Law
200 McAllister Street
San Francisco, CA 94102
415-565-4703

Health and Welfare Agency Data Center
1651 Alhambra Blvd.
Sacramento, CA 95816
916-739-3187

Office of Statewide Health Planning and Development
1600 Ninth Street
Sacramento, CA 95814
916-324-6439

Department of Health Services
714 P Street
Sacramento, CA 95814
916-324-1308

Other Offices In: Bakersfield, Berkeley, Burbank, Chico, Emeryville, Fresno, Long Beach, Los Angeles, Modesto, Oakland, Rancho Cordova, Redding, Salinas, San Bernardino, San Diego, San Francisco, San Jose, Santa Ana, Santa

Barbara, Santa Rosa, Stockton, Suisun City, Terminal Island

Department of the California Highway Patrol
2555 First Avenue
Sacramento, CA 95818
916-322-5380

Other Offices In: Altadena, Alturas, Antelope Valley, Aptos, Arcata, Bakersfield, Baldwin Park, Banning, Barstow, Bishop, Blythe, Bridgeport, Buellton,, Chico, Coalinga, Corte Madera, Crescent City, El Cajon, Fairfield, Ft. Tejon, Fresno, Gilroy, Gold Run, Goleta, Grass Valley, Hanford, Hayward, Imperial, Indio, Jamestown, Kelseyville, King City, Lake Valley, Lancaster, Los Angeles, Los Banos, Madera, Malibu, Mariposa, Martinez, Merced, Modesto, Mojave, Mt. Shasta, Napa, Needles, Newcastle, Newhall, Oakland, Oceanside, Ontario, Oroville, Placerville, Porterville, Quincy, Rancho Cordova, Red Bluff, Redding, Redwood City, Riverside, Rohnert Park, Running Springs, San Andreas, San Bernardino, San Diego, San Francisco, San Juan Capistrano, San Jose, San Luis Obispo, Santa Ana, Santa Fe Springs, Santa Maria, South Lake Tahoe, Stockton, Susanville, Sutter Creek, Temecula, Templeton, Tracy, Truckee, Ukiah, Ventura, Victorville, Visalia, Weaverville, Westminster, Williams, Willows, Winterhaven, Woodland, Woodland Hills, Yreka, Yuba City

California Horse Racing Board
1010 Hurley Way, Suite 190
Sacramento, CA 95825
916-920-7165

Other Offices In: Los Alamitos, San Mateo

Department of Housing and Community Development
921 Tenth Street
Sacramento, CA 95814
916-445-4807

Other Offices In: Fresno, Inglewood, La Mesa, Redding, San Bernardino, San Jose, San Luis Obispo, Santa Ana, Santa Rosa, Winnetka

---

California Housing Finance Agency
1121 L Street, 7th Floor
Sacramento, CA 95814
916-322-3966

California Housing Insurance
1121 L Street, Suite 203
Sacramento, CA 95814
916-322-8936

California Industrial Development Financing Advisory Commission
915 Capitol Mall, Suite 280
Sacramento, CA 95814
916-323-9860

Department of Industrial Relations
525 Golden Gate Avenue
San Francisco, CA 94102
415-557-0450

Other Offices In: Arcadia, Bakersfield, Cerritos, Costa Mesa, Downey, El Centro, Eureka, Fresno, Hollywood, Inglewood, Long Beach, Los Angeles, Marysville, Napa, Norwalk, Oakland, Pomona, Redding, Sacramento, Salinas, San Bernardino, San Diego, San Francisco, San Jose, San Mateo, San Rafael, Santa Ana, Santa Barbara, Santa Monica, Santa Rosa, Stockton, Truckee, Van Nuys, Ventura, Whittier, Woodland Hills

---

Department of Insurance
200 Van Ness Avenue, 17th Floor
San Francisco, CA 94102
415-557-0366

Other Offices In: Los Angeles, Sacramento, San Diego, Vallejo

Department of Justice
1515 K Street, Suite 511
Sacramento, CA 95814
916-324-5044

Other Offices In: Chico, Eureka, Fresno, Los Angeles, Modesto, Orange, Redding, Riverside, Salinas, San Diego, San Francisco, San Jose, San Rafael, Santa Barbara, Stockton.

State Lands Commission
1807 13th Street
Sacramento, CA 95814
916-322-3587

Other Offices In: Goleta, Huntington Beach, Long Beach

California Law Revision Commission
4000 Middlefield Road, Suite D-2
Palo Alto, CA 94303-4739
415-494-1335

Legislative Counsel Bureau
3021 State Capitol
Sacramento, CA 95814
916-445-3796

Office of the Lieutenant Governor
State Capitol, Room 1114
Sacramento, CA 95814
916-445-8994

Other Offices In: Los Angeles, San Francisco

California State Lottery
600 North Tenth Street
Sacramento, CA 95814
916-323-8098

Other Offices In: Anaheim, Bakersfield, Fresno, Redding, Riverside, Sacramento, San Diego, San

Francisco, San Jose, Sylmar, Ventura Whittier

Commission on State Mandates
1130 K Street, Suite LL50
Sacramento, CA 95814
916-323-3562

California Maritime Academy
P.O. Box 1392
Vallejo, CA 94590
707-648-4230

California Medical Assistance Commission
1121 L Street, Suite 300
Sacramento, CA 95814
916-324-2726

Department of Mental Health
1600 Ninth Street
Sacramento, CA 95814
916-323-8253

Other Offices In: Atascadero, La Mesa, Napa, Norwalk, Patton, San Francisco, Santa Fe Springs, Stockton, Vacaville

Military Department
2829 Watt Avenue
Sacramento, CA 95821-4405
916-973-3474

California Mortgage Bond and Tax Credit Allocation Committee
915 Capitol Mall, Suite 280
Sacramento, CA 95814
916-324-7419

Department of Motor Vehicles
2415 First Avenue
Sacramento, CA 95818
916-732-7623

Other Offices In: Alhambra, Alturas, Arleta, Arvin, Auburn, Bakersfield, Banning, Barstow, Bellflower, Bell Gardens, Bishop, Blythe, Brawley, Campbell, Capitola, Carmichael, Chico, Chula Vista, Clovis, Coalinga, Colusa, Compton, Concord, Corona, Corte Madera, Costa Mesa, Crescent City, Daly City, Davis, Delano, El Cajon, El Centro, El Cerrito, Escondido, Eureka, Fairfield, Fall River Mills, Fontana, Fort Bragg, Fremont, Fresno, Fullerton, Garberville, Gilroy, Glendale, Goleta, Grass Valley, Hanford, Hawthorne, Hayward, Hemet, Hollister, Hollywood, Indio, Inglewood, Jackson, King City, Laguna Hills, Lakeport, La Mesa, Lancaster, Lodi, Lompoc, Long Beach, Los Angeles, Los Banos, Los Gatos, Madera, Manteca, Mariposa, Merced, Modesto, Montebello, Mount Shasta, Mountain View, Napa, Needles, Newhall, North Hollywood, Northridge, Oakland, Orland, Oroville, Oxnard, Palmdale, Palm Springs, Paradise, Pasadena, Paso Robles, Petaluma, Pittsburg, Placerville, Pleasanton, Pomona, Porterville, Poway, Red Bluff, Redding, Redlands, Redwood City, Reedley, Ridgecrest, Riverside, Rocklin, Roseville, Salinas, San Andreas, San Bernardino, San Clemente, San Diego, San Francisco, San Jose, San Luis Obispo, San Mateo, San Pedro, Santa Ana, Santa Barbara, Santa Clara, Santa Maria, Santa Monica, Santa Paula, Santa Rosa, Seaside, Shafter, Simi Valley, Sonora, South Lake Tahoe, Spring Valley, Stockton, Susanville, Taft, Thousand Oaks, Torrance, Tracy, Truckee, Tulare, Tulelake, Turlock, Twenty Nine Palms, Ukiah, Upland, Vacaville, Vallejo, Van Nuys, Ventura, Visalia, Watsonville, Weaverville, West Covina, Westminster, Whittier, Willows, Winnetka, Woodland Hills, Yreka, Yuba City

---

Museum of Science and Industry
700 State Drive
Los Angeles, CA 90037
213-744-7477

Native American Heritage Commission
915 Capitol Mall, Room 288
Sacramento, CA 95814
916-322-7791

California Occupational Informational Coordinating Committee
800 Capitol Mall, MIC-67
Sacramento, CA 95814
916-323-6544

Board of Osteopathic Examiners
921 11th Street, Suite 1201
Sacramento, CA 95814
916-322-4306

Department of Parks and Recreation
1416 Ninth Street
Sacramento, CA 95814
916-445-6911

Other Offices In: Aptos, Arnold, Arroyo Grande, Big Sur, Borrego Springs, Calistoga, Carlsbad, Chico, Columbia, Concord, Descanso, Duncans Mills, Eureka, Felton, Folsom, Friant, Goleta, Grass Valley, Half Moon Bay, Hesperia, Hollister, Huntington Beach, Idyllwild, Kelseyville, Lancaster, Lodi, Lompoc, Mendocino, Monterey, Newbury Park, North Shore, Oroville, Perris, Rio Vista, Riverside, San Clemente, San Diego, San Francisco, San Juan Bautista, San Luis Obispo, San Rafael, San Simeon, Santa Nella, Shasta, Sonoma, Ventura, Weott, Winterhaven.

Commission on Peace Officer Standards and Training
1601 Alhambra Blvd.
Sacramento, CA 95816-7083
916-739-5354

Department of Personnel Admininstration
1515 S Street, North Building
Suite 400
Sacramento, CA 95814
916-324-0463

State Personnel Board
801 Capitol Mall
Sacramento, CA 94244-2010
916-445-5808

Other Offices In: Los Angeles, San Francisco

Board of Pilot Commissioners
World Trade Center, Room 339
San Francisco, CA 94111
415-397-2253

Office of Planning and Research
1400 Tenth Street
Sacramento, CA 95814
916-322-3170

California Postsecondary Education Commission
1020 12th Street, 3rd Floor
Sacramento, CA 95814
916-323-0809

Board of Prison Terms
545 Downtown Plaza, Suite 200
Sacramento, CA 95814
916-323-0936

State Public Defender
1107 Ninth Street, 3rd Floor
Sacramento, CA 95814
916-322-2130

Other Offices In: Los Angeles, San Francisco

Public Employees' Retirement System
400 P Street
Sacramento, CA 95814
916-326-3065

Public Employment Relations Board
1031 18th Street
Sacramento, CA 95814
916-322-3088

Public Utilities Commission
505 Van Ness Avenue
San Francisco, CA 94102
415-557-2324

Other Offices In: Bakersfield, Campbell, Downey, El Centro, El Monte, Eureka, Fresno, Los Angeles, Oakland, Redding, Sacramento, San Bernardino, San Bruno, San Diego, Santa Ana, Santa Barbara, Santa Rosa, Stockton, Van Nuys

Department of Real Estate
2201 Broadway
Sacramento, CA 95818
916-739-3620

Other Offices In: Fresno, Los Angeles, San Diego, San Francisco, Santa Ana

Department of Rehabilitation
830 K Street Mall
Sacramento, CA 95814
916-445-2142

Other Offices In: Albany, Anaheim, Antioch, Auburn, Bakersfield, Barstow, Bell, Berkeley, Blythe, Burbank, Campbell, Canoga Park, Chico, Chula Vista, Compton, Corona, Crescent City, Culver City, Delano, Downey, El Cajon, El Centro, Escondido, Eureka, Fairfield, Fremont, Fresno, Fullerton, Gardena, Glendale, Grass Valley, Hacienda Heights, Hayward, Hemet, Hollywood, Indio, Lancaster, LaVerne, Long

Beach, Los Angeles, Merced, Modesto, Monterey, Mountain View, Napa, Newport Beach, Norwalk, Oakland, Oceanside, Oxnard, Placerville, Pleasant Hill, Pomona, Redding, Redondo Beach, Ridgecrest, Riverside, Salinas, San Bernardino, San Diego, San Francisco, San Jose, San Luis Obispo, San Pablo, San Rafael, Santa Ana, Santa Barbara, Santa Cruz, Santa Maria, Santa Monica, Santa Rosa, South Lake Tahoe, Stockton, Susanville, Thousand Oaks, Torrance, Ukiah, Upland, Vallejo, Van Nuys, Victorville, Visalia, Watsonville, Westminster, Woodland, Yreka, Yuba City

---

San Francisco Bay Conservation and Development Commission
30 Van Ness Avenue, Suite 2011
San Francisco, CA 94102
415-557-3686

Santa Monica Mountains Conservancy
107 South Broadway, Suite 7117
Los Angeles, CA 90012
213-620-2021

Department of Savings and Loan
350 Sansome Street, 2nd Floor
San Francisco, CA 94104
415-557-3666

Other Offices In: Los Angeles

Secretary of State
1230 J Street
Sacramento, CA 95814
916-445-6223

Other Offices In: Los Angeles, San Diego, San Francisco

Seismic Safety Commission
1900 K Street, Suite 100
Sacramento, CA 95814
916-322-4917

Department of Social Services
744 P Street
Sacramento, CA 95814
916-445-2010

Other Offices In: Berkeley, Chico, Emeryville, Fresno, Los Angeles, Oakland, Riverside, San Diego, San Francisco, Santa Ana, Santa Barbara, Santa Rosa,

Commission on the Status of Women
1303 J Street, Suite 400
Sacramento, CA 95814-4000
916-445-3173

Stephen P. Teale Data Center
2005 Evergreen Street
Sacramento, CA 95815
916-920-6002

Student Aid Commission
1515 S Street, North Building, 5th Floor
Sacramento, CA 95814
916-322-3165

California State Summer School for the Arts
2012 H Street, Room 201
Sacramento, CA 95814
916-445-8919

California Tahoe Conservancy
2161 Lake Tahoe Blvd.
South Lake Tahoe, CA 95731
916-542-2940

Commission on Teacher Credentialing
1812 Ninth Street
Sacramento, CA 95814
916-322-5773

State Teachers' Retirement System
7667 Folsom Blvd.
Sacramento, CA 95826
916-386-3757

Office of Traffic Safety
7000 Franklin Blvd., Suite 330
Sacramento, CA 95823
916-445-0527

California Transportation Commission
1120 N Street, Room 2230
Sacramento, CA 95814
916-445-1690

Department of Transportation
1120 N Street
Sacramento, CA 95814
916-445-3618

Other Offices In: Alturas, Bakersfield, Banning, Barstow, Bishop, Boonville, Chula Vista, Colton, Crescent City, El Centro, Eureka, Foster City, Fresno, Garberville, Lakeport, Los Angeles, Marysville, Monrovia, Needles, Newhall, Oakland, Ontario, Orange, Orinda, Petaluma, Quincy, Red Bluff, Redding, Redwood Valley, Riverside, San Diego, San Francisco, San Jose, San Leandro, San Luis Obispo, Santa Ana, Stockton, Susanville, Victorville, Walnut Creek, Westwood, Whittier, Willow Creek, Woodland Hills, Yreka

State Treasurer
915 Capitol Mall, Room 110
Sacramento, CA 95814
916-445-2247

Other Offices In: Los Angeles, San Francisco

University of California
Office of the President
300 Lakeside Drive
Oakland, CA 94612-3550
415-987-0700

Other Offices In: Sacramento; Campuses: Berkeley, Davis, Irvine, Los Angeles, Riverside, San Diego-La Jolla, San Francisco, Santa Barbara, Santa Cruz

---

Department of Veterans Affairs
1227 "O" Street
Sacramento, CA 95814
916-445-5666

Other Offices In: Bakersfield, Concord, Citrus Heights, Fresno, Los Angeles, Redding, San Bernardino, San Diego, San Francisco, Santa Clara, Santa Fe Springs, Ventura

---

California State Council on Vocational Education
501 S Street, Suite 2
Sacramento, CA 95814
916-445-0698

California Waste Management Board
1020 Ninth Street, Suite 300
Sacramento, CA 95814
916-322-3330

State Water Resources Control Board
901 P Street
Sacramento, CA 95814
916-322-4142

Other Offices In: Fresno, Los Angeles, Oakland, Palm Desert, Redding, Riverside,San Diego, San Luis Obispo, San Marcos, Santa Rosa, South Lake Tahoe, Victorville

Department of Water Resources
1416 Ninth Street, Room 304-2
Sacramento, CA 95814
916-445-4281

Other Offices In: Bakersfield, Bryte, Byron, Castaic, Coalinga, Eureka, Fresno, Lancaster, Los Angeles, Oroville, Pearblossom, Red Bluff, Santa Nella, Sutter

Wildlife Conservation Board
1416 Ninth Street
Sacramento, CA 95814
916-445-8448

California State World Trade Commission
1121 L Street, Suite 310
Sacramento, CA 95814
916-324-5511

Other Offices In: Long Beach, Los Angeles, San Francisco, Washington, D.C.

Department of the Youth Authority
4241 Williamsbourgh Drive
Sacramento, CA 95823
916-427-4722

Other Offices In: Bakersfield, Camarillo, Chico, Compton, Covina, El Centro, Glendale, Fresno, Ione, Long Beach, Los Angeles, Mariposa, Montebello, Nevada City, Norwalk, Oakland, Ontario, Panorama City, Pasadena, Pine Grove, Riverside, San Francisco, San Jose, San Leandro, Santa Cruz, Stockton, Valyermo, Yucaipa

Youthful Offender Parole Board
4241 Williamsbourgh Drive
Sacramento, CA 95823
916-427-4873
Other Offices In: Glendale

Appendices

A. California Cities That Have State Civil Services Opportunites

Acton
Albany
Alhambra
Alturas
Anaheim
Anderson
Angels Camp
Antelope Valley
Antioch
Aptos
Arcadia
Arcata
Arleta
Arnold
Arroyo Grande
Arvin
Astascadero
Auburn
Avenal
Azusa
Bakersfield
Baldwin Park
Banning
Barstow
Bell Gardens
Bell
Bella Vista
Bellflower
Bento
Berkeley
Big Sur
Bishop
Blythe
Boonville
Borrego Springs
Brawley
Bridgeport
Bryte
Buellton
Burbank

Byron
Calexico
Calistoga
Camarillo
Camino
Campbell
Canoga Park
Capitola
Carlsbad
Carson
Castaic
Castroville
Cedarville
Ceres
Cerritos
Chatsworth
Chicago, IL
Chico
Chicoot
Chino
Chula Vista
Citrus Heights
City of Industry
Cloverdale
Clovis
Coachello
Coalinga
Colton
Columbia
Compton
Concord
Corcoran
Corona
Corte Madera
Costa Mesa
Cottonwood
Covina
Crescent City
Crestline
Culver City
Daly City

Davis
Del Mar
Delano
Descanso
Dinuba
Dorris
Downey
Duncans Mills
El Cajon
El Centro
El Cerrito
El Monte
Elk Creek
Emeryville
Escondido
Eureka
Exeter
Fairfield
Fall River Mills
Fallbrook
Felton
Folsom
Fontana
Fort Bragg
Fort Jones
Fort Tejon
Fortuna
Foster City
Fresno
Friant
Fullerton
Garberville
Garden Grove
Gardena
Georgetown
Gilroy
Glendale
Gold Run
Goleta
Grass Valley
Hacienda Heights

Half Moon Bay
Hanford
Hawthorne
Hayward
Hemet
Hesperia
Hollister
Hollywood
Hornbrook
Houston, TX
Huntington Beach
Huntington Park
Huron
Idyllwild
Imperial
Indio
Inglewood
Ione
Irvine
Jackson
Jamestown
Kelseyville
King City
Klamath
La Jolla
La Mesa
La Verne
Laguna Hills
Lake Valley
Lakeport
Lakewood
Lamont
Lancaster
Lemoore
Lodi
Lompoc
Long Beach
Los Alamitos
Los Angeles
Los Banos
Los Gatos
Lower Lake
Madera
Magalia
Malibu
Mammoth Lakes
Manhasset, NY
Manhattan, NY
Manteca
Mariposa
Martinez
Marysville
McCain Valley
Mendocino
Mendota
Menlo Park
Merced
Mill Valley
Miramonte
Modesto
Mojave
Monrovia
Montague
Montebello
Morro Bay
Mountain View
Mt. Shasta
Napa
Needles
Nevada City
New York, NY
Newbury Park
Newcastle
Newhall
Newport Beach
Norco
North Highlands
North Hollywood
North Shore
Northridge
Norwalk
O'Brien
Oakdale
Oakland
Oceanside
Ontario
Orange
Oregon
Orland
Orinda
Oroville
Oxnard
Pacoima
Palm Desert
Palm Springs
Palmdale
Panorama City
Paradise
Paskenta
Paso Robles
Patton
Pearblossom
Perris
Petaluma
Pico Rivera
Pittsburg
Placerville
Pleasant Hill
Pleasanton
Plymouth
Pomona
Porterville
Poway
Quincy
Rancho Cordova
Rancho Mirage
Red Bluff
Redding
Redlands
Redondo Beach
Redway
Redwood Valley
Reedley
Represa
Richmond
Ridgecrest
Rio Vista
Riverside
Rocklin
Rohnert Park
Rosemead
Roseville
Running Springs
Sacramento
Salinas
San Andreas
San Bernardino
San Bruno
San Clemente
San Diego
San Fernando
San Francisco
San Gabriel Valley
San Jose

San Juan Bautista
San Juan Capistrano
San Leandro
San Luis Obispo
San Marcos
San Mateo
San Pablo
San Pedro
San Quentin
San Rafael
San Simeon
San Ysidro
Sanger
Santa Ana
Santa Barbara
Santa Clara
Santa Cruz
Santa Fe Springs
Santa Maria
Santa Monica
Santa Nella
Santa Paula
Santa Rosa
Seaside
Shafter
Simi Valley
Smith River
Soledad
Sonora
South Gate
South Lake Tahoe
South San Francisco
Spring Valley
Springville
St. Helena
Stockton
Suisun City
Susanville
Sutter Creek
Sutter
Sylmar
Taft
Tahoe Paradise
Tehachapi
Temecula
Templeton
Terminal Island
Thousand Oaks
Topaz
Torrance
Tracy
Truckee
Tulare
Tulelake
Turlock
Tustin
Twenty Nine Palms
Ukiah
Upland
Vacaville
Valencia
Vallejo
Valyermo
Van Nuys
Ventura
Victorville
Vidal
Visalia
Walnut Creek
Warner Springs
Wasco
Washington, D.C.
Watsonville
Weaverville
Weoot
West Covina
West Los Angeles
West Sacramento
Westminster
Westwood
Whittier
Williams
Willow Creek
Willows
Winnetka
Winterhaven
Woodland Hills
Woodland
Yermo
Yreka
Yuba City
Yucaipa
Yucca Valley

B. Civil Service Classifications Which are Peace Officers

Air Operations Officer I, II & III
Air Operations Officer I, II & III, Maintenance
Aquatic Specialist
Arson/Bomb Investigator
Board Coordinating Parole Agent, Youthful Offender Parole Board
Case Work Specialist, Youth Authority
Community Services Consultant I
Correctional Case Worker Trainee
Correctional Counselor I & II
Correctional Officer
Correctional Officer Trainee
Correctional Program Supervisor
Deputy Registrar of Contractors I & II
Deputy State Fair Marshal Intern
Deputy State Fire Marshal I & II
Deputy State Fire Marshal III, Specialist
District Representative I & II, Division of Codes and Standards
Fire Apparatus Engineer
Fire Captain
Fire Control Aide
Fire Crew Supervisor
Fire Prevention Officer I & II
Fire Service Training Specialist I, II & III
Firefighter
Firefighter, California Department of Forestry
Firefighter, Correctional Institution
Firefighter/Security Guard
Fish and Game Patrol, Lieutenant
Fish and Game Warden
Food and Drug Investigator I, II & III
Food and Drug Program Coordinator
Food Technology Specialist
Forester I
Forestry Aide
Forestry Helicopter Pilot
Group Supervisor
Group Supervisor Trainee
Heavy Fire Equipment Operator
Hospital Peace Officer I
Investigator Assistant

Investigator Trainee
Investigator, Structural Pest Control Board
Junior Forester
Life Guard
Lottery Agent
Lt. Fish and Game Patrol Boat
Medical Technical Assistant, Correctional Facility
Museum Security Officer I
Park Safety/Enforcement Specialist
Parole Agent I & II, Adult Parole
Parole Agent I & II, Youth Authority
Parole Services Associate
Polygraph Examiner, Youth Authority
Seasonal Firefighter, Department of Forestry
Senior Investigator, Structural Pest Control Board
Senior Medical Technical Assistant
Senior Special Investigator
Sergeant, California State Police
Sergeant, State Fair Police
Special Investigator
State Park Ranger I
State Park Ranger Trainee
State Park Technician
State Police Officer
State Security Officer
Supervisor Firefighter/Security Guard
Transportation Officer, Youth Authority
Warden/Pilot, Fish and Game
Youth Counselor

Glossary

Adverse Action - Any demotion or disciplanary action; dismissal or suspension from State service.

Alternate Range - A different—usually higher salary level—than the general entry rate, or monthly salary for a particular class. Employees with additional experience and/or education may be eligble for movement between salary ranges to a higher monthly salary if they meet the established Alternate Range Criteria.

Appeal - A written request for review of a personnel action which is filed with the State Personnel Board.

Career Credits - Three points added to the final score of successful open exam competitors who have permanent civil service status or mandatory reinstatement rights.

Career Executive Assignment - A high administrative and policy influencing position within California State civil service. These positions can only be established in the top managerial levels of State service, and assume broad responsibility for implementing policies.

Certification - Process for referring the names of qualified persons on an employment list to a hiring department. The names are referred in rank order, based on the Rule of Three Ranks.

Classification - (Also known as class) the title used to designate a group of State positions which are very similar in terms of duties and responsibilities (ie: Office Assistant and Staff Services Analyst).

Comparable Class - A class that has substantially the same salary range or duties of another class. Substantially the same means a maximum rate of two salary steps higher or lower than or the same as the maximum salary rate of another class.

Demotion - Any transfer of an employee from a position in a higher class to a position in a lower class. A lower class is considered two salary steps lower than the existing maximum salary rate.

Departmental Exam - A civil service exam offered by an individual department or group of departments. Usually a department administers such an exam when it anticipates future vacancies in the testing class.

Employment List - Also known as an eligible list: A group of persons who have been successful in an open civil service exam and are eligible for certification for a specific class.

Exam Announcement - The one to two-page notice which informs potential exam applicants of an upcoming exam for a particular class. The announcement lists, among other things, the exam title, the monthly salary range, the duties of the class and minimum qualifications for admittance into the exam.

Final Filing Date - This is the date by which an appllicant for any civil service examination must have his application postmarked (if the application is mailed) or date stamped by the testing department (if the application is delivered in person).

Inactive List - A group of names of persons who were on an employment list, but who have sent a written request to the State Personnel Board to temporarily remove their names from the employment list because they are unable to accept State employment at this time.

Lateral Transfer - The transfer of an employee from a position in one class to a position in another (comparable) class without having to take a civil service exam.

Limited Examination and Appointment Program (LEAP) - A program that provides for the hiring of persons with disabilities into State civil service where accommodation can be provided.

Limited Term - A civil service position that exists for a specified period of time of two years or less.

Merit Salary Adjustment - The one salary step (5%) increase in monthly salary which occurs once every 12 months until an employee has reached the maximum monthly salary for a particular class.

Open Exam - A state civil service exam which is not restricted to state employees. Anyone who meets the minimum qualifications may apply to take the exam. You don't have to be a State employee.

Opportunity Bulletin - A flyer distributed by individual State departments announcing one or more job vacancies for specific classes. These bulletins usually list position duties, desirable qualificiations and the application deadline.

Permanent Intermittent - A State civil service position in which the employee works periodically or for a changing portion of a full time work schedule.

Probationary Period - The six to 12 month "evaluation" period a new State employee serves. If, at the end of this period an employee performs satisfactorily, the employee acquires permanent civil service status. There is also a probationary period for each new position you accept thereafter.

Promotion - Any transfer of an employee from a position in a lower class to a position in a higher class. A higher class is considered two salary steps higher than the existing maximum salary rate.

Promotional Exam - A civil service exam limited to State employees who meet the minimum qualifications. The exam is usually given by an individual department or a group of departments.

Qualifications Appraisal Interview - The portion of a civil service exam in which a group of representatives from State service review your qualifications for a class based on your experiences, education and an oral interview.

Rank - Position on employment list for a group of persons having the same exam score.

Reinstatement - The mandatory right of return to their departments that former or current state employees with permanent civil service status. Such employees have the right to return to the same or similar position.

Rule of Three Ranks - When providing certification for any employment list resulting from an open exam, only the names of persons in the first three ranks will be certified to the hiring department.

Salary Range - The minimum and maximum monthly salary rate authorized for a particular class.

Salary Step - Five percent differential above or below a salary rate, rounded to the nearest whole dollar. For hourly rate employees, it is rounded to the nearest cent.

Seasonal Position - A temporary position in a State department which does not require a civil service exam.

Specification - A brief State Personnel Board publication that explains the minimum qualifications required for admittance into an exam for a particular class. The specification details typical duties of an employee in the class and provides overall insight into the qualifications necessary to be eligible for the class.

Student Assistant - A position in State government, not requiring an exam, occupied by a high school, college or graduate school student paid at an hourly rate.

Veterans Preference - Extra points added to the final score of successful open exam participants who have requested and qualified for the preference.

Waiver - When a job applicant is offered temporary or permanent state employment but does not accept, the name of such applicant's name is placed on the inactive list.

Bibliography and Sources

California State Civil Service Pay Scales. Department of Personnel Administration, July 1, 1989.

Governor's Budget Summary, 1989-90. Department of Finance, 1989.

The Great State Employee. Department of Personnel Administration, 1989.

Laws and Rules Governing California State Personnel Administration. Department of Personnel Administration, February, 1988.

Laws and Rules Governing the California State Civil Service. State Personnel Board, January, 1989.

Merchandising Your Job Talents. Employment Development Department, August, 1987.

State of California Telephone Directory 1989. Department of General Services, 1989.

Assorted publications produced by:
California State Employees Association
Department of Education
Department of Health Services
Department of Justice
State Personnel Board.

Index

E

F

G

H

I

J

L

T

U

V

W

Y

Please send me ______ additional copies of **Jobseeker's Guide to California State Employment** at $14.95 per book. Add $1.40 for shipping and handling. California residents add 6.75% sales tax. Immediate shipment guaranteed. Note: 10% discount for purchases of 10 or more books.

NAME ____

ADDRESS ____

CITY ______________________ STATE ________ ZIP ________

TELEPHONE ____

Payment enclosed: ❑ Check ❑ Money Order

Mail To:
Columbia Publishers
709 Columbia Drive, Suite 1200
Sacramento, CA 95864

Also available from Columbia Publishers: "A helpful 'how to' book for small businesses interested in the State of California business. I recommend it highly."

Kirk West, President
California Chamber of Commerce

BOTTOM LINE BIDDING: A Small Business Guide to Lucrative California State Contracts

Yes! I am a small business person who wants to become more aware of the marketing opportunities available with the State of California. Send me **BOTTOM LINE BIDDING** for $45.00 plus $4.50 shipping and handling. Send check or money order to:

Columbia Publishers
709 Columbia Drive, Suite 1200
Sacramento, CA 95864

NAME ____

ADDRESS ____

CITY ______________________ STATE ________ ZIP ________

TELEPHONE ____